D062464

ABOUT ISLAND PRESS

Island Press is the only nonprofit organization in the United States whose principal purpose is the publication of books on environmental issues and natural resource management. We provide solutions-oriented information to professionals, public officials, business and community leaders, and concerned citizens who are shaping responses to environmental problems.

In 2006, Island Press celebrates its twenty-second anniversary as the leading provider of timely and practical books that take a multidisciplinary approach to critical environmental concerns. Our growing list of titles reflects our commitment to bringing the best of an expanding body of literature to the environmental community throughout North America and the world.

Support for Island Press is provided by the Agua Fund, The Geraldine R. Dodge Foundation, Doris Duke Charitable Foundation, The William and Flora Hewlett Foundation, Kendeda Sustainability Fund of the Tides Foundation, Forrest C. Lattner Foundation, The Henry Luce Foundation, The John D. and Catherine T. MacArthur Foundation, The Marisla Foundation, The Andrew W. Mellon Foundation, Gordon and Betty Moore Foundation, The Curtis and Edith Munson Foundation, Oak Foundation, The Overbrook Foundation, The David and Lucile Packard Foundation, The Winslow Foundation, and other generous donors.

The opinions expressed in this book are those of the author(s) and do not necessarily reflect the views of these foundations.

ABOUT THE CONSERVATION FUND

The Conservation Fund is a national, nonprofit land conservation organization that forges partnerships to protect America's legacy of land and water resources. Through land acquisition, community planning, and leadership training, the Fund and its partners demonstrate sustainable conservation solutions emphasizing the integration of economic and environmental goals. Since 1985, the Fund has protected more than five million acres of open space, wildlife habitat, and historic sites across America. For more information, visit www.conservationfund.org.

Green Infrastructure

Green Infrastructure

Linking Landscapes and Communities

MARK A. BENEDICT

EDWARD T. MCMAHON

The Conservation Fund

Washington • Covelo • London

Library of Congress Cataloging-in-Publication data.

Benedict, Mark A.
  Green infrastructure : linking landscapes and communities / Mark A. Benedict, Edward T. McMahon.
      p. cm.
  Includes bibliographical references (p.   ) and index.
    ISBN 1-59726-027-4 (cloth : alk. paper) — ISBN 1-55963-558-4 (pbk : alk. paper)
    1. Land use, Urban. 2. Cities and towns—Growth. 3. Natural areas. 4. Cultural property—Protection. I. McMahon, Edward T., 1947– II. Title.
  HD1391.B46 2006
  333.73—dc22   2005031588

British Cataloguing-in-Publication data available.

Printed on recycled, acid-free paper ✹

Design by Amy Stirnkorb

Manufactured in the United States of America
10 9 8 7 6 5 4 3 2 1

I dedicate this book to my parents, Paul and Phyllis,
who nurtured my love of nature and of places outdoors,
and to my wife and son, Georgia and Skylar, who help me
remember the joy and exhilaration that comes from
natural open spaces close to home and far away.

—MARK A. BENEDICT

I dedicate this book to Sherry, Megan, and Sean McMahon
for all of their encouragement, love, and support
during my many years of exploring America's
green spaces and special places.

—EDWARD T. MCMAHON

Each of us is an artist whose task it is to shape life
into some semblance of the pattern he dreams about.
The molding is not of the self alone but of shared tomorrows
and times we shall never see. So let us be about our task.
The materials are very precious and perishable.

—ARTHUR GRAHAM

CONTENTS

FOREWORD

The protection of land is an expression of faith in the future: it is a pact between generations. For more than two centuries, Americans have been creating public spaces that inspire and enrich our lives. Today, Americans of all ages, races, and backgrounds rely on these natural areas and open spaces for recreation, reflection, and relaxation or, as in the case of working forests and farms, for a way of life. These lands also provide vital ecological services such as clean air and water.

Ironically, as much as we value our special places—national parks and wildlife refuges, working farms, and urban green spaces—we do not always act consistently with these values. In recent decades, the rate of development in many parts of the nation has been breathtaking. In fact, each year we lose more than 2 million acres of land to development. Many protected areas have literally become islands of nature surrounded by a sea of development. The results are having a dramatic and adverse impact on our health and well-being as well as on the essential functioning of natural systems that support both our environment and economy.

To protect the landscapes and waterways that sustain us as a nation and define us as a people, we need a new way of looking at ourselves and the land around us. Natural areas are not simply lands that have yet to be developed. Parks are not simply beautiful places. Working landscapes are not merely sites for producing food and fiber. These open spaces form a natural tapestry that connects us to our outdoor heritage, to one another, and to the communities in which we live. Unfortunately, subdivisions, parking lots, and highways are tearing apart the very fabric that binds us together.

But great challenges often present great opportunities. To be successful we must broaden the conservation community to engage all Americans. We must reach out to new audiences that in the past have not been part of the traditional environmental movement including communities of color, recent immigrants, rural landowners, planning officials, and even developers. If we are to build a lasting network of land and water, we simply must have all hands on deck.

For its part, The Conservation Fund has been a national leader in bringing diverse groups together to find common ground and to demonstrate the powerful, and sometimes profitable, link between nature and people. *Green Infrastructure: Linking Landscapes and Communities* is a groundbreaking publication that introduces a balanced, strategic, and comprehensive approach to conservation expressed as a new concept called green infrastructure. It explains the need to implement sensible, sustainable land use plans in the states, counties, communities, and neighborhoods in which we live.

This bold vision is greater than any one organization or any one project. Collectively, we must see the broader landscape and develop conservation programs that link to one another as well as strive to connect natural lands, heritage areas, and open spaces.

Working together and using green infrastructure as our guide, we can conserve our essential resources and create a lasting, and linked, land and water legacy for present and future generations. From our towns and communities, to our states and regions, to our country as a whole, this network of natural and cultural landscapes will support our way of life and connect all Americans to their land, from sea to shining sea.

We invite you to join in partnership with us to make this vision a reality. The time to act is now and the need is ongoing.

Charles Jordan
Chairman, The Conservation Fund

Lawrence Selzer
President, The Conservation Fund

PREFACE

There is a land-use crisis in the United States. We are consuming our open space with subdivisions, strip malls, and highways and we are fragmenting natural systems so that they no longer function effectively. According to a recently released USDA Forest Service study, "every day, America loses more than 4,000 acres of open space to development; that's more than 3 acres per minute, and the rate of conversion is getting faster all the time." Landscapes that yesterday were inhabited by bears, moose, or cougars today serve as shopping centers and parking lots. Traditional routes enjoyed by long-distance hikers and horseback riders have been degraded by the noise and pollution that comes with changing land use and ownership. Lands once appreciated for their quiet beauty are being transformed into tract housing or industrial parks. Many urban areas are bursting at their seams, gobbling up the once vacant lands that surrounded them. Others are experiencing a slow trickle, growing a few houses at a time. Of course there remain rural communities that have not yet experienced the pangs of growth. But if current trends continue, it won't be long before change comes to even the most remote areas.

In all regions of the country, the rate at which we are developing forests, farms, and other open space far exceeds population growth. And the conversion of land is occurring faster than ever before. This trend is a direct result of haphazard development that results in sprawl—a development pattern that many Americans dislike. People complain that sprawl is ugly. It creates traffic jams. It undermines the character that once gave their community its charm. It gobbles up rural landscapes and cherished landmarks. It reduces opportunities for hunting, fishing, and other forms of outdoor recreation. It is an expensive land-use pattern for governments to build and maintain. But sprawl has even more devastating effects: it fragments wildlife habitats, endangers the viability of forests and farms, pollutes the air, and threatens our water supplies.

Americans have consistently supported funding to protect land for conservation and outdoor recreation. Between 1996 and 2004, voters passed 1,065 bond referenda, providing over $27 billion for conservation. The approval rate for these land conservation initiatives—1,065 of the proposed 1,376 conservation ballot measures, 77 percent—is greater than for any other type of ballot measure. Encouraged by this support, all levels of government and a diversity of nonprofits are implementing a wide range of programs to protect open space and preserve our natural resources. A myriad of nongovernmental organizations are furthering these goals by adopting and applying strategic conservation planning at the regional and community levels.

So, can we sit back and celebrate our success? Are our land conservation efforts achieving our vision and goals? Are we maximizing the resources dedicated to land conservation? Have our efforts succeeded in preserving key ecological sites and functions, in shaping and directing the patterns of growth, and in protecting forestry and farming as vital economic engines for America? We believe the answer to all of these questions is a resounding "No."

Although current policies and programs have achieved much toward protecting natural systems and processes and improving environmental quality, there remain three key challenges to today's land and water conservation efforts. First, many of today's conservation activities are haphazard: largely reactive, site specific, and narrowly focused. Second, conservation action is often undertaken in isolation from land-use planning and growth management efforts. And finally, funding for conservation efforts are cut whenever there is an economic downturn. Unlike our roads, storm water systems, schools, and other types of public infrastructure, green infrastructure—natural lands and processes—is perceived as an amenity, not as a necessity—a "nice to have" rather than a "must have."

Our haphazard, reactive approach to conservation is not working. It does not help us prioritize our needs or focus our energies on the land and resources of greatest value. We need to plan in a more proactive and comprehensive way. As Albert Einstein said, "the significant problems we face today cannot be solved by the same level of thinking that created them." Or, as the adage goes, "If you do what you've always done, you'll get what you've always gotten."

American communities of all sizes face the same challenge: How to grow without sacrificing the natural, historic, and cultural features that improve quality of life for residents and bolster the economy. Smart growth has emerged as a powerful tool to strategically direct and influence the pattern of growth and land development. But just as we need smart growth, we also need smart conservation to strategically direct our nation's conservation practices. Our conservation programs need to promote systematic thinking and integrated action related to planning, protection, and long-term management of conservation lands and other open space. We need new ways to think about and address the natural resource and environmental management problems that have plagued us for decades. To paraphrase Buckminster Fuller, we need to be architects of the future, not its victims.

Green infrastructure uses the identification, protection, and long-term management of interconnected networks of conserved lands and other open spaces that cross political boundaries and span diverse landscapes to promote strategic conservation. Furthermore, green infrastructure makes the argument that the conservation, restoration, and maintenance of functioning natural systems not only protects ecosystem values and functions, but also provides diverse recreational, social, and economic benefits to people.

Green infrastructure goes beyond traditional conservation strategies and approaches to promote and support conservation action that is undertaken in concert with development, infrastructure planning, and smart growth efforts. It provides a process to bring diverse interests together to identify shared values and goals that can be used to guide land-use decision-making. Green infrastructure provides objective and scientific rationale that enables communities to put politics aside to focus on the greater good. It encourages people to focus on the benefits of holistic land-use planning and emphasizes the congruence of environmental and economic goals. By elevating the importance of long-term funding of open space conservation and management, green infrastructure can guarantee that our plans are realistic and realizable.

We need a new approach. We need a way to involve people on all sides of the land-use issue in defining a common vision and crafting solutions to the challenges brought about by population growth. We need conservation networks across this nation and around the world that link lands for nature and people. We believe that strategic conservation through green infrastructure is the best way to achieve this new conservation vision for the twenty-first century.

Mark A. Benedict
The Conservation Fund

Edward T. McMahon
Urban Land Institute

ACKNOWLEDGMENTS

Just like green infrastructure, this book is the culmination of years of work by countless individuals. Originally conceived of as an update of existing materials developed for a course on green infrastructure first piloted by The Conservation Fund in 2001 at the U.S. Fish and Wildlife Service's National Conservation Training Center, the book expanded far beyond its initial scope to include new information on green infrastructure concepts and practices from across the United States and beyond. It is impossible for us to mention everyone who has influenced and supported us in writing the book or touched the manuscript in one way or another, but we would like to specifically acknowledge a few of the people and organizations without whom this book would never have been published.

First, we would like to acknowledge the generosity of our funders. Specifically, we extend our thanks to the USDA Forest Service and to the Surdna Foundation, which have provided funding for our work in green infrastructure and have supported strategic conservation programs throughout the country. We would also like to thank the Doris Duke Charitable Foundation's support of the Consortium on Biodiversity and Land Use, which further helped to underwrite this book.

We extend our sincere thanks to Lydia Bjornlund, who, in collaboration with the authors, wrote and rewrote much of the material in this book. A freelance writer and consultant in Oakton, Virginia, Lydia provided ongoing support from the initial concept and outline through the research, writing and editing, to the preparation of the final manuscript.

We also would like to acknowledge the many people who contributed to and/or reviewed specific chapters. Bill Jenkins of the Maryland Department of Natural Resources (currently on assignment to the Environmental Protection Agency, Region 3) and Wink Hastings of the National Park Service's Rivers, Trails, and Conservation Assistance Program prepared course materials on which parts of this book were based and provided excellent guidance during the review of various chapters. Peggy Carr and Tom Hoctor of the University of Florida, Jeff Lerner of Defenders of Wildlife, and Brad Meiklejohn and Ted Weber of The Conservation Fund all provided invaluable insights. Freelance environmental science writer Joy Drohan wrote the green infrastructure case studies on which many of the Green Infrastructure in Action descriptions are based, and freelance designer Jo Gravely and Margarita Carey of The Conservation Fund helped with graphics and other technical issues.

Thank you to Erik Meyers and Will Allen at The Conservation Fund for your support during the writing of this book; Heather Boyer, Jeff Hardwick, Shannon

O'Neill, and Cecilia González at Island Press for your guidance and skills in making this book a reality; Daniel Montero whose copyediting strengthened the manuscript; and the many people working on the green infrastructure projects included in this book for answering our questions, updating and amending information, and providing graphics so that we could tell your story. We would also like to acknowledge the work of the design team members who originally crafted the green infrastructure course that provided inspiration for and has served as the cornerstone of this book.

Finally, we wish to thank Larry Selzer, president of The Conservation Fund, for his leadership in supporting strategic conservation efforts throughout America, and Pat Noonan, founder and former president of The Conservation Fund, for his inspiration and long-term support of our work. The ongoing commitment of The Conservation Fund and other organizations to green infrastructure is helping communities large and small fulfill the promise of strategic conservation.

chapter one

Why Green Infrastructure?

Green infrastructure is a term that is appearing more and more frequently in land conservation and land development discussions across the United States and the world. The term, however, means different things depending on the context in which it is used: for some it refers to trees that provide ecological benefits in urban areas; for others it refers to engineered structures (such as storm water management or water treatment facilities) that are designed to be environmentally friendly.

Our definition of green infrastructure is loftier and broader. We define it as an interconnected network of natural areas and other open spaces that conserves natural ecosystem values and functions, sustains clean air and water, and provides a wide array of benefits to people and wildlife. Used in this context, green infrastructure is the ecological framework for environmental, social, and economic health—in short, our natural life-support system.

Green infrastructure challenges popular perceptions about green-space planning and protection. To many people, open space is simply land that is not yet developed, and green space refers to isolated parks, recreation sites, or natural areas. *Webster's Dictionary* defines "infrastructure" as "the substructure or underlying foundation on which the continuance and growth of a community or state depends." Green infrastructure emphasizes the importance of open and green space

Figure 1.1
Green infrastructure provides an opportunity to protect our nation's valuable lands and natural beauty. The John Heinz National Wildlife Refuge is a welcome respite from urban life for Philadelphians. Credit: John and Karen Hollingsworth, U.S. Fish and Wildlife Service.

as parts of interconnected systems that are protected and managed for the ecological benefits they provide. While green space is often viewed as something that is *nice* to have, green infrastructure implies something that we *must* have. Protecting and restoring our natural life-support system is a necessity, not an amenity. While green space is often viewed as self-sustaining, green infrastructure implies that green space and natural systems must be actively protected, managed, and in some cases restored.

Green infrastructure differs from conventional approaches to land conservation and natural resources protection because it looks at conservation in concert with land development and man-made infrastructure planning. Other conservation methods typically are undertaken in isolation from—or even in opposition to—development, but green infrastructure provides a framework for conservation and development that acknowledges the need for providing places for people to live, work, shop, and enjoy nature. Green infrastructure helps communities identify and prioritize conservation opportunities and plan development in ways that optimize the use of land to meet the needs of people and nature.

WHAT IS GREEN INFRASTRUCTURE?

Used as a noun, green infrastructure refers to an interconnected green space network (including natural areas and features, public and private conservation lands, working lands with conservation values, and other protected open spaces) that is planned and managed for its natural resource values and for the associated benefits it confers to human populations. Used as an adjective, green infrastructure describes a process that promotes a systematic and strategic approach to land conservation at the national, state, regional, and local scales, encouraging land-use planning and practices that are good for nature and for people.

Taking a green infrastructure approach provides benefits both as a concept and as a process. As a concept, the planning and management of a green infrastructure network can guide the creation of a system of open space hubs and links that support conservation and associated outdoor recreational and other human values, connect existing and future green space resources, and "fill in" gaps. As a process, the approach provides a mechanism for diverse interests to come together to identify priority lands for protection. Green infrastructure provides a framework that can be used to guide future growth and future land development and land conservation decisions to accommodate population growth and protect and preserve community assets and natural resources. Taking a green infrastructure approach facilitates systematic and strategic conservation activities, adds value to project results, and provides predictability and certainty for both conservationists and developers. In areas anticipating growth, a green infrastructure plan can pre-identify key lands for future

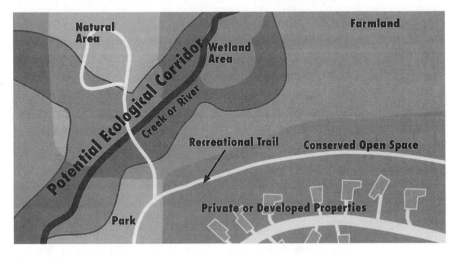

Figure 1.2
By focusing on the lands to be conserved as well as developed, green infrastructure helps communities plan for land conservation and land development in a way that optimizes land use to meet the needs of nature and people. Credit: Conservation Resource Alliance, Michigan.

Table 1.1

Advances in the History of American Infrastructure

Era	Growth Issue	Infrastructure Solution
Mid–Late 1800s	Public health and welfare	Sanitation, hospitals, parks, schools
	Communication	Telegraph
	Industrialization	Planned communities, company towns
	Energy	Coal, oil, gas, electricity
	Transportation	Canals, railways
Early 1900s	Automobiles	Roads
	Food production (Dust Bowl)	Crop rotation, agricultural practices
	Communication	Radio, telephone
Mid-1900s	Energy	Hydro and nuclear power
	Nuisances	Community zoning and planning
	Pollution	Air/water/sewage treatment
	Transportation	Interstate system, airports
	Mass communication	Television
Late 1900s	Garbage	Recycling
	Traffic congestion	Mass transit, alternative transportation
	Flooding	Storm water management, detention
	Information management	Computers/Internet
2000+	Sprawl, globalization	Sound land use, smart growth
	Sustainability	Green infrastructure

Source: Karen S. Williamson, *Growing with Green Infrastructure*, Heritage Conservancy, 2003, 1.

conservation and restoration efforts and help shape the pattern and location of future growth.

Green infrastructure uses planning, design, and implementation approaches similar to those used for roads, water management systems, and other community support facilities. The approach can be applied at multiple scales (e.g., across landscapes, watersheds, regions, jurisdictions) and can help move communities beyond jurisdictional and political boundaries.

Green infrastructure also provides a strong rationale for funding green space conservation and management. Just as roads, sewer systems, hospitals, and other aspects of the built or gray infrastructure provide for the critical needs of communities, green infrastructure is integral to a community's health and viability. Like gray infrastructure, green infrastructure has evolved to meet specific needs that have resulted from growth (see Table 1.1).

The Need for a New Approach
to Conservation and Development

The first European explorers who saw the New World wrote poetically about its vast wilderness. Land was plentiful; the challenge was to tame it, to make way for towns, roads, and farms. Americans today experience a far different landscape from that seen by these explorers. Wilderness and natural areas are no longer plentiful; in fact, they have become scarce. Less than 10 percent of the land in the United States remains in a wild state, and only 4 percent has been set aside in nature reserves.[1]

While previous generations of Americans had the foresight to protect some of America's most beautiful and vital landscapes, our public lands have proven to be inadequate to meet the needs of both people and wildlife. The conditions that existed when the National Park Service and other resource agencies were founded have changed dramatically, but the assumptions that guide our land conservation decisions remain stuck in the past. The rural lands that once surrounded public lands are fast disappearing. National and state parks and wildlife refuges are becoming ecological islands in an increasingly fragmented landscape. Population growth and development in communities that serve as gateways to public lands are creating problems for many pristine and protected lands. Many public lands lack the capacity to handle the increasing number of visitors seeking to connect with nature. Population growth also means more cars, which means more roads, which in turn produces more air pollution, water pollution, and noise. Road construction often means the loss of natural areas, the obstruction of critical wildlife migration routes, and the erosion of historic and natural landscapes.

Growth and Development

In the last fifty years, the amount of urban land in the United States quadrupled. Between 1982 and 2001, about 34 million acres—an area the size of Illinois—were converted to developed uses (see Table 1.2). Between 1997 and 2001, almost 9 million acres were developed, of which 46 percent had been forestland, 20 percent cropland, and 16 percent pasture (see Table 1.3). Much that has been developed for houses, stores, offices, and parking lots was once productive working lands—the farms and forests on the outskirts of America's cities, towns, and suburbs. From 1982 to 1997, an average of 680,000 acres per year of nonfederal forest land, most of which is private, were converted to developed uses, but the rate of conversion "jumped to 1 million acres per year during the last five years of this period" and is expected to continue to increase exponentially in many parts of the country.[2] Because farmland is relatively flat and has rich soils for building—as well as plowing—it is particularly at risk for development. Between 1992 and

2001, the United States witnessed the loss of more than 6 million acres of prime farmland,[3] which accounts for approximately 28 percent of the land developed during this time.[4]

Today, almost 2 million acres of farmland and 500,000 acres of private forestland is lost to development each year.[5] The American Farmland Trust warns that America is losing over seventy-four acres of prime farmland every hour of every day and that 86 percent of America's fruit and vegetables and 63 percent of our dairy products come from farmland that is directly in the path of development.[6] Moreover, the USDA indicates that 44.2 million acres—over 11 percent of our nation's private forestland—may be converted to housing by 2030. Private forests provide over 90 percent of the nation's timber harvests and nearly 30 percent of our freshwater resources; they are critical to water quality and to the survival of many fish and wildlife resources. The conversion of private forestland may be particularly significant in the Southeast, considered the "wood basket" of the United States and an area rich in biodiversity.[7]

Perhaps more alarming than the total number of acres being developed is the escalating rate of land consumption. Between 1992 and 1997, land was converted at a rate of 2.2 million acres per year—a rate that is more than 1.5 times the rate of the previous ten-year period.[8] Today's rates are estimated to be even higher.

The population of the United States is growing. Don't we need houses and commercial areas to support this population growth? Yes. But the rate of open space conversion exceeds population growth. From 1982 to 1997, the nation experienced a 47 percent increase in urbanized land, despite the fact that population grew only 17 percent (see Table 1.4). The situation is often most evident in urban areas. Between 1960 and 1990 populations of metropolitan areas grew by 50 percent, while developed land area increased by 100 percent. From 1970 to 1990, Cook County and the five other counties closest to Chicago experienced a 35 percent increase in developed land, but population increased by only 4 percent. From 1975 to 1995, the population of the New York City metropolitan area increased 8 percent while its urban area increased by 65 percent; and the Cleveland metropolitan area increased 33 percent while it experienced an 11 percent *decrease* in its population.[9]

Census 2000 figures show the average size of the nation's one hundred most populated cities is about 168 square miles, more than triple the size in 1950. Much of this increase has come as cities have annexed the farms and open space around them to convert to housing developments and strip shopping centers.[10] But rapid development—and the sprawl associated with it—is not only an urban problem. Sixty percent of new homes built from 1994 to 1997 were built in communities of less than forty thousand people.[11] In recent years, rural counties with federally designated wilderness areas grew six times faster than counties without such areas.[12]

In and of itself, such urbanization is not a problem. Many poor communities benefit from the renewal and economic recovery made possible by growth. When land

Table 1.2

Developed Land (in millions of acres)

Year	Large urban and built-up areas	Small built-up areas	Rural transportation land	Total developed land
1982	46.9	4.7	21.2	72.8
1987	52.6	5.1	21.3	79.0
1992	59.6	5.4	21.5	86.5
1997	69.8	6.1	21.6	97.5
2001	77.6	6.7	22.0	106.3

Source: Reprinted from 2001 Annual National Resources Inventory: Urbanization and Development of Rural Land (July 2003).

Table 1.3

Sources of Newly Developed Land (in thousands of acres)

Year	Cropland	Pastureland	Rangeland	Forest land	All other land uses	Total
1982–1992 (10 years)	3,900	2,270	1,950	5,600	360	14,080
1992–1997 (5 years)	2,880	1,930	1,270	4,740	470	11,290
1997–2001 (4 years)	1,830	1,470	1,210	4,150	280	8,940

Source: Reprinted from 2001 Annual National Resources Inventory: Urbanization and Development of Rural Land (July 2003).

Table 1.4

Population Growth and Land Development, 1982–1997

U.S. region	Change in population	Change in urbanized land
Midwest	7.06%	32.23%
Northeast	6.91%	39.10%
South	22.23%	59.61%
West	17.02%	48.94%
Total U.S.	17.02%	47.14%

Source: William Fulton, Rolf Pendall, Mai Nguyen, and Alicia Harrison, *Who Sprawls Most? How Growth Patterns Differ Across the U.S.*, The Brookings Institution, Survey Series, July 2001, www.brook.edu/es/urban/publications.

Figure 1.3
All across America farmland is being converted to housing developments at an
increasingly rapid (and often alarming) rate. Credit: Lynn Betts, USDA Natural
Resources Conservation Service.

is developed without adequate planning, however, governments find themselves
paying for infrastructure improvements needed to support far-flung development
and residents suddenly discern the loss of once-cherished natural resources and rural
landscapes.

In part, this rapid consumption of land is the result of a growing demand
for ever-larger lots. As the footprint of development increases, more land is converted. Almost 90 percent of the land converted for single-family homes from
1993 to 1997 was made into lots of one acre or larger, purchased by just over 33
percent of new homebuyers; since 1994, house lots of ten acres or larger have
accounted for 55 percent of the land developed.[13] The nation's largest and fastest
growing metropolitan areas risk total eradication of their natural areas—except
perhaps those owned by government.

All of these factors contribute to the sprawl that plagues America's suburbs and
threatens our rural areas. Without clear plans to check the natural proclivity to sit-
uate residential neighborhoods and commercial uses on land that is less expensive—
and farther and farther from existing communities—we will continue to threaten
plant and animal communities and natural ecological functions and processes.

The Environmental, Social, and Economic Impacts of Sprawl

As natural areas give way to haphazard development, habitat diversity diminishes, resulting in a decline both in the number of species and the number of individuals in those species that survive. The development of wetlands, riparian areas, and other native ecosystems also reduces their capacity to perform their natural functions—control floods, trap sediment, and filter out toxins and excess nutrients. Today, 40 to 50 percent or more of the total land in urban areas is covered by impervious surfaces—roads, parking lots, and buildings. This dramatically increases the rate and volume of storm water runoff and reduces nature's ability to clean our water and cool our air. A significant increase in impervious land cover and the loss of forestland increases the risk of flooding. Worse yet, land clearing and grading add chemicals, sediments, and other substances that degrade water quality. A 2002 study published in *Science* concludes that the destruction of habitat costs the world the equivalent of about $250 billion each year. The research team further estimates that a network of global nature reserves would provide an annual net benefit of over $4.4 trillion.[14]

In addition, as we convert open land, we fragment it into smaller and more isolated patches. Fragmentation significantly affects landscapes in many critical ways, including resource availability, environmental degradation, and recreational and aesthetic quality. Among the negative effects of fragmentation is the reduction in the amount of habitat of sufficient size to sustain plant and animal species. Moreover, as the distance between undisturbed habitat patches increases, wildlife populations become isolated. This interferes with the ability of animals to move from one habitat to another, decreasing diversity among species and, for some, jeopardizing their survival.

The development and fragmentation of green space puts at risk already endangered plant and animal species. Ninety-five percent of species listed under the federal Endangered Species Act are threatened by habitat loss, fragmentation, or other forms of alteration.[15] Sprawl is the primary cause of habitat loss and fragmentation in California, where 188 of 286 imperiled or endangered species are in areas vulnerable to development.[16] Here, and elsewhere, endangered plants and animals are not confined to remote wilderness areas; their habitat is often intertwined with human settlements. In fact, three-fifths of the nation's rarest and most imperiled species are found within designated metropolitan areas; the thirty-five fastest growing large metropolitan areas are home to nearly one third (29 percent) of these species. A total of 287 imperiled species are found in thirty-seven counties that were expected to lose half or more of their nonfederal open space between 2000 and 2025. The Tampa-St. Petersburg-Clearwater metropolitan area, for example, which is home to twenty-six imperiled species, is expected to lose 40 percent of its remaining natural lands by 2025.[17]

The effects of development on animals and our natural environment extend beyond jurisdictional boundaries; development that occurs in one jurisdiction can have a profound impact on the habitat and wildlife in another. In the Florida Everglades, for example, development has had a profound effect on the entire ecosystem. The Everglades National Park and the Big Cypress National Preserve protect a significant portion of the south Florida peninsula, but the alteration of surface water flows and related natural fire and other landscape processes in upstream areas has had a drastic impact on birds and other wildlife in protected areas downstream.

Many other related negative effects of sprawl are associated with an increased reliance of people on the automobile. Communities along our nation's highways and roadways are often inaccessible by public transportation systems. As commuters travel greater distances to work, their automobiles produce more carbon dioxide and other toxic gasses. These greenhouse gasses block the sun's radiant energy from escaping back into space, which raises the temperature here on earth. In the past twenty-five years, the earth's average temperature has risen about one degree and the temperature of the Pacific Ocean has risen three degrees. Related effects include urban heat islands, ozone depletion, and urban dust plumes.

There are also social and economic repercussions of sprawling development. When homes and businesses are spread farther apart, it costs more to provide them with utility and government services. A study by the Center for Urban Studies at Rutgers University reports a region's capital costs over a twenty-year period (for roads, schools, and water and sewer facilities) attributable to sprawl development patterns to be in the billions, with additional annual operating and maintenance

Figure 1.4
Each year, more and more of our nation's historic lands are lost to sprawl. Preserving our history requires protecting not only important historical sites but also the lands that surround them. Credit: Ed McMahon.

costs of $400 million. Some suburban communities have found that the inefficient infrastructure created by years of sprawling development cannot be supported at a tax level that citizens are willing to pay.

Finally, changes in the landscape are disruptive to a person's sense of history, continuity, and stability. The places that are dearest to our hearts are often among those destined for development. According to the Civil War Preservation Trust, an acre of battlefield land disappears beneath asphalt or concrete every ten minutes. Each year sees further erosion of other historic resources through demolition, neglect, increasing sprawl, highway construction, inefficient use of existing infrastructure, and development occurring in areas increasingly distant from urban centers.

STRATEGIC CONSERVATION THROUGH GREEN INFRASTRUCTURE

The American public recognizes the accelerated consumption of land and its associated ecological and social consequences as a leading land-use issue. In a February 2000 poll by the Pew Center for Civic Journalism, Americans rated sprawl and traffic congestion equal to crime and violence as the top problems facing communities. Asked to name "the most important problem facing the community where you live," 18 percent of respondents across the United States cited sprawl and traffic as their top concern—the same percentage as those citing crime. In suburban communities, sprawl outranked crime and other problems; over 26 percent of respondents said it was their community's most pressing problem.[18]

In response to the increasing development of land, many communities are attempting to conserve natural resources and influence future growth by developing new programs and strategies. *Smart growth* has become a popular tool for influencing the pattern of growth and land development. Smart growth has been defined as development that is economically sound, environmentally friendly, and supportive of healthy communities—growth that enhances quality of life. The sprawl that results from our growing dependence on the automobile, the haphazard spread of strip malls, and the proliferation of nondescript subdivisions are the opposite of smart growth. Smart growth advocates emphasize that we can have development that is more attractive, more efficient, more affordable, and more environmentally sensitive. State and local governments are beginning to use smart growth as a unifying concept for growth and development. In 1997, for example, the state of Maryland launched a smart growth initiative with these goals in mind. Maryland's Smart Growth policy was designed to redirect the state's financial resources to communities and areas approved for growth while taking a more aggressive and strategic approach to preserving remaining open space. The state's GreenPrint program, which emerged from this initiative, aims to identify and protect the state's most ecologically sensitive lands through a comprehensive statewide green infrastructure assessment. Several other states and communities have used urban growth boundaries and other legislation to achieve smart growth goals. (These and other regulatory tools are discussed in chapter 6.)

Green Infrastructure: Smart Conservation for the Twenty-first Century

Just as we need smart growth to address haphazard development, we also need *smart conservation* to address haphazard conservation. Land conservation is too often piecemeal, site specific, and narrowly focused. Conservation efforts are seldom coordinated with one another or integrated into land-use planning or growth-management efforts. Smart conservation overcomes these obstacles.

Just as smart growth focuses holistically, strategically, and systematically on the development needs of a community, smart conservation focuses holistically, strategically, and systematically on conservation needs. Smart conservation promotes large-scale thinking and integrated action related to the planning, protection, and long-term management of conservation and other open space lands.

Green infrastructure capitalizes on what is best about smart growth and smart conservation strategies. It promotes a strategic approach to land and water conservation that is systematic and well integrated. Green infrastructure also addresses a community's development needs. Simply put, some places are better for development than others. The first principle of better development is determining where not to develop. Green infrastructure can help identify these areas. Mapping natural systems, for example, can help communities to direct development away from floodplains, reducing the cost of flood mitigation and control, as well as the vulnerability of human settlements to flood damage. It is sometimes less expensive—and more effective—to move entire communities away from a floodplain than to build levees and other structures to contain the floodwaters. Of course, the best solution of all is to never build on the floodplain in the first place—and green infrastructure can help to make this happen.

What Does Green Infrastructure Look Like?

Green infrastructure encompasses a wide variety of natural and restored native ecosystems and landscape features, including conserved natural areas such as wetlands, woodlands, waterways, and wildlife habitat; public and private conservation lands such as national and state parks, nature preserves, wildlife corridors, and wilderness areas; working lands of conservation value such as forests, farms, and ranches; and other protected open spaces such as parks, viewsheds, and greenways.

A green infrastructure network connects these ecosystems and landscapes in a system of *hubs*, *links*, and *sites*. Hubs anchor green infrastructure networks and provide space for native plants and animal communities, as well as an origin or destination for wildlife, people, and ecological processes moving through the system. Hubs come in all shapes and sizes, including large reserves and protected areas, such as national wildlife refuges or state parks; large publicly owned lands, including national and state forests, which are managed for resource extraction (e.g., mining or timber) as well as natural and recreational values; private working lands, including farmland, forests, and ranch lands; regional parks and reserves; and community parks and green spaces where natural features and processes are protected and/or restored.

Links are the connections that tie the system together. These connections are critical to maintaining vital ecological processes and the health and biodiversity of wildlife populations. Landscape linkages, which are especially long and wide links, connect existing parks, preserves, or natural areas and provide sufficient space for native plants and animals to flourish while serving as corridors connecting ecosystems and landscapes. Landscape linkages may also provide space for the protection of historic sites and opportunities for recreational use. Links and conservation corridors, such as river and stream floodplains, serve as biological conduits for wildlife and may also provide opportunities for outdoor recreation, while greenways and greenbelts

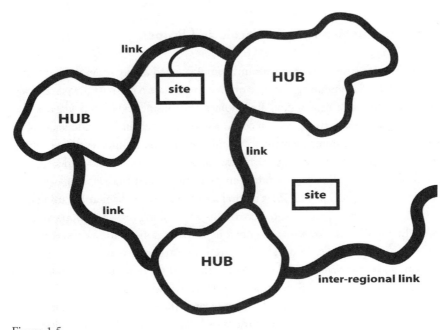

Figure 1.5
A green infrastructure network connects ecosystems and landscapes in a system of hubs, links, and sites. Credit: Maryland Department of Natural Resources.

create a framework for development, preserve native ecosystems and/or farms or ranches, and often provide a place for hiking, biking, or simply enjoying nature.

Green infrastructure networks also include sites. Sites are smaller than hubs and may not be attached to larger, interconnected community and regional conservation systems, but like the other components of a green infrastructure network, they can contribute important ecological and social values, such as protecting wildlife habitat and providing space for nature-based recreation and relaxation.

Protecting natural systems and biodiversity is an important goal of green infrastructure, but green infrastructure networks can include a wide diversity of elements that may not be related directly to this goal. Greenways and trails that provide recreational and health values for people; historical, cultural, and archeological sites that are valued community resources; and farms, orchards, ranches, and forests that provide people with important economic yields can also be elements of a green infrastructure network.

It is important to realize that hubs, links, and sites vary in size, function, and ownership. Some are public conservation lands; others are private working lands. Moreover, the natural systems protected by a green infrastructure network are not all green. Rivers and streams are critical elements of almost any green infrastructure system. The deserts of the American Southwest and snowy mountain ranges of Alaska also provide all the critical functions of green infrastructure hubs and corridors, although one would be hard-pressed to find many "green" elements within them.

Green Infrastructure at Any Scale and Scope

The green infrastructure approach can be implemented at any scale: the individual parcel, the local community, the state or even multi-state region. At the parcel scale, green infrastructure means designing homes and businesses around green space. Conservation developments that incorporate green space and include walking or nature trails are becoming increasingly popular. At the community level, green infrastructure could mean creating greenways to link existing public parks. At the statewide or regional level, it could mean protecting broad landscape linkages that connect forests, prairies, and other natural areas and provide habitat for animals.

Creating a green infrastructure network means looking for where opportunities exist. In some areas, there may be obvious lands of conservation value that can serve as hubs and links. In others, the green infrastructure network may need to rely on lands that were once—or are still—reserved for other uses. In addition to the "ecologically based" green infrastructure hubs and links mentioned above, a green infrastructure network could include large tracts of public land, including land on military installations; large tracts of forested land, fallow land, desert, or other open land; riparian lands, including rivers, streams, creek corridors, and floodplains; fragile lands, including steep slopes, coastal areas, wetlands, and

Box 1.1

What Green Infrastructure Is Not

- **A program.** Green infrastructure is a philosophy or organizational strategy that provides a framework for planning conservation and development.
- **A panacea.** Green infrastructure cannot be everything to everyone. Like any planning effort, green infrastructure requires tradeoffs among priorities to be made.
- **A short-term solution.** The planning, design, and management of green infrastructure require a long-term commitment.
- **An isolated effort.** Green infrastructure requires the coordination of many people.
- **A government program.** Although often led by state, regional, or local government, green infrastructure relies on all sectors of the community, including private landowners.
- **Smart growth, no growth, or antidevelopment.** Used in conjunction with other planning processes, green infrastructure may be used to guide the pattern of growth, but it does not dictate whether growth will occur. Unlike other conservation approaches, green infrastructure provides for development and other changes in land use.
- **Elitist.** All people within a community or region benefit from green infrastructure planning and implementation.
- **A system of greenways.** Greenways may be an important component of green infrastructure, but green infrastructure has broader ecological goals.
- **Schoolyards, playgrounds, or other parcels of green space.** These may be part of a green infrastructure initiative, but they may not share the ecological or environmental goals of green infrastructure.

hydric soils; working lands, including lands used for agriculture, forestry, hunt clubs, and preserves; recreation lands, such as parks, golf courses, and hiking or walking trails; private lands, including corporate/industrial properties, utility company rights-of-way, and railroad corridors; abandoned or underutilized sites, including brownfields; or transportation corridors.

Appropriate green infrastructure strategies depend on the setting in which green infrastructure takes place. In rural areas, designing a green infrastructure network can help the community protect its most ecologically valuable land while directing development toward areas best suited for human use and nature-based recreation. In an urban setting, green infrastructure might include backyard habitat, street trees, or setting aside buffers along rivers and streams that protect against flooding. Near national parks and wildlife refuges, it might mean encouraging compatible adjacent land uses such as agriculture or forestry and seeking out connections to conservation lands. In all cases, green infrastructure means looking at the landscape in relation to the many uses it could serve—for nature and people—and determining which use makes the most sense.

   Green infrastructure is not a new concept. It has its origins in two fundamental initiatives: (1) protecting and linking parks and other green spaces for the benefit of people (recreation, health, aesthetics, and urban design), and (2) preserving and linking natural areas to benefit biodiversity and counter habitat fragmentation (protecting native plants, animals, natural processes, and ecosystems). Understanding the origins of the green infrastructure movement can help people understand the principles behind designing and implementing green infrastructure networks and engage others in working together toward more strategic conservation.

GREEN INFRASTRUCTURE IN ACTION: MARYLAND GREENWAYS AND THE GREEN INFRASTRUCTURE ASSESSMENT

Like many green infrastructure initiatives, the groundbreaking work in Maryland began with an emphasis on greenways. In 1991 Governor William Donald Schaefer signed an executive order formally establishing the Maryland Greenways Commission as part of the effort to address the rapid growth occurring in the state and the resulting disappearance of woods, marshes, and meadows that served as critical habitats. The commission was charged with creating a statewide network of greenways that would provide natural pathways for wildlife movement and, where compatible, trails for recreation and transportation alternatives for the state's residents. The greenways network was intended not only to provide trails from one place to another, but also to provide environmental benefits by buffering waterways and enhancing the protection of the Chesapeake Bay.

   Maryland's Greenways Program proved popular, but its focus on greenways and trails soon overshadowed its ecological goals. Several natural resource proponents, including the Maryland Department of Natural Resources (MD-DNR), advocated a more strategic and comprehensive approach to land conservation. To address these concerns, the state embarked in the mid-1990s on an ambitious effort to map and prioritize its ecological lands. A statewide green infrastructure assessment was an integral part of this effort.

   To complete the green infrastructure assessment, MD-DNR, in conjunction with the Maryland Greenways Commission and the Baltimore County Department of Environmental Protection and Resource Management, developed a sophisticated modeling program based on geographic information system (GIS)

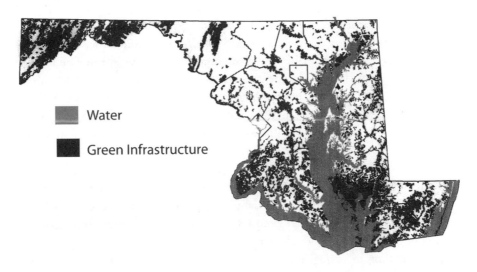

Water

Green Infrastructure

Figure 1.6
The results of Maryland's statewide Green Infrastructure Assessment. Credit: Maryland Department of Natural Resources.

tools. Using data layers of land cover, wetlands, sensitive species, roads, streams, terrestrial and aquatic conditions, floodplains, soils, and development pressure, MD-DNR identified a network of hubs and corridors that contained the most ecologically critical remaining undeveloped lands in the state. Much of the corridor system consists of protected river valleys and riparian corridors, which Maryland has been protecting since the early twentieth century.

The green infrastructure assessment provides a powerful tool for identifying and prioritizing lands that should be targeted for acquisition, protection, and/or restoration. MD-DNR staff has used GIS data sets to identify priority areas for restoration—those places where significant ecological benefit will result from limited investment because the land is connected to or part of the green infrastructure network. The idea is to marry restoration priorities with the green infrastructure assessment to fill in the gaps in the network.

"It's a fundamental shift in thinking . . .
to get governments to regard green infrastructure
as they do other infrastructure investment."

JOHN GRIFFIN
FORMER MARYLAND SECRETARY OF NATURAL RESOURCES

In May 2001, the state of Maryland created GreenPrint, a program designed to protect the state's most valuable ecological lands—the 2 million acres of green infrastructure lands identified in the green infrastructure assessment. The results of the green infrastructure assessment also helped to focus some of the state's other land conservation programs and funding, including Program Open Space and the Rural Legacy Program. Between 1999 and 2002, 88,000 acres were protected in accordance with green infrastructure assessment information. About one-third of that land was protected with GreenPrint funding, which has been targeted mostly toward network hubs.

When GreenPrint was established, it was expected to boost the state's land conservation capacity by about ten thousand acres per year for the next five years— focused on protecting the state's most valuable ecological lands. Unfortunately, state budget problems interfered with these desired outcomes, leaving state officials scrambling to leverage other resources and reach out to find new resources and engage other partners. Some experts believe that Maryland's lack of funding support for the implementation of its green infrastructure assessment may lie in the fact that citizens were not actively engaged at the outset of the program. Citizens who perceive the green infrastructure program as a state government-run initiative with little relation to community needs may lack the impetus to ensure that it survives budget shortfalls and cutbacks. The state is seeking to rectify this situation and plans to work with citizens, land trusts, and conservation groups to implement protection and restoration activities.

Local and Regional Efforts Based on Maryland's Model

The statewide green infrastructure effort has spawned local initiatives in Maryland, particularly in communities facing rapid growth and development pressure. County governments and local land trusts are using the state's green infrastructure methodology to identify and prioritize conservation lands. In Queen Anne's County, a rapidly developing yet still rural county, the commissioners recently passed a resolution of support for incorporating green infrastructure into the planning decisions of all communities. Talbot County, a largely rural county located on Maryland's Eastern Shore of the Chesapeake Bay, engaged The Conservation Fund to produce a county-scale green infrastructure plan identifying key areas and methods for protection and incorporated a green infrastructure element into its comprehensive plan. Prince George's County is among the many other counties in Maryland that are building on the statewide green infrastructure assessment to develop their own local green infrastructure plans.

Anne Arundel County was the first county in the state to base its officially adopted greenways plan on the concept of green infrastructure and the results of the statewide green infrastructure assessment. The county adapted many of the procedures developed by the state to accommodate its unique goals and needs. For example, the county set the minimum threshold size for hubs at 50 acres, rather than the 250 acres used in the statewide assessment. The county's parks and recreation department staff diligently engaged the public to get feedback on the plan and to educate citizens about conservation ecology. The county created a Web site with information about the plan and the analysis process, a questionnaire, newsletters, and an e-mail address to provide feedback. Radio, cable TV, and newspaper coverage further educated citizens about the plan, and the county held public meetings, which featured large-scale maps on which people could identify the green infrastructure elements for their area of the state.

The public response to Anne Arundel County's green infrastructure plan, which the county officially adopted in 2002, has been overwhelmingly favorable. A coalition of private land trusts in the county agreed to use the plan to set their priorities for land protection. Anne Arundel County has also received several hundred acres of donated land in response to these efforts.

Several nonprofit organizations are also building on the state's work. Like many other private land trusts, Catoctin Land Trust, which was formed in 2000 to protect land in and near the Catoctin Mountains in western Maryland, lacked both the expertise to manipulate GIS data and the funds to purchase expensive GIS-capable computers and software. To compensate, the Catoctin Land Trust worked with staff of The Conservation Fund and MD-DNR to create the Catoctin Mountain Explorer, a GIS-based tool that does not require GIS capability. The Explorer allows the land trust to work with data at any scale down to the individual parcel level and to highlight those characteristics of greatest interest. The trust has used the Explorer to identify the most strategic green infrastructure lands for riparian forest restoration in the Catoctin area and to determine which lands are in the viewshed of a highway that cuts through the Catoctin Mountains, enabling the trust not only to target lands for protection and restoration, but to identify potential funding sources as well.

Maryland's green infrastructure approach also has been used on the Delmarva Peninsula, an effort that has been undertaken in cooperation with the states of Delaware and Virginia. The Delmarva Conservation Corridor project is focused on sustaining a network of working lands and protecting the rural character and biodiversity of the Peninsula. A team consisting of staff from MD-DNR, the U.S. Fish and Wildlife Service, Delaware's natural resources department, and regional planners in Virginia adapted the existing green infrastructure methodology to create a hub and corridor network model that crosses the peninsula's jurisdictional boundaries. The partners are currently engaged in planning how to make the vision a reality by protecting the priority lands that have been identified in the model.

Maryland's green infrastructure work has dovetailed with efforts to protect and preserve the 64,000-square-mile Chesapeake Bay Watershed. In the 1980s,

Maryland joined Virginia, Pennsylvania, the District of Columbia, the Chesapeake Bay Commission, and the U.S. Environmental Protection Agency in a compact to protect and restore the bay's ecosystem. The Chesapeake 2000 Agreement committed these states to permanently protect from development 20 percent of the lands in the watershed by 2010. The agreement also committed the partners to "complete an assessment of the Bay's resource lands including forests and farms, emphasizing their role in the protection of water quality and critical habitats, as well as cultural and economic viability." The resource lands assessment was intended to identify the forests, farms, and wetlands that have the highest values related to water quality, habitat, economy, and culture; are most vulnerable to loss; and based on this information are of the highest priority to preserve. The resource lands assessment task force modeled the ecological component of this assessment after the approach used for the state of Maryland and the Delmarva Peninsula and has used the methodology to identify a network of hubs and corridors for the watershed.

Finally, MD-DNR has expanded on its green infrastructure assessment to create a Strategic Forest Lands Assessment. MD-DNR adapted the GIS-based approach used for the statewide green infrastructure assessment to take a more comprehensive look at forests by examining all forestlands of the state (not just those within the green infrastructure network) and assessing these lands for their long-term economic potential as well as their ecological value. To identify forest areas of high ecological value, a GIS-based computer model was developed that considers both the regional and local ecological significance of the forest. Socioeconomic and policy factors were taken into account to assess the economic values of the forestlands, and similar factors were used to evaluate their vulnerability to development.

The resulting identification of priority forestlands can be used to establish forest conservation priorities in the state and to align geographically conservation strategies with high ecological and economic resource values and high or moderate vulnerability to development. The result is a more efficient application of the tools and limited resources available to influence forest conservation and management.

The Advantages of Green Infrastructure

Maryland's groundbreaking work in developing a GIS-based model and tools for assessing the relative ecological—and economic—value of lands and their vulnerability to development has furthered the science and practice of strategic conservation through green infrastructure and has inspired similar efforts in a number of other states and regions in and beyond the United States.

The results in Maryland prove that the ability to represent visually the interrelationship of lands in the green infrastructure network is critical to establishing conservation priorities. Already, the map of green infrastructure lands has helped finalize funding commitments for some large land purchases in the state of Maryland. The biggest one-seller land protection transaction in the state—the 1999 Chesapeake Forest Products property acquisition—protected 58,000 acres of mostly high-value forestland on the Lower Delmarva Peninsula. The land, which consisted of about 460 different parcels, was bought with the assistance of private foundations. Staff credits the green infrastructure assessment with the success: being able to show how the properties fit together as part of the green infrastructure network helped to convince funders of the land's importance and to overcome obstacles and complications in the deal.

   • *For more information about the Maryland Greenways and the Green Infrastructure Assessment, see www.dnr.state.md.us/greenways/greenprint/.*

Notes

   1. Edward O. Wilson, in his introduction to Richard T. T. Forman, *Land Mosaics: The Ecology of Landscapes and Regions* (Cambridge: Cambridge University Press, 1995), quoted in Funders' Network for Smart Growth and Livable Communities, *Translation Paper #10: Biodiversity and Smart Growth*, October 2002. Translation papers can be downloaded from www.fundersnetwork.org.

   2. Susan M. Stein, et al., *Forests on the Edge: Housing Development on America's Private Forests*, USDA Forest Service, Pacific Northwest Research Station, General Technical Report PNW-GTR-636, May 2005.

   3. As defined by the U.S. Department of Agriculture, prime farmland has the best combination of physical and chemical characteristics for producing food, feed, forage, fiber, and oilseed crops and is available for these uses. See http://soils.usda.gov/technical/handbook/contents/part622.html.

   4. USDA Natural Resources Conservation Service, *2001 Annual National Resources Inventory*. See www.nrcs.usda.gov/technical/NRI.

   5. American Farmland Trust, *Farming on the Edge: Sprawling Development Threatens America's Best Farmland*, 2001. See www.farmland.org/farmingontheedge.

   6. Ibid.

   7. Susan M. Stein, et al., *Forests on the Edge.*

   8. USDA Natural Resources Conservation Service, *2001 Annual National Resources Inventory*. See www.nrcs.usda.gov/technical/NRI.

   9. William Fulton, Rolf Pendall, Mai Nguyen, and Alicia Harrison, *Who Sprawls Most? How Growth Patterns Differ across the U.S.*, The Brookings Institution, Survey Series, July 2001. See www.brook.edu/es/urban/publications.

   10. Genaro C. Armas, "Cities Are Filling Out Faster Than Up," *Seattle Times* (September 28, 2002).

   11. American Housing Survey, 1997, conducted by the Census Bureau and the Department of Housing and Urban Development, see www.census.gov/prod/99pubs/h150-97.pdf. See also American Farmland Trust, www.keepamericagrowing.org.

12. The President's Council on Sustainable Development, *Towards a Sustainable America: Advancing Prosperity, Opportunity, and a Healthy Environment for the 21st Century*, U.S. Government Printing Office, 1999.

13. American Housing Survey, 1997, conducted by the Census Bureau and the Department of Housing and Urban Development.

14. Aaron Bruner, et al., "Economic Reasons for Conserving Wild Nature." *Science* 297 (August 9, 2002), 5583.

15. Statistics from EPA, in Funders' Network for Smart Growth and Livable Communities, *Translation Paper #10: Biodiversity and Smart Growth.*

16. National Wildlife Federation, *Paving Paradise: Sprawl's Impact on Wildlife and Wild Places in California.* February 2001.

17. Reid Ewing and John Kostyack, *Endangered by Sprawl: How Runaway Development Threatens America's Wildlife*, National Wildlife Federation, Smart Growth America and NatureServe 2005. *Endangered by Sprawl* integrates widely accepted measures of development density and projections of population growth with a new analysis of the comprehensive data on rare and endangered species that is compiled by the NatureServe network of state natural heritage programs.

18. Pew Center for Civic Journalism, *Straight Talk from Americans*, 2000. See www.pewcenter.org/doingcj/research/r_ST2000.html.

chapter two

The Green Infrastructure Approach: Principles from Past to Present

T he term *green infrastructure* is relatively new, but the concept is not. The green infrastructure movement is rooted in studies of the land and the interrelationship of man and nature that began over 150 years ago. Myriad disciplines have contributed theories, ideas, research, and conclusions to what has become a growing field of knowledge. Specifically, the origins of green infrastructure planning and design relate to the ideas and actions taken to conserve nature through national and state parks; wildlife refuges; forest, river, wetland, and wilderness protection; and development planning in relation to nature in the disciplines of urban planning, landscape design, and environmentally sensitive development. A third major impetus for green infrastructure is the greenways movement, which focuses attention on the impact of development on the landscape. Green infrastructure gains its strength from these interdisciplinary roots. It is a scientific approach to determining the best use of the land to support both the natural processes that exist on the landscape and the infrastructure and recreational needs of the people who live there.

Table 2.1

The Rise of Green Infrastructure

Time period	Milestones	Key ideas
The Formative Years: 1850–1900	• Henry David Thoreau writes about the "importance of preserving some portions of nature herself unimpaired." Frederick Law Olmsted "invents" concept of linked systems of parks and parkways. • The first urban open-space network, the Minneapolis-St. Paul metropolitan park system, is completed. • The idea of a greenbelt is introduced in England "to prevent one town from growing into another." • *Man and Nature*, by George Perkins Marsh, is published.	• The intrinsic character of land should guide its use.
Experimentation and evolution: 1900–1920s	• The Bronx River Parkway becomes the first parkway designed for recreational motor use. • Warren Manning uses the overlay technique to analyze natural and cultural information about a site. • President Theodore Roosevelt's love for the great outdoors brings land conservation to the forefront of the national agenda. • Yellowstone National Park sets the stage for our national park system. • The greenbelt concept is included in the 1920s plan for Radburn, New Jersey.	• Experimentation with large-scale planning methodologies. • Conserving natural places for future generations.
Environmental design comes of age: 1930s–1950s	• Biologist/ecologist Victor Shelford calls for the preservation of natural areas and buffer zones. • As part of the New Deal, several greenbelt communities are planned with an emphasis on including green space in urban design and buffering the community from adjacent land uses. • Benton MacKaye "invents" the discipline of regional planning and promotes the Appalachian Trail as a wide belt of open land to buffer the West from expanding settlement. • Aldo Leopold introduces the concept of a land ethic, focusing on the fundamental principles of ecology.	• Linkage between ecology and design. • Ethical principles of land use. • Preservation of nature in its "wild" state.
A decade of ecology: 1960s	• Town planner and landscape architect Ian McHarg argues that ecology should serve as the basis for design. • Philip Lewis creates a method of landscape analysis that looks at environmental corridors and features such as vegetation and scenery. • William H. Whyte introduces the term and concept of a "greenway." • Landscape ecology emerges with a focus on the interactions between biological communities and the physical environment. • Island biogeography explores the relationships between species and landscapes. • Congress passes the Wilderness Act. • Rachel Carson publishes *Silent Spring*, bringing attention to man's impact on nature.	• Landscape and suitability analysis. • Scientific, definable process for land-use planning. • Protecting core areas of wilderness.

Time period	Milestones	Key ideas
Refinement of key concepts: 1970s–1980s	• The Man and Biosphere Program promotes the concept of core areas surrounded by zones of compatible land use. • Conservation biology is introduced as a discipline that applies the principles of ecology to the maintenance of biological diversity. • The Conservation Fund establishes the American Greenways Program to promote greenways and greenway systems across the U.S. • Richard T. T. Foreman leads the way in landscape ecology and ethics. • Larry Harris and Reed Noss formulate and promote the design and protection of regional reserve systems. • GIS is introduced as a tool for regional planning. • The UN World Commission on Environment and Development concludes that sustainable development requires population size and growth to be in harmony with the changing productive potential of the ecosystem.	• Science and a process are needed to guide complex land-use planning that takes ecological features into account. • Preserving isolated natural areas is not enough to protect biodiversity and ecosystem processes. • Linkages between natural areas are needed.
A growing emphasis on linkages: 1990s and beyond	• The states of Maryland and Florida initiate planning efforts to create statewide systems of greenways and green spaces. • The Wildlands Project is created to establish a North American system of interconnected wildlands. • The President's Commission on Sustainable Development identifies green infrastructure as one of five strategic areas that provide a comprehensive approach for sustainable community development. • Interest grows in green infrastructure as a tool to guide land conservation and development.	• A focus on the landscape scale. • Understanding landscape patterns and processes. • Green infrastructure planning requires identifying and linking priority conservation areas. • Participatory and consensus-based decision-making.

EARLY INTEREST IN LAND CONSERVATION

Concern for land conservation and the preservation of natural resources dates from the early days of the United States. In an 1847 speech to the Agricultural Society of Rutland County, Vermont, George Perkins Marsh called attention to the destructive impact of human activity on the land, especially through deforestation, and called for a conservationist approach to the management of forested lands. This speech became the basis for Marsh's book *Man and Nature*, published in 1864.[1] At about the same time, Henry David Thoreau wrote of the "importance of preserving some portions of nature herself unimpaired." Thoreau applied his ideas to urban design. "I think that each town should have a park," he wrote, "or rather a primitive forest, of five hundred or a thousand acres, either in one body or several—where a stick should never be cut for fuel—nor for the navy, nor to make wagons, but stand and decay for higher uses—a common possession forever, for instruction and recreation."[2]

Landscape architect Frederick Law Olmsted agreed with Thoreau's opinion that an urban, "biologically artificial" environment is detrimental to our mental and physical health and incorporated parks and greenways into the plans he created for cities and towns throughout the country. In the 1868 plan for Riverside, Illinois, for example, Olmsted provided ample green space for recreation and made sure that scenic areas were available to all residents. To accomplish this, he preserved the floodplain and the riverbanks as well as two open areas of upland. Olmsted planned a shaded parkway to connect Riverside to Chicago. He paid particular attention to making the inner roads of the community as scenic as possible and designed streets to follow the curve of the land.

Olmsted recognized that nature could provide peace of mind and an "enlarged sense of freedom" while preserving natural scenery and water quality. But Olmsted concluded that no single park, no matter how large or well designed, could provide people with all the beneficial influences of nature. Designed by Olmsted to tie together a series of parks in 1887, Boston's Emerald Necklace is one of the nation's oldest systems of linked public parks and parkways. The network—which includes the Boston Public Garden, the Boston Common, Commonwealth Avenue, the Back Bay Fens, the Riverway, Olmsted Park, Jamaica Park, Arnold Arboretum, and Franklin Park—is strung together with a series of parkways. Today, the Emerald Necklace provides a welcome respite from city life and serves as a home to many kinds of wildlife seldom found in an urban environment. White-tailed deer, eastern red fox, muskrats, wild turkeys, herons, snapping turtles, barred owls, ducks and geese, songbirds, and even an occasional coyote make their home in Boston's parks.

The Emerald Necklace also provides valuable water storage, flood protection, and other environmental benefits. In fact, many of Olmsted's parks were not designed for human use, but rather were attempts to tame nature. Olmsted's plan to restore the Back Bay Fens as a saltwater marsh was driven by the fact that it was so contaminated that it posed a health hazard for people in neighboring areas. Recognizing that the Fens could function as a stormwater basin, Olmsted placed pedestrian and horse paths around its perimeter. In this way, Olmsted balanced the needs of people and nature: people could use Back Bay for recreation while the Fens was restored to its natural functions.

This emphasis on preserving and connecting open space took hold in communities throughout the country. Landscape architect Horace W. S. Cleveland's 1890s plans for park systems in both Minneapolis and St. Paul included a network of interlinked scenic drives, parks, and river boulevards. He also preserved land around the cities' lakes and natural areas along the Mississippi River. Cleveland's legacy is a Minneapolis park system comprising almost 6,400 acres and fifty-eight miles of parkways and a St. Paul park system of 4,207 acres and forty-six miles of parkways.

The benefit of preserving green space in urban environments was recognized in Europe as well. England's garden city movement, led by town planner Ebenezer

Howard, focused on the importance of balancing development with the need for nature. His original plan for Victoria, England, proposed a thousand-acre town surrounded by a nine-thousand-acre agricultural greenbelt. The town also had 120-foot-wide radiating boulevards planted on each side of the pathways with trees and in many places with shrubs and evergreens. Howard's vision was for "a Garden City that, as it grows, the free gifts of Nature—fresh air, sunlight, breathing room and playing room—shall be retained in all needed abundance."[3]

By the late 1800s in the United States, federal and state governments were becoming involved in land conservation and resource preservation. In 1864, Congress passed legislation giving Yosemite Valley to the state of California to be set aside as a public park to protect its natural beauty. Just eight years later, President Ulysses S. Grant signed a law making Yellowstone our first national park "dedicated and set apart as a public park or pleasuring ground for the benefit and enjoyment of the people." This was not only the first area of wild land devoted to recreational use and enjoyment under federal management, but also the pilot model for perfecting that management.

At the turn of the century, naturalist and Sierra Club founder John Muir, forester Gifford Pinchot, and President Theodore Roosevelt brought conservation to the forefront of the national agenda. President Roosevelt's abundant love for the outdoors led to the origin of the National Park System, designed to "conserve the scenery and the natural and historic objects and the wildlife therein and to provide for the enjoyment of the same by means as will leave them unimpaired for the enjoyment of future generations." During his presidency, Roosevelt designated 150 National Forests, fifty-one Federal Bird Reservations, five National Parks, eighteen National Monuments, four National Game Preserves, and twenty-one Reclamation Projects. Altogether, between 1901 and 1909, he provided federal protection for almost 230 million acres, an area equivalent to all the East Coast states from Maine to Florida.

LAND CONSERVATION IN THE INDUSTRIAL AGE

The early twentieth century witnessed the rise of a movement to preserve "self-willed" wildlands where nature reigns unimpaired by man. In 1920, biologist and ecologist Victor Shelford called for the preservation of "areas of natural conditions."[4] He wrote, "Biologists are beginning to realize that it is dangerous to tamper with nature by introducing plants and animals, or by destroying predatory animals or by pampering herbivores. . . . The reserved areas in the National Parks are possibly too small, but in any event should be zoned about by (buffer) areas of complete or partial protection of the roaming animals."[5] A 1932 study reiterated the limitations of the National Parks as habitat for some species and concluded that most of the parks were not large enough for sustainability. "The preponderance of unfavorable wildlife conditions . . . is traceable to the insufficiency of park areas as self-contained biological units. . . . At present, not one park is large enough to provide year-round sanctuary for adequate populations of all resident species."[6]

Throughout America, the rise of the automobile was changing the nature of the landscape. As automobiles became commonplace, the need to accommodate them grew. The first automotive parkways were often designed with a dual purpose in mind: to meet the transportation needs of people traveling from one place to another and to meet the recreation needs of the nation's growing urban populations. In an effort to create a recreational network for New Yorkers, Robert Moses designed automotive parkways in Westchester County and Long Island. The parkways on Long Island linked public parks (such as Jones Beach, a popular beachside park) to form part of today's Brooklyn-Queens Greenway.

Parkways were seen as one way to mitigate the negative effects of urbanization. In designing the twenty-three-mile parkway between New York City and Westchester County, the Bronx River Commission took care to preserve the nature of the open space. Construction requirements declared that the roadway should "display to the traveler the principle interesting features"[7] and that bridges and other features should be designed in harmony with their natural surroundings, using natural materials wherever possible. Painstaking efforts were made to preserve natural features, including existing trees, and to plant native species. Requirements further dictated: "In planning the planting, therefore, as in the rest of the design, a humanized naturalness has been aimed at, sufficiently diversified to create woodland groups and vistas of all of the types that belong; broad enough that he who runs (or rides) may see; with intimate bits for those who wish to pause; with material prevailingly indigenous, but always suitable to the situation and its requirements."[8] The idea of allowing the public to use portions of the Bronx River Parkway for recreation was an attempt to spark interest in the parkway. The Bronx River Parkway Reservation, which parallels the parkway, was the first parkland in Westchester County.

While some people saw the automobile as progress, others considered its ability to bring people into once remote areas a threat to the nation's natural resources. In 1935, the Wilderness Society was founded. In the first issue of its magazine, *Living Wilderness*, editor Robert Sterling Yard wrote, "The Wilderness Society is born of an emergency in conservation which admits of no delay. The craze is to build all the highways possible everywhere while billions may yet be borrowed from the unlucky future."[9] In 1946, the Wilderness Society proposed "a national system of wildland belts" along rivers and mountains "to preserve for the information and inspiration of posterity representative areas of our county in a primitive condition, and to foster a deeper appreciation of the natural features of the earth which are characteristics of the United States."[10] This early proposal for a wilderness system is different from the system that exists today; it more closely resembles the concept of a nationwide green infrastructure network.

Benton MacKaye was among those who began to focus on the need for regional planning. His concern about urban encroachment led to a staunch defense of green space, and his recommendations combined the need for recreation with the use of green space corridors following natural landforms. He is perhaps most famous for promoting the Appalachian Trail not just for hiking, but as a buffer against development from Eastern cities. MacKaye envisioned cities that used natural landscapes —hills, mountains, and rivers—to surround and contain development. MacKaye included systems of open space and low-intensity land uses, such as dairies and managed woodlands, that would "form a linear area, or belt, around and through the locality." These natural lands were not only to protect the scenery in undeveloped areas and encourage local "wildland patches" but also to provide city dwellers with space for recreation.[11] In calling for the use of maps as conservation tools, MacKaye was among the first to recognize the importance of topography in determining the path of human settlement.

A few community planners also began to focus on creating a boundary between community growth areas and agricultural or rural lands. During the 1930s, several "greenbelt" communities were designed, drawing on the idea of using green space as a buffer zone around an urban core. Greenbelt, Maryland, was the first of three "green towns" built from scratch by the Resettlement Administration as part of President Franklin D. Roosevelt's New Deal. From the beginning Greenbelt was designed as a complete city, with businesses, schools, roads, and facilities for recreation and town government. In addition to this gray infrastructure, green infrastructure was included as an integral part of the design. Modeled after the nineteenth-century English garden cities, Greenbelt's plan included a system of interior walkways and corridors, a forest buffer around the town, and belts of green between neighborhoods that offered easy contact with nature. (Many more green towns were planned during the New Deal, but only two others were built: Greendale, Wisconsin, and Greenhills, Ohio.)

LANDSCAPE ECOLOGY AND CONSERVATION BIOLOGY

Spearheaded by Frederic Edward Clements, Henry Chandler Cowles, and Henry Allen Gleason, new scientific concepts focused on the distribution of plant communities and gave rise to a new science: ecology. In the 1920s, while working for the National Forest Service in Arizona, Aldo Leopold began to think about the land as a living organism. His "land ethic" envisioned a concept of community that embraced all the living things within it. Often credited as the founding father of wildlife ecology, Leopold's *Game Management* defined the fundamental skills and techniques for managing and restoring wildlife populations. This landmark work created a new science that intertwined forestry, agriculture, biology, zoology, ecology, education, and communication.[12]

It would take several decades before the principles of ecology would be applied to urban planning and landscape architecture. Ian McHarg introduced the idea of "physiographic determinism," claiming that natural processes should be the basis for determining development (or nondevelopment) priorities. In his landmark 1969 book, *Design with Nature*, McHarg spelled out the need for urban planners to consider an environmentally conscious approach to land use, and provided a new method for evaluating and implementing this approach. McHarg argued that form must follow more than just function; it must also respect the natural environment in which it is placed. "[The engineer's] competence is not the design of highways," McHarg explained, "merely of the structures that compose them—but only after they have been designed by persons more knowing of man and the land."[13]

The environment played a small role in land-use planning and urban design in part because there was no way to quantify and display information about the natural environment in any meaningful way: researchers lacked the means to store, process, or present large amounts of spatial data. To overcome this limitation, McHarg used map overlays. A picture is worth a thousand words, as the adage goes, and McHarg felt that visually displaying spatial data could convey large amounts of information in a way that was easy to understand.

Like McHarg, Philip Lewis, a professor of landscape architecture, emphasized the importance of understanding the potential of land and responding to it. Lewis focused particular attention on the importance of setting aside fertile soil for agricultural use and stressed the importance of environmental corridors along stream valleys, arguing that natural corridor planning can play a crucial role in the protection of wildlife. He created a method of landscape analysis with 220 environmental values that looks at perceptual features, such as vegetation and scenery, in addition to environmental corridors.[14]

As these diverse threads began to weave together, they gave rise to new ways to look at the landscape. Carl Troll, a German geographer who was applying aerial photograph interpretation to studies of interactions between environment and vegetation, coined the term *landscape ecology* to describe a new field of knowledge that focused holistically on the spatial arrangement of elements in the landscape (such as fields, woodlots, rivers, or towns) and how their distribution affected the distribution and flow of energy and individuals in the environment.

Others were using aerial photography to explore the relationship between species and their habitats and the effect that changes in the landscape had on the animals that lived there. *Island biogeography*, a theory proposed by biologists E. O. Wilson and Robert MacArthur, helped to frame this thinking. In studying animal populations, Wilson and MacArthur found that the number of species on an island reflects a balance between the rate at which new species colonize it and the rate at which populations of established species become extinct. They also discovered relationships that linked the size of the island to the number of species inhabiting the space. In the mid-1900s, as urban development spread across the

Figure 2.1
Philip Lewis was among the early advocates of considering land's potential value in
land-use planning, focusing particular attention on the importance of environmental
corridors. Shown here is an analysis of environmental corridors in Wisconsin.
Credit: Philip Lewis.

landscape and habitats became more fragmented, the theory of island biogeography
became a tool for understanding the nature and pattern of species diversity for these
isolated habitats.

The discipline of conservation biology evolved from this new field of research.
Based on the theories of ecology, genetics, biogeography, and wildlife ecology,
conservation biology focuses on the protection of biological diversity and related
critical habitats. Conservation biology strives to provide information to manage
the dynamic evolutionary processes in a changing ecological background. Together,
the fields of landscape ecology and conservation biology provide green infrastructure with the scientific knowledge and tools to plan for viable plant and animal
populations over the long term.

Among the tools that landscape ecologists and conservation biologists promoted
to meet biodiversity goals is the design of reserves. The purpose of reserves is to
protect areas of high biological value that would otherwise likely be degraded and
to preserve biodiversity and protect rare, threatened, and endangered species. The

initial focus of reserve design was on protecting individual species, but reserve design can also incorporate a diversity of biological scales (species, communities, and ecosystems), informing the design of green infrastructure networks. (This is discussed more fully in chapter 5.)

ENVIRONMENTALISM

In the 1960s, interest in conservation and land use was fueled by growing concern among the general public about the impact that people were having on the environment. The 1962 publication of Rachel Carson's *Silent Spring* alerted the American public to the dangers of pesticides and the effect that humans were having on nature. Carson, a renowned nature author and a former marine biologist with the U.S. Fish and Wildlife Service, wrote, "The 'control of nature' is a phrase conceived in arrogance, born of the Neanderthal age of biology and philosophy, where it was supposed that nature exists for the convenience of man."[15] Carson's proposal was radical: At times, technological progress is so fundamentally at odds with natural processes that it must be curtailed. *Silent Spring* fostered new public awareness that nature was vulnerable to human intervention. For the first time, the need to regulate industry in order to protect the environment became widely accepted, and environmentalism was born.

The federal government continued to be involved in preserving resource lands and open space. In 1964, Congress passed the Wilderness Act: "In order to assure that an increasing population, accompanied by expanding settlement and growing mechanization, does not occupy and modify all areas within the United States and its possessions, leaving no lands designated for preservation and protection in their natural condition, it is hereby declared to be the policy of the Congress to secure for the American people of present and future generations the benefits of an enduring resource of wilderness."[16]

Five years later, the National Environment Policy Act (NEPA)—the first major U.S. environmental legislation—established the Environmental Protection Agency. NEPA declared "that it is the continuing policy of the Federal Government, in cooperation with State and local governments, and all other concerned public and private organizations, to use all practicable means and measures, including financial and technical assistance, in a manner calculated to foster and promote the general welfare, to create and maintain conditions under which man and nature can exist in productive harmony, and fulfill the social, economic, and other requirements of present and future generations of Americans."[17] The next years witnessed the passage of several major pieces of legislation strengthening the federal government's commitment to environmental protection, including the Clean Air Act (1970), the Water Pollution Control Act (1972), and the Endangered Species Act (1973). As the U.S. population has continued to grow and development to expand, the nation's environmental laws have been revised and updated to address the wide range of effects of development on the environment.

Of course, the United States was not alone in grappling with geopolitical environmental issues. In 1983, the United Nations' World Commission on Environment and Development held a conference to discuss the importance of sustainable development in the changing world economy. The Commission concluded that sustainable development required population size and growth to be in harmony with the changing productive potential of the ecosystem. Countries and communities throughout the world began to focus increasing attention on planning for sustainable development and integrating sustainability into their land-use programs.

Box 2.1

Green Infrastructure in Europe

As in the United States, wildlife protection and resource conservation in European countries traditionally have focused on the protection of specific sites. In the 1970s, however, a new approach began to focus on "ecological networks." This approach goes beyond simply protecting important wildlife sites; it amplifies them through the restoration of habitats and the creation of corridors and stepping stones for the dispersal and migration of species.

The European ecological network typically comprises four main components:

- Core areas representing key habitat types and ensuring their conservation
- Corridors or stepping stones that allow species to disperse and migrate between the core areas, thus reducing isolation and improving the coherence of natural systems
- Buffer zones that protect the network from potentially damaging external influences such as pollution or land drainage
- Natural restoration areas adjoining or close to core areas that will expand the network to an optimum size.

The Life ECOnet Project is advocating this approach by working with local constituents in Cheshire, United Kingdom, and Abruzzo and Emilia-Romagna, Italy, to create networks connecting areas for wildlife and demonstrating how these networks can contribute to sustainable land-use planning and management. The project is using GIS and other technologies to identify concentrations of habitats of high value for wildlife as well as areas that have the potential for the creation of new habitats and corridors for the movement of wildlife.

Source: Life ECOnet Web site, www.lifeeconet.com.

THE ADVENT OF AN INTEGRATED APPROACH

Over the next two decades, interest grew in the concepts of green infrastructure planning and design and refinement of land conservation practices. Conservation strategies became more holistic and comprehensive, and regulatory approaches gave way to nonregulatory approaches like ecosystem management, sustainable development, and regional planning.

In addition, the greenways movement began to involve an increasing number and variety of organizations, agencies, and people at the community, regional, state, and national levels. Many concerned people began to think seriously about the urban landscape and how best to plan to protect connected networks of green space in the future. In 1987, The Conservation Fund established the American Greenways Program to promote and support the concept of greenways throughout the United States.

A number of professors took the lead in promoting an integrated approach to green space conservation. For example, Richard T. T. Forman, a landscape architect, wrote, "[I]n land use decisions and actions, it is unethical to evaluate an area in isolation from its surroundings or from its development over time. Ethics impel us to consider an area in its broadest spatial and temporal perspectives."[18] Larry D. Harris, a University of Florida ecologist, focused attention on the effects of fragmentation and isolated patches, including their devastating impact on wildlife and the extinction of species. He argued that protecting wildlife corridors and linking them to large hubs of biodiversity are the best ways to counter the impact of habitat fragmentation. Harris and Reed Noss are among those who begin to formulate and promote the design and protection of regional reserve systems consisting of core reserves, multiple-use (buffer) zones, and corridors.[19] (This approach is discussed in more detail in chapter 5.)

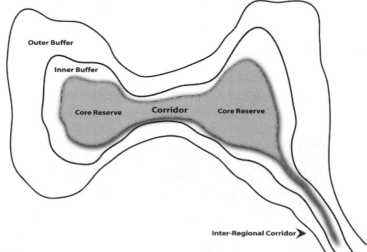

Figure 2.2
The regional reserve system proposed by Larry Harris and Reed Noss includes core reserves, buffer zones, and corridors. Credit: Adapted from Noss and Cooperrider (1994).

> **Box 2.2**
>
> ## Greenways and Green Infrastructure
>
> Although green infrastructure initiatives often begin from greenways efforts, there are some important differences. Green infrastructure differs from greenways in three major ways:
> - Green infrastructure emphasizes ecology, not recreation
> - Green infrastructure includes ecologically important hubs, as well as key landscape linkages
> - Green infrastructure can be designed to shape urban form and provide a framework for growth—a framework that pre-identifies ecologically significant lands and suitable development areas.

THE RISE OF GREEN INFRASTRUCTURE AS A STRATEGIC CONSERVATION TOOL

By the 1990s, sustainability was becoming a national and international goal. In 1993, President Clinton called for further study on sustainable development. The resulting President's Council on Sustainable Development initiated efforts to apply the concept of sustainable development in the United States. In its May 1999 report, the Council identified green infrastructure as one of several key strategies for achieving sustainability.

There was growing interest in finding a mechanism for addressing the complexity of sustainability and land conservation. Conservationists and planners alike recognized that preserving isolated natural areas is not enough—that natural areas need to be connected at the regional and landscape scales to protect biodiversity and ecosystem processes.

The first broadscale, integrated green infrastructure design effort in the United States was born in 1990, when Maryland began a statewide greenways planning initiative, which gave rise to a statewide ecological analysis and green infrastructure maps. The state of Florida also undertook a major green infrastructure initiative in the 1990s. In 1994, the Florida Greenways Commission issued a report recommending the creation of a statewide greenways system by linking existing and proposed conservation lands, trails, urban open spaces, and private working landscapes. In 1998, the Florida Greenways Coordinating Council and the Florida Department of Environmental Protection released draft GIS-generated maps depicting statewide ecological and recreational/cultural networks, which together make up the Florida Greenways System. (These initiatives are discussed in more detail as Green Infrastructure in Action case studies at

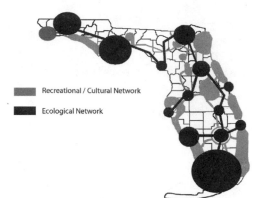

Figure 2.3
Florida used GIS information to develop two statewide
networks: one focusing on the ecological value of the land
and the other on lands with recreational or cultural value.
Together, these networks make up the Florida Greenways
System. Credit: Executive Summary, The Florida Statewide
Greenways System Planning Project, 1999.

the end of chapters 1 and 2 as well as in chapter 5.) In addition to these two
statewide efforts, a growing number of regions and communities began to
undertake green infrastructure planning, design, and implementation efforts.

The diversity of these initiatives reflects their origins. Some were initiated to
complement a smart growth initiative; others evolved as grassroots movements following a community visioning forum. Some began as recreation-based greenways
programs and expanded to include ecological goals; others began with a focus on
the conservation of biological and natural resources. Some have been spearheaded
by national or community nonprofit organizations; local government or regional
planning units have initiated others.

All share a common interest, however, and recognize the importance of land-use
planning based on landscape value. All also focus on making the optimum use of land
by setting aside land for conservation before the threat of development is imminent.

GREEN INFRASTRUCTURE PRINCIPLES

From the many green infrastructure initiatives underway across the country and
the world, a common set of assumptions and principles have emerged as being
critical to success. These principles, outlined below, provide a strategic approach
to and a framework for conservation that can advance sustainable use of land while
benefiting people and nature. The principles can be used as benchmarks for incorporating a green infrastructure approach into existing planning activities and for
strengthening existing efforts to protect and conserve ecologically valuable lands.

Principle 1: Connectivity Is Key

Green infrastructure draws its strength from its focus on connectivity—between natural lands and other open spaces, between people, and between programs. Most land conservation programs in the United States have focused on protecting individual sites with important natural or cultural resources (parks, nature preserves, Civil War battlefields, etc.). Conservation biology, however, has demonstrated that linkage is essential for natural systems to function properly and for wildlife to thrive. The strategic connection of ecosystem components—parks, preserves, riparian areas, wetlands, and other green spaces—is critical to maintaining the values and services of natural systems (such as carrying and filtering storm-water runoff), and to maintaining the health and diversity of wildlife populations.

Green infrastructure can help establish land acquisition priorities that ensure adequate connectivity among already preserved lands. The Corkscrew Regional Ecosystem Watershed (CREW) project in southwest Florida, for example, focuses on preserving the large, interconnected wetlands which the Florida panther and the Florida black bear need to survive. The project will conserve connections between the Florida Panther National Wildlife Refuge, the Fakahatchee Strand State Preserve, and the National Audubon Society's Corkscrew Swamp Sanctuary. The

---

Box 2.3

Ten Principles of Green Infrastructure

1. Connectivity is key.
2. Context matters.
3. Green infrastructure should be grounded in sound science and land-use planning theory and practice.
4. Green infrastructure can and should function as the framework for conservation and development.
5. Green infrastructure should be planned and protected *before* development.
6. Green infrastructure is a critical public investment that should be funded up front.
7. Green infrastructure affords benefits to nature and people.
8. Green infrastructure respects the needs and desires of landowners and other stakeholders.
9. Green infrastructure requires making connections to activities within and beyond the community.
10. Green infrastructure requires long-term commitment.

CREW project also supports at least two species of rare and endangered orchids, and includes an unusual stand of dwarf bald cypress. In addition to providing this critical protection for rare wildlife, the project protects the waters feeding these areas and provides opportunities for citizens to learn about and enjoy these natural resources, even as the area around them continues to undergo rapid development.

Successful green infrastructure also requires linkages among the programs and staff of different agencies, nongovernmental organizations, and the private sector. Chicago Wilderness is an example of a collaborative conservation effort involving diverse community agencies and organizations. Chicago Wilderness began in 1996, when organizations in the greater Chicago area came together to discuss what they could do collectively to study, protect, restore, and manage the precious natural ecosystems of the region. In less than ten years, the so-called Chicago Wilderness coalition has grown from 34 to more than 170 member organizations. Member institutions include landowners; local, state, and federal agencies; centers of research and education; conservation organizations; and others who have pledged their commitment to restore the region's natural communities to long-term viability, enrich local residents' quality of life, and contribute to the preservation of global biodiversity. The resulting regional system of nature reserves

Figure 2.4
This wet prairie is part of the Corkscrew Regional Ecosystem Watershed Project, which is designed to help protect the habitat of the Florida panther, the Florida black bear, and other plant and animal species increasingly threatened by encroaching development. Credit: David Addison.

includes more than two hundred thousand acres of protected natural lands from southeastern Wisconsin through northeastern Illinois and into northwestern Indiana. The protected lands include forest preserves, state parks, federal lands, county preserves, and privately owned lands.

Principle 2: Context Matters

A fundamental concept of landscape ecology is that the study of content alone (the study of flora, fauna, and processes within a single site or managed area) is not sufficient. Understanding and predicting change in native ecosystems and landscapes requires an analysis of the context in which these ecosystems exist—the biological and physical factors of the surrounding areas.

Strategic conservation requires an integrated landscape approach that takes context into account. A county's conservation plan, for example, needs to consider how the county's natural resources contribute to, interact with, and are influenced by the ecosystems of neighboring areas. The managers of public parks, wildlife refuges, and other conservation lands within a region need to consider what is happening outside their borders, in terms of both how land-use changes may impact their resources and how to link up with other conservation areas and natural resource initiatives to meet common goals at a landscape scale.

The public land planning processes provide an opportunity—and a responsibility—for public land managers to look at the broader landscape to consider how changes beyond their borders affect the lands they manage. In 2002, the Sherburne National Wildlife Refuge in Minnesota held a series of scoping meetings. In answer to the question, "What is the primary conservation issue for the Sherburne National Wildlife Refuge in the next 25 years?" 79 percent of respondents identified off-site issues related to the loss of natural areas: for example, "human population growth and demands," "how to contribute to the conservation of the ecosystem in the face of increasing development pressure," "the isolation of the Refuge as an island within suburban sprawl," "loss of habitat surrounding the Refuge," and "working with local planning entities to engender a sustainable ecosystem." Based on the input gained from stakeholders, Refuge managers worked with citizens to develop goals and to identify a management scenario that recognized the rapidly changing environment surrounding the refuge and that focused on the refuge as part of a larger landscape. The scenario called for discretionary funding and new staff to be directed toward off-refuge land conservation efforts and the pursuit of a strong land conservation ethic in the local community. The Sherburne Refuge also embraced green infrastructure as a means to encourage a proactive approach, to engage stakeholders, and to put the natural environment and the services at the front of the planning process.

Principle 3: Green Infrastructure Should Be Grounded in Sound Science and Land-Use Planning Theory and Practice

As we have discussed, green infrastructure is not a new concept. Various disciplines have contributed theories, ideas, research, and conclusions to what has become a growing field of knowledge and continue to contribute to the successful planning and design of green infrastructure systems.

Successful green infrastructure initiatives build on the foundation of many disciplines and engage experts from various fields in network design and review. Conservation biology, landscape ecology, urban and regional planning, landscape architecture, geography, and civil engineering all contribute to the successful design and implementation of green infrastructure systems. Drawing from the theories, practices, and opinions of a variety of professions helps to ensure the appropriate balance and integration of ecological, cultural, social, and practical considerations.

In the mid-1990s, New Jersey, the most densely populated state in the country, was losing twenty-six thousand acres of wildlife habitat each year. In 1994, the state attempted to address this habitat loss through the Landscape Project, which provides scientific information about the distribution of biodiversity across the state. The project's goal is "to protect New Jersey's biological diversity by maintaining and enhancing rare wildlife populations within healthy functioning ecosystems."[20] The project aims to make scientifically sound information easily accessible to planning and protection programs throughout the state. This information includes maps that may serve as the basis for developing habitat protection ordinances, zoning, or land acquisition projects, as well as for planning new development. This information also helps to inform the state's Green Acres program, which provides funding for land acquisition at the state and local levels.

The Garden State Greenways program, undertaken by the New Jersey Conservation Foundation, has served to support the state's effort. Garden State Greenways is an interactive statewide map of undeveloped lands (forest, farmland, and wetland hubs) and potential connectors between these lands. The program identifies and ranks potential corridors in terms of connecting existing open space and value for protecting watersheds, habitat, and recreational opportunities. The interactive tool can help coordinate the planning efforts of private groups and government agencies by providing maps illustrating the Garden State Greenways concept and vision, as well as map-based information that can assist in open space planning on the local, county, regional, and statewide levels.[21]

In planning for future growth, Anne Arundel County, Maryland, also has focused on objective, scientific criteria to make land-use decisions. The goal for its greenways network is to protect ecologically valuable lands and to provide adequate habitat to support healthy populations of a diversity of naturally occurring plant and animal species. The county capitalized on the state of Maryland's green infrastructure initiative, using the methodology that had been used statewide. Anne Arundel County focused primarily on ecological principles to select five criteria to use to assess land as potential greenways: habitat value, size, connections to other land with ecological value, future potential (i.e., the potential to create greenways where they do not currently exist), and national and countywide trails.

During the process leading up to the development of the Sonoran Desert Conservation Plan, Pima County, Arizona, focused on establishing clear, scientific criteria for the preservation of species and habitat. In addition, scientists completing the plan were deliberately isolated from politics. The experts who reviewed the plan cited these elements as one of the SDCP's main strengths. (The SDCP is the topic of the Green Infrastructure in Action case study at the end of chapter 4.)

Principle 4: Green Infrastructure Can and Should Function as the Framework for Conservation and Development

Green infrastructure planning can help communities prioritize conservation needs and determine where to direct new growth and development. By making green infrastructure the framework for conservation and development, communities can plan for green space systems that maintain essential ecological functions and provide a host of ecological services. Green infrastructure also provides a tool that helps communities develop a framework for shaping where growth will go and make better use of existing infrastructure to encourage more compact, walkable communities. In short, green infrastructure plans can provide a framework for future growth while also ensuring that significant natural resources will be preserved for future generations. Green infrastructure plans can even reduce opposition to new development by assuring civic groups and environmental organizations that growth will occur only within a framework of expanded conservation and open space lands.

Principle 5: Green Infrastructure Should Be Planned and Protected *before* Development

Restoring natural systems is far more expensive than protecting undeveloped land. Moreover, man-made wetlands and other restoration projects often fail to function over the long term, particularly in comparison to their natural counterparts. Green infrastructure provides communities with a framework that takes into account the ecological characteristics of the landscape, enabling communities to identify and protect critical ecological hubs and linkages in advance of development. Protecting green infrastructure up front ensures that existing open spaces and working lands are seen as essential community assets and not left vulnerable to development.

Box 2.4

The Southeastern Ecological Framework

The southeastern United States has large areas of unique ecological character—
areas that are being fragmented by agricultural, silvicultural, and road development practices and threatened by sprawling development. Research shows a host
of natural ecosystem types, including long-leaf pine forests and wetlands that
provide habitat for many endangered species and protect water quality for the
growing population.

The Southeastern Ecological Framework Project is a GIS-based analysis to
identify ecologically significant areas and connectivity in the southeast region
(Florida, Georgia, Alabama, Mississippi, South Carolina, North Carolina,
Tennessee, and Kentucky). The project began in October 1998 and was completed in December 2001 by the University of Florida GeoPlan Center and
sponsored by the U.S. Environmental Protection Agency (EPA) Region 4. EPA's
Region 4 Planning and Analysis Branch continues to use this data to facilitate
EPA programs and to work with state and federal agencies and local groups to
make sound conservation decisions.

The Southeastern Ecological Framework provides a basic regional landscape
and natural resource planning tool. This is not a map of areas that must be protected, nor does the framework suggest that these are the only places that need
protection. Rather, the framework provides a tool for the many federal, state, and
local government agencies, nonprofit organizations, and business groups involved
in natural resource protection to coalesce their efforts.

Some communities have done a great deal to protect open space in advance of
development. Montgomery County, Maryland, for example, initiated green infrastructure planning for its stream valley park system in advance of the county's rapid
growth. In the 1940s, the county began buying land along all of its major stream
corridors—well before land development had made it impossible to preserve these
ecologically important areas. Today the county's system of stream valley parks
encompasses over twenty-five thousand acres. The county has begun adding to this
system with a ten-year, $100 million initiative to complete a countywide network
of open space comprised of protected farmland, stream valley parks, ecological
reserves, trail corridors, and green space preserves.

The city of Anchorage, Alaska's, trail and greenbelt system is another example.
Based on an innovative concept plan from the 1950s, the city has protected greenbelt parks and over three hundred miles of trails. Although there is more work to

be done, efforts to date represent the start of a green infrastructure network that will support future growth in Anchorage and the surrounding suburbs.

In places where development has already occurred, a green infrastructure approach can help communities determine where green space protection or restoration could benefit people and nature. Green infrastructure plans should set acquisition and restoration priorities and help communities identify opportunities to reconnect isolated habitat islands as redevelopment possibilities surface.

Principle 6: Green Infrastructure Is a Critical Public Investment that Should Be Funded Up Front

Green infrastructure should be funded up front using the full range of available financing options. Our nation's gray infrastructure—transportation, water, sewer, electricity, telecommunications, and other essential community support systems— are publicly financed as primary budgetary line items, in part to spread the costs of development and upkeep across a large pool of users and to ensure that all parts connect to one another to achieve the design function. State and local governments use dedicated gasoline taxes and other public funding mechanisms to pay for the planning, rights-of-way acquisition, construction, maintenance, and improvement of our highway systems.

> "Just as we must carefully plan for and invest in our capital infrastructure—our roads, bridges and waterlines, we must invest in our environmental or green infrastructure—our forests, wetlands, streams and rivers."
>
> PARRIS GLENDENING
> FORMER MARYLAND GOVERNOR

Green infrastructure is likewise an appropriate and necessary use of public funds and should be funded in the same way as our nation's built infrastructure— as primary budgetary items for which the costs are spread across a large pool of users and all parts connect to achieve maximum functionality. A city, county, or state would never build a road, water system, or utility network piece by piece with no advance planning or coordination between different components and jurisdictions. We should plan, design, and invest in our green infrastructure following the same approaches that are used for built infrastructure.

An increasing number of states and communities are using conventional mechanisms to finance green infrastructure projects—including bond referenda, real estate transfer taxes, lottery proceeds, dedicated development fees, direct appropriations,

Box 2.5

Growing, or Simply Spreading Out?

The following excerpt from the GreenSpace Alliance of Southeastern Pennsylvania's Web site demonstrates the argument for addressing conservation as a critical public investment.

> Unfortunately, while we spend billions of dollars to plan and build our highway infrastructure, our failure to plan for and to protect our green spaces condemns them to inevitable destruction. While over the past few decades the region's population has continued to stagnate, we have increased the amount of land we've developed by leaps and bounds. In other words, rather than growing, southeastern Pennsylvania is simply spreading out.
>
> Large areas of contiguous, or "linked," green spaces are particularly important to the region's economy and ecology. Linear greenways provide important habitat for wildlife, buffer streams from pollution and runoff, and create tranquil settings for recreation close to home, with minimal intrusion from the "outside world."

To address these problems, the GreenSpace Alliance of Southeastern Pennsylvania, a coalition of more than a hundred organizations, advocates an approach that uses GIS data and mapping to create an integrated system of open spaces in a five-county area and to help define the physical design for livable communities in the region. The alliance has used GIS-based analysis to develop a composite regional map and identify high-priority open space and urban/suburban areas. In the report on its findings, the alliance advocated setting priorities for protection on two kinds of lands: Open Space Priority Lands, where regional protection should be focused, and Suburban/Urban Priority Lands, where local community needs should predominate. The report continued, "A balance should be maintained between protection of critical open space, managed growth in undeveloped areas, and community revitalization." Using the information and following the recommendations of the Alliance can help communities protect the region's critical assets while directing growth and development to areas where it is most desirable.

• *For more information, see the GreenSpace Alliance of Southeastern Pennsylvania's Home Page at www.greenspacefun.org.*

and other mechanisms. States and communities have also made creative use of federal programs to further their green infrastructure initiatives, by including street tree programs as line items in the local government budget, for example. For green infrastructure to succeed, public funding must continue to be made available.

Principle 7: Green Infrastructure Affords Benefits to Nature and People

Interconnected green space systems benefit people, wildlife, ecological systems, and community quality of life. Strategic land-use decision making that protects green infrastructure reduces the need for gray infrastructure, freeing public funds for other community needs. Green infrastructure also reduces a community's susceptibility to floods, fires, mudslides, and other natural disasters.

The first step to reduce the vulnerability of human settlements to natural disasters is to identify high-risk areas. This is done by risk mapping—relating a natural hazard, such as a flood, to the terrain and to the probability that such an event will occur. When incorporated into a green infrastructure planning and implementation process, risk mapping can ensure the best use of the land and direct development away from floodplains and other areas at high risk of natural disasters.

There are many examples of the dangers of building communities without consideration of the surrounding environs. Building on floodplains has been shown time and again to be a dangerous and expensive proposition. After the devastating floods of 1993 along the Mississippi and Missouri rivers, the U.S. Soil Conservation Service purchased flood-prone farmlands for conversion to natural conditions at the cost of $25 million, protecting the floodplain to perform its natural function to avoid future devastation.

When development occurs too close to fire-prone forests, people again put themselves in harm's way. The traditional response is often to suppress fires in forests near residential areas, but scientists warn that forests in which fires are suppressed often burn much hotter and more dangerously when a fire finally erupts. Moreover, naturally occurring forest fires provide a valuable ecological function by reducing dead wood and ground brush, and they rejuvenate the landscape by recycling nutrients, providing ideal conditions for trees to grow. Fire also improves the forest floor as habitat for many species that prefer relatively open spaces to a dense thicket of brush and dead branches.

It is far less expensive to plan development away from where natural hazards are likely to occur than to try to combat a flood or forest fire that is threatening a residential area on the urban-wildland interface. Just as satellite maps and sophisticated computer simulations are helping scientists pinpoint places in danger of wildfires well before the blazes begin, these tools can be used as part of a green infrastructure effort to identify high-hazard areas first and then help locate residential and commercial neighborhoods away from these areas.

The ecological, social, and economic benefits of green infrastructure need to be documented and explained. Just as all forms of built infrastructure are promoted for the wide range of public and private benefits they provide, we need to promote green infrastructure systems actively for the wide range of essential ecological and social functions, values and benefits that accrue to people and nature. Effective green infrastructure initiatives describe and define the values and functions of interconnected networks of open space in a context that enables citizens to understand the ecological, human, and economic benefits. As an integral part of its efforts to preserve and protect green space in Wisconsin, the Community Open Space Partnership published *Paint the Town Green: Green Infrastructure for Tomorrow*, a plan for open space in which it clearly outlined the multiple ecological, social, and economic benefits of an interconnected system of green spaces for Wisconsin's communities and provided concrete steps for taking action.[22]

Principle 8: Green Infrastructure Respects the Needs and Desires of Landowners and Other Stakeholders

Green infrastructure does not require all the land in a green infrastructure network to be under public ownership. Privately owned land, particularly working farms and forests, can play an important role in any green space system. Successful green infrastructure initiatives require considering the perspectives of various stakeholders in the public, private, and nonprofit sectors and incorporating the concerns of citizen groups into the design.

Strategic conservation can meet with opposition from those who think it is antigrowth or antidevelopment. Success depends on sharing plans with the wide range of stakeholders, including those who may be in opposition to a proposed green infrastructure initiative. When green infrastructure is presented as a concept that will help plan development, the most vociferous opponents sometimes become the strongest allies.

In some parts of the country, strong feelings about private property rights may be at odds with a community's desire to protect landscapes, direct development, and preserve the rural way of life. Care must be taken to ensure that landowners feel their voices are heard, their opinions are valued, and their rights are respected. As it revised its land-use planning system in 1994, Larimer County, Colorado, developed a system it dubbed the Partnership Land Use System (PLUS) "to maintain and enhance . . . [the] county's quality of life and to be fundamentally fair to all our citizens and to respect their individual rights."[23] PLUS has been used to identify conservation sites for rare species, habitats for economically important species, areas of high species richness, and rare plan communities were worked into a map of the county to identify areas requiring habitat mitigation plans. Before

Box 2.6

The Threat of Wildfires

In a report discussing the causes and effects of the wildfires that raged throughout the West in 2000, the Congressional Research Service concluded that two major factors contributing to the threat were "the decline in forest and rangeland health and the expansion of residential areas into wildlands—the urban-wildland interface." The report goes on to discuss the impact of humans on natural ecosystems: "Over the past century, aggressive wildfire suppression, as well as past grazing and logging practices, have altered many ecosystems, especially those where light, surface fires were frequent. Many areas now have unnaturally high fuel loads (e.g., dead trees and dense thickets) and an historically unnatural mix of plant species (e.g., exotic invaders)." [1]

> [W]e should recognize that people who construct homes in fire-prone environments are just as imprudent as someone who parks a car on a railroad track. Fighting fires to "save" homes in the woods—often built by wealthy people—is a subsidy of immense proportions. Such fire-prone sites should be zoned off-limits to home construction, just as we attempt to zone construction away from river floodplains. [2]

Nationwide, wildfire damage to homes and property increased sixfold from the 1980s to the 1990s, to a total of $3.2 billion. In an average year between 1991 and 2000, 1,200 homes burned—more than double the number over the previous decade. The main reason for the escalating risk of fire damage is development in remote canyons and on hillsides near forest boundaries. The Forest Service estimates that over 40 million Americans live in what it calls the urban-wildland interface, directly adjacent to or scattered within unpopulated areas with wildland vegetation. [3]

1. Ross W. Gorte, *Forest Fire Protection, CRS Report for Congress*, Washington, D.C.: Congressional Research Service, 2000, 1.

2. George Wuerthner, "What Ever Happened to Letting Fires Burn?" *High Country News*, September 16, 1996.

3. Douglas Jehl, "Wildfire Damage Swells Sixfold as Rural Population Increases," *New York Times*, May 30, 2000, cited at Forest Guardians Web site, www.fguardians.org.

changes in land use may occur, developers must determine to what extent changes will affect these land features and how mitigation will be accomplished. These requirements provide developers with predictability and information about environmentally sensitive lands prior to application for a permit. Colorado Open Lands, which has been working since 1981 "to preserve the significant open lands and diminishing natural heritage of Colorado," also credits its success to the active involvement of landowners and public and private partnerships. Since its founding, Colorado Open Lands has permanently protected over seventy-six thousand acres.

As more communities gain awareness that not only wildlife and rare species are at risk, but also their way of life—whether ranching, farming, or simply enjoying nature—they will likely embrace green infrastructure as a means for protecting what they have come to cherish. Moreover, as landowners begin to understand how green space can increase the value of adjacent development, more people will become active supporters of green infrastructure initiatives.

Principle 9: Green Infrastructure Requires Making Connections to Activities within and beyond the Community

The success of green infrastructure requires bringing together people and programs engaged in various conservation initiatives and focuses on bridging the gap between conservation activities and other planning efforts. Considering green infrastructure in conjunction with smart growth helps government and communities provide a useful and beneficial framework for development while protecting vital agricultural and other working lands. Green infrastructure affords opportunities for and can build on programs related to everything from flood mitigation planning and river or waterfront management to environmental education and historic or cultural heritage, to outdoor recreation, to greenways or trails, to downtown revitalization or brownfield redevelopment.

The desired outcome for all green infrastructure initiatives is a green space network that functions as an ecological whole. Green infrastructure sees beyond political boundaries to focus on the natural landscape. This requires making connections with related activities not only within a community or jurisdiction but well beyond it—to those communities upstream or downstream that play a vital role in the ecosystem of the green space network.

Principle 10: Green Infrastructure Requires Long-Term Commitment

A green infrastructure plan and network design should be considered "living" documents that need to be modified and updated periodically to remain relevant as the community and region continue to grow and evolve. This requires

Box 2.7

Making Connections: Linking Hazard Mitigation to Community Conservation and Recreation Objectives, Kinston/Lenoir County, North Carolina

Developed by graduate students at the University of North Carolina in 2001, the Kinston/Lenoir County Green Infrastructure Plan for the Neuse River Floodplain seeks to identify opportunities to maintain, restore, and provide new green infrastructure along the Neuse River floodplain and adjacent areas in Lenoir County and the city of Kinston. The area suffered considerable damage from flooding caused by hurricanes Fran and Floyd. The local governments have used Federal Emergency Management Agency (FEMA) disaster relief funds to purchase many damaged properties lying in the floodplain.

The plan uses green infrastructure principles and complements existing community projects and goals such as the Kinston-Lenoir County Parks and Recreation Master Plan and the Greater Kinston Urban Area Growth Plan. The components of the Green Infrastructure Plan present ideas for how the Neuse River and its floodplain can provide Lenoir County and Kinston with additional recreational and environmental amenities. The governments can use the plan as a way to continue their flood mitigation work by turning vacant buyout areas into a network of parks, trails, and habitats along the Neuse River and the Adkin Branch stream that connects downtown Kinston and other areas in the community.

In accordance with the plan, the city of Kinston has purchased eight junkyards in the floodplain and one of the biggest has been turned into soccer fields. The "checkerboard" properties identified by the green infrastructure plan were bought with money from the Clean Water Management Trust Fund and converted to a large recreation and ecotourism area.

considering land management issues at the outset of the initiative, as well as how restoration and ongoing maintenance of various elements will be funded.

If a green infrastructure initiative is spearheaded by an elected official or group, preparing for the long term requires thinking about how to ensure that activities will outlast political changes. Bipartisan support and endorsement by a legislative body can help ensure that green infrastructure will have staying power, as can a strategic plan that extends beyond the term of office. In Florida, for example, control of the green infrastructure initiative spearheaded by Governor Lawton Chiles and the Greenways Commission was turned over to the Florida Greenways Coordinating Council, a bipartisan group with representatives from state government, regional agencies, nonprofit conservation organizations, industry, and other public and private organizations with a stake in the issue. The greenway initiative has persisted to this day and has had an enormous impact on Florida's landscape. Engaging citizens from the beginning also can help ensure that a program has the momentum to survive changes in government and priorities.

Each of the initiatives discussed in this book adhere to the principles discussed in this chapter, but perhaps none more closely than Florida. The following description of Florida's effort to design a statewide greenways system illustrates these principles in action.

GREEN INFRASTRUCTURE IN ACTION: FLORIDA GREENWAYS AND THE STATEWIDE ECOLOGICAL NETWORK

Florida's work in strategic conservation planning and green infrastructure extends back several decades. In fact, as early as the 1970s, University of Florida professor Larry Harris was among the preeminent scientists who, after studying the effects of fragmentation and isolation on wildlife populations, emphasized the importance of wildlife corridors for the survival of species. In the 1980s, Harris, Reed Noss, and others at the University of Florida became early advocates of landscape connectivity and the design of integrated conservation systems consisting of core preserves, buffer zones, and corridors. Harris continued to lead the state's efforts as an active and vocal member of the Florida Greenways Commission.

The state of Florida's green infrastructure efforts began in 1991, when several nonprofit organizations and concerned citizens collaborated on the development of the Florida Greenways Program. The Conservation Fund and 1000 Friends of Florida led the effort to protect the state's diminishing resources from the threat of development. Program advocates believed that a statewide system of greenways could help public agencies and nonprofit organizations develop and use clearly defined criteria to prioritize conservation needs and make land purchases strategically, rather than continuing to focus reactively under threat of development.

In 1993, Governor Lawton Chiles created the Florida Greenways Commission, a forty-member group charged with assessing the status of Florida's greenways, developing a vision for a statewide system of linked green spaces and greenways, drafting recommendations for state agency leadership of the program, and collecting public input on proposed plans for the future of the statewide system of greenways. The commission's membership represented conservation nonprofits; recreation groups; state, regional, and local government agencies; educational organizations; working lands advocates; and the business sector. Lead staff from 1000 Friends of Florida and facilitators from Florida State University's Growth Management Conflict Resolution Center supported the commission's work.

In its 1994 report, "Creating a Statewide Greenways System: For People . . . for Wildlife . . . for Florida," the commission recommended a greenways system

Box 2.8

Florida Greenways Commission Vision Statement, 1994

In the twenty-first century, Florida has a protected system of greenways that is planned and managed to conserve native landscapes, ecosystems, and their species and to connect people to the land . . . Florida's diverse wildlife species are able to move . . . within their ranges with less danger of being killed on roadways or becoming lost in towns or cities. Native landscapes and ecosystems are protected, managed, and restored through strong public and private partnerships. Sensitive riverine and coastal waterways are effectively protected by buffers of green, open space and working landscapes. . . . Florida's rich system of greenways helps sustain Florida's future by conserving its green infrastructure, by providing continuing economic benefits, by connecting people with their natural, historic and cultural heritage, and by improving the quality of life for people.

comprised of two networks: an Ecological Network, consisting of ecological hubs, linkages, and sites along rivers and coastlines and across watersheds; and a Recreational/Cultural Network, consisting of trail corridors that would connect parks to each other and to urban areas, working landscapes, and cultural/historic sites.

In 1995, Florida's greenways initiative transitioned from an NGO-led program to a government-based program, funded by the Florida legislature and led by the Florida Greenways Coordinating Council (FGCC). The Florida Department of Environmental Protection, which was designated as the statewide program's lead agency, contracted with the University of Florida to develop the physical design of a statewide greenways system and worked with the FGCC to prepare a five-year implementation plan that was released in September 1998. At this time, the leadership role was taken over by the Florida Greenways and Trails Council.

The Design Process for the Ecological Network

The Florida Ecological Network was designed by University of Florida faculty and graduate students in consultation with the Florida Greenways Commission, the Florida Greenways Coordinating Council, and the Florida Department of Environmental Protection (see Figure 5.5). The design goals for the Florida Ecological Network were to conserve critical elements of native ecosystems and landscapes, restore and maintain connectivity among native ecological systems and processes, facilitate the ability of ecosystems and landscapes to function as dynamic systems, and maintain the evolutionary potential of the components of the ecosystems to adapt to future environmental changes.

Florida used a GIS-based network design model to categorize both natural and built landscape features for their significance and compatibility with ecological conservation objectives. This information was used to identify hubs, the areas with the highest ranked ecological features, and linkages between these hubs. These hubs and linkages were combined to create a preliminary design for the Ecological Network. After the preliminary network design was finished, "human benefit areas" were added, such as lands connecting the trail network to urban areas and cultural sites.

The University of Florida team used coarse and fine filters in designing the Ecological Network so that it would support the greatest level of biodiversity. The coarse filter identified and protected entire ecosystems or communities and all of the associated species. Fine filters targeted the habitat needs of specific threatened or endangered species, such as the Florida panther. This type of analysis helped to ensure protection for species with particularly large or specific habitat requirements.

The Ten Principles Applied

The resulting network, particularly its ecological component, meets the green infrastructure criteria and adheres to the principles outlined in this chapter. The ecological network was designed so that land acquisition decisions could be made proactively *before* development—or the threat of development.

Florida's green infrastructure initiative engaged a diverse group of stakeholders and fostered collaboration among groups with disparate interests. The composition of all three leadership groups in Florida was purposely formulated to represent all the interests in the program, from the tourism and agricultural industries to private landowners, conservationists, and outdoor recreation advocates.

Public outreach and citizen involvement were a major focus of the groups tapped to lead the initiative. All phases of the green infrastructure network planning, design, and implementation featured extensive public involvement and education. Newsletters, fact sheets, a Florida Greenways poster, a Florida Greenways slideshow and video, workshops and roundtables, and press releases were used to disseminate information about greenways planning and to celebrate project milestones.

Linkage is a key aspect of Florida's green infrastructure efforts. The statewide greenways program and its successive leadership forums made critical links to other organizations—private and public—that played a role in making the vision a reality. The network design process involved people with many divergent interests. Whether people were interested in resource conservation, water management, environmental education, historic and cultural resource management, or recreation, the green infrastructure initiative reached people where their passions lay and provided a common vision for them to rally around and work toward.

The importance of linkage is also evident in the greenways system that was developed. The Ecological Network connects hubs and sites using ecologically important links such as rivers and wetlands. The Florida Greenways and Trails Council identified ten critical linkages as the highest priority for state protection, believing that linking protected areas in regions with heavy growth pressure would be critical to the ultimate success of the greenways initiative.

The Florida Ecological Network functions at different scales and cuts across county and other political jurisdictions, as well as watershed boundaries. Having a holistic visual representation of the entire landscape helps people appreciate that natural ecosystems rarely align with jurisdictional boundaries and therefore require joint management.

The GIS-based network design model developed by the University of Florida allowed unbiased analysis of the ecological value of various pieces of land. The model accounted for many landscape features, including vegetation, land use, water management potential, connectivity to other natural areas, and human population patterns. The model also focused on specific ecological goals, such as protecting the Florida's native wildlife. By providing planners and decision makers with clear criteria for making decisions, the resulting ecological network provides a sound rationale for and justification for land-use planning and land acquisition decisions.

By reaching into state coffers to fund the network design and implementation, the state of Florida demonstrated its commitment to strategic planning for land and water conservation. With start-up money provided by private foundations, $2 million was secured from the Florida Department of Transportation. The Department of Environmental Protection was named the lead state agency, building on its long history of support for public land acquisition.

The Success of the Network Design

The design results demonstrate that Florida's ecological network modeling approach was effective in identifying the land that should be conserved statewide. The Ecological Network protects Florida's native biodiversity, provides landscape linkages for wildlife and healthy fisheries, protects the supply of drinking water, guards against flooding and erosion, purifies the air, and protects natural viewsheds. But the benefits extend beyond these natural functions. By enhancing the natural environment and providing recreational opportunities, the network increases tourism, which generates $3 billion in revenues in the state, improves community quality of life for Floridians, and increases property values and the tax base in the state.

Support for greenways and green infrastructure principles has increased developers' interest in sustainable growth models, strengthened the connection to the land, and fostered support for natural resource conservation. Finally, Florida's approach to green infrastructure planning and its GIS-based model have served as prototypes for several other statewide and regional green infrastructure programs, extending the benefits far beyond the state.

• *For more information about Florida Greenways and the Statewide Ecological Network, visit www.dep.state.fl.us/gwt/about/ or www.dep.state.fl.us/gwt/network/ network.htm, as well as the other Web page links for the Florida Office of Greenways and Trails.*

Notes

1. See George Perkins Marsh, *Man and Nature—Or Physical Geography as Modified by Human Action* (Cambridge, MA: Harvard University Press, 1965 [1864]).

2. As discussed in Thoreau's classic, *Walden Pond*, originally published in 1860.

3. Howard discussed this in *Garden Cities of Tomorrow*, published in 1902. Quoted at The Effect of Ebenezer Howard and the Garden City Movement on Twentieth-Century Town Planning, www.rickmansworthherts.freeserve.co.uk/howardl.htm.

4. Victor E. Shelford, "Preserves of Natural Conditions," *Transactions of the Illinois Academy of Science* 13:1 (1920), 37–58.

5. Victor E. Shelford, "The Preservation of Natural Biotic Communities," *Ecology* 14 (1933), 240–245. For more information on Shelford's work see Robert A. Croker, *Pioneer Ecologist: The Life and Work of Victor Ernest Shelford, 1877–1968* (Washington, DC: Smithsonian Institution Press, 1991).

6. George M. Wright, Joseph S. Dixon, and Ben H. Thompson, *Fauna of the National Parks of the United States* (Washington, DC: National Park Service, May 1932), 37.

7. Bronx River Parkway, Historic Overview. See www.nycroads.com/roads/bronx-river/.

8. Ibid.

9. Ecology of Fame, Environmental Movement Timeline, www.ecotopia.org/ehof/timeline.html.

10. Ed Zahniser, "Walk Softly and Carry a Big Map: Historical Roots of Network Planning," *Wild Earth* 10:2 (Summer 2000): 33–38.

11. Benton MacKaye, *The New Exploration: A Philosophy of Regional Planning* (New York: Harcourt Brace, 1928).

12. Aldo Leopold, *Game Management* (New York: Charles Scribner's Sons, 1933).

13. Ian McHarg, *Design with Nature* (Philadelphia: The Falcon Press, 1969).

14. Phil Lewis and his colleagues have applied his environmental corridors approach repeatedly over the last fifty years for projects in Illinois, Wisconsin, Alaska, the Upper Mississippi River Valley, and the Great Lakes Basin.

15. Rachel Carson, *Silent Spring* (Boston: Houghton Mifflin Co. 1962).

16. Public Law 88-577, quoted in *The Wilderness Act Handbook* (Washington, D.C.: The Wilderness Society, 1998).

17. Public Law 90-190, Sec 101. See http://ceq.eh.doe.gov/nepa/regs/nepa/nepaeqia.htm.

18. Richard T. T. Forman, "The Ethics of Isolation, the Spread of Disturbance, and Landscape Ecology," in *Landscape Heterogentry and Disturbance* (New York: Springer-Verlag, 1987), 213.

19. See, for example, Reed F. Noss and Larry D. Harris, "Nodes, Networks, and MUMs; Preserving Diversity at All Scales," *Environmental Management* 10:299–309.

20. Defenders of Wildlife, *Integrating Land Use Planning and Biodiversity* (Washington, D.C.: Defenders of Wildlife, 2003), 38.

21. For more information, see www.gardenstategreenways.org.

22. The full report can be viewed at www.ouropenspaces.org.

23. Defenders of Wildlife, *Integrating Land Use Planning and Biodiversity* (Washington, D.C.: Defenders of Wildlife, 2003), 54.

chapter three

The Benefits of a Green Infrastructure Approach

A comprehensive, proactive, green infrastructure approach to land conservation and development provides a number of immediate benefits to communities and regions. Green infrastructure networks ensure that critical habitats and the connections between them are protected, conserving the rich biodiversity present on Earth today. Green infrastructure helps to sustain forests, farms, and other working lands and allows natural systems to function as intended, saving communities millions of dollars in flood mitigation, water purification, and a host of other savings resulting from avoiding expensive man-made solutions.

Green infrastructure also provides people with mental and physical health benefits derived from living near nature. Green infrastructure provides opportunities for outdoor recreation, from biking to fishing, and protects valuable natural amenities that attract tourists and the dollars they have to spend. Green infrastructure also helps to direct growth away from areas prone to forest fires, floods, and other natural hazards, saving lives, as well as the millions of dollars needed for recovery. Finally, by providing predictability and certainty about growth and the patterns of development, green infrastructure helps reduce opposition to development and mediate the opposing viewpoints of "developers" and "conservationists." Communities that want more housing, more jobs, *and* more open space can use green infrastructure to achieve all of these goals.

GREEN INFRASTRUCTURE AND BIODIVERSITY

Across the country a battle is being waged between people and wildlife. The daily newspapers tell the story: In suburban Philadelphia and the Virginia suburbs of Washington, D.C., people are frightened by the sudden appearance of cougars in their backyards. In the Midwest, black bears dig through trashcans in suburban neighborhoods. Western ranchers complain that the reintroduction of wolves and grizzly bears threatens their flocks. In Florida, alligators sun themselves in streams near where children play. And all across the nation, traffic fatalities result from people hitting deer, antelope, wolves, and other "wild" animals. Road kills are a leading cause of death for animals—and of injury to humans. Researchers estimate that at least a million animals are killed on U.S. highways each day.[1]

This is a fight that animals are destined to lose. Ninety-five percent of the species listed under the federal Endangered Species Act are endangered by habitat loss, fragmentation, or other alteration to the landscape.[2] Exotic plants used to landscape new developments invade disturbed habitat, creating another threat to species. In California, sprawl is threatening 188 of 286 imperiled or endangered species;[3] in Florida, the encroachment of residential and commercial development on panther habitat has occurred so frequently that biologists estimate that there are fewer than eighty adult panthers left; in the Seattle area, the Chinook (king) salmon—symbol of the Pacific Northwest and a huge economic resource—is at risk of extinction because of haphazard development.

If current trends continue, scientists warn, we may experience an unprecedented wave of extinctions that put at risk the rich web of life present today. Biodiversity—the variability among living organisms on the earth—sustains human life. Biodiversity includes the diversity within and between species and within and between ecosystems. Biodiversity among ecosystems not only provides for a wide range of animal species, it also provides people with food, medicine, and shelter. It is biodiversity that provides us with the wide array of food we enjoy. It is biodiversity that leads to new breakthroughs in medical science. Today, roughly half of all prescription medicines are derived from natural resources.

The two greatest threats to biodiversity are habitat loss/degradation and invasive species, both of which are strongly correlated with sprawling growth. Unfortunately, many wildlife conservation programs focus on protecting a single site or a single species without providing an alternative plan for growth or development. Green infrastructure offers a solution. By directing growth away from important habitats, green infrastructure helps to protect the biodiversity present today.

Green infrastructure protects the forests and wetlands that provide habitat for the vast array of species on earth today. Wetlands, for example, serve as reservoirs of biodiversity and support a wide range of wildlife, from shorebirds to alligators. Although freshwater ecosystems cover only 1 percent of the Earth's surface, they hold more than 40 percent of the world's species and 12 percent of all animal species. A range of products can be gleaned from the system of marshes and bogs, including cranberries and other fruits, fish and shellfish, resins, timber and fuel wood, and reeds that can be woven into baskets. Two-thirds of all species used for seafood are dependent on coastal wetlands at some stage in their life cycle, a critical function that far surpasses the actual area covered by these wetlands. Wetlands also support large rice plantations, the staple diet of over half the world's population.

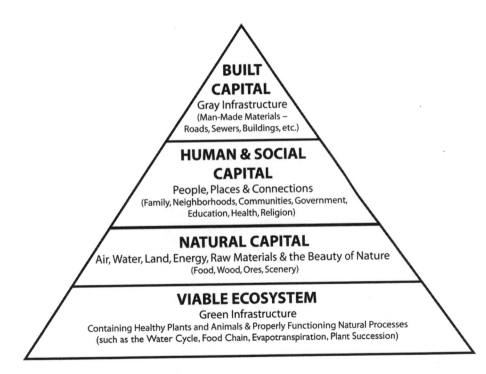

Figure 3.1
This sustainability pyramid illustrates how viable ecosystems preserved as green infrastructure serve as society's foundation by providing the natural resources that support our human systems and man-made surroundings. A variety of natural processes interact to create a healthy environment and allow us to harvest the food we eat and obtain the raw materials to build our communities. Credit: Adapted from Karen S. Williamson, *Growing with Green Infrastructure*, © 2003 by Heritage Conservancy. All rights reserved.

Figure 3.2
Wetlands provide habitat for wildlife, serve as natural basins for storm water, and purify groundwater of pesticides and other toxins. Credit: Mark Benedict.

By providing a place for nature—a place that accommodates the needs of wildlife—green infrastructure is a tool for saving species from extinction. Careful selection of where to set aside open space helps to ensure that animals have sufficient space, the right climate, and the appropriate ecosystem to survive. Many green infrastructure network designs focus on protecting the critical habitats of rare, threatened, or endangered (RTE) species and providing adequate room for them to thrive.

Animals also need pathways to get from one habitat location to another. In the Rockies, for example, elk, deer, and grizzly bears migrate in the fall from higher to lower elevations where they spend their winters. Green infrastructure initiatives help meet the migration needs of animals by linking the places where they live. This is key to maintaining strong wildlife populations. In the Pinhook Swamp, for example, a priority for protection was a vital travel route for the Florida black bear between the Osceola National Forest in north Florida and the Okeefenokee Swamp in southern Georgia. Officials estimate the bear's population to be from 1,200 to 3,000; the subspecies that lives in Osceola is considered threatened in Florida. Because the national forest is too small to sustain them, experts argue that protecting the Pinhook is critical to the bears' survival. In 2001, 60,000 acres of the 170,000-acre swamp passed from private to public ownership at a cost of $60 million.

The federal government recognizes and protects species through the Endangered Species Act and other legislation; state and local governments have followed suit by including environmental impact statements as part of their planning requirements. Green infrastructure offers an opportunity to take biodiversity protection a step further. When biodiversity is included in network design goals, the resulting green infrastructure network and plan gives policymakers and land-use planners the

Box 3.1

Wildlife Corridors

Wildlife corridors are stretches of land that connect otherwise disconnected wildlife habitat. First espoused by Harvard biologist Edward O. Wilson in the 1960s, the wildlife corridor concept has become an important technique for managing at-risk wildlife populations. Corridor projects are in place throughout the United States. In California, for example, more than 160 scientists, conservationists, and land managers came together for a one-day mapping charrette. The resulting atlas and report identified more than three hundred *linkages* that needed immediate protection.

Several nonprofit organizations have initiated projects to address the need for wildlife corridors. One example is American Wildlands' Corridors of Life project, which uses scientific modeling to locate the best potential public and private lands for conversion to wildlife corridors throughout the Northern Rocky Mountains. The Wildland Project's Room to Roam campaign is working to protect the most endangered wildlife linkages in the Rocky Mountains, along the spine of the continent. In 1990, the Wildlife Conservation Society launched the Paseo Pantera ("path of the panther"). The purpose of the initiative is to establish a biological corridor of parks and protected areas throughout the length of Central America—an effort that would not only protect the panther but a wealth of other species that require unbroken blocks of habitat to survive.

Ecologists consider wildlife corridors crucial because they increase the total amount of habitat available for species, while counteracting the fragmentation that has resulted from human activity. The benefits include greater biodiversity, larger wildlife populations, wider ranges of food sources and shelter, and increased long-term genetic viability due to population interbreeding. Corridor projects throughout the United States and beyond are critical building blocks for green infrastructure networks.

information they need to make decisions that will minimize the impact of development on habitat and animals. Biodiversity is protected by identifying, undertaking scientific analysis of, and preserving the natural diversity within a landscape; diverting development away from rare landscape elements; protecting large contiguous, connected areas that contain critical habitats; and reducing negative *edge effects* and the invasion of nonnative species. With the green infrastructure approach, the interface between humans and animals is no longer a win/lose proposition, but rather, a mutually satisfactory solution.

Box 3.2

Carbon Sequestration through Reforestation

For companies that need to comply with regulations concerning greenhouse gas emissions, carbon sequestration through reforestation has emerged as a cost-effective way to offset emissions and generate carbon credits. Carbon sequestration is based on the fact that, as plants grow, they incorporate carbon from the atmosphere into their structure through photosynthesis. Carbon sequestration through reforestation is relatively inexpensive and yields quantifiable results. It also provides benefits beyond carbon sequestration (e.g., wildlife and fish habitat, enhanced water quality, etc.), which is perhaps the main reason that companies are beginning to see it as a way to comply with environmental laws while also enhancing their public image.

Catahoula Lake, a scenic haven for migratory birds located in the Mississippi Delta in Louisiana, is the site of a groundbreaking carbon sequestration project in which The Conservation Fund, American Electric Power (AEP), and the U.S. Fish and Wildlife Service (USFWS) have partnered to acquire, protect, and restore a hardwood forest on more than eighteen thousand acres.

After acquiring the acreage from Tensas Delta Land Co., the Fund in turn conveyed 10,257 acres to AEP for $3.2 million and 8,115 acres to the USFWS for $1.5 million from the Migratory Bird Conservation Fund, which provides federal funding for land acquisitions. AEP has planted native trees on its property and a portion of the property owned by the USFWS. Eventually, 3 million trees will be planted. The entire 18,372 acres will be managed by the USFWS as part of the Catahoula National Wildlife Refuge, benefiting birds, deer, and other wildlife.

AEP will submit data on carbon sequestration annually to the U.S. Department of Energy. Over the seventy-year period of the project, it is estimated that more than 5 million tons of carbon dioxide will be sequestered and converted into biomass.

The Lower Mississippi River Valley is also home to another carbon sequestration partnership between The Conservation Fund, the Tex Corp., and Environmental Synergy. This project will contribute to the USFWS's long-term goal of reforesting lands that have been cleared for other uses but have now become fallow and of marginal economic value. As a result of the seventy-year project, it is estimated that more than eight hundred thousand metric tons of CO_2 will be removed from the atmosphere. Other environmental benefits will include reduced soil erosion and agricultural runoff, and enhanced biodiversity.

Farther north, a similar sequestration effort has established America's newest national wildlife reserve: the Red River National Wildlife Refuge in northwest Louisiana. Entergy has partnered with The Conservation Fund, Environmental Synergy, Inc., and the USFWS to acquire six hundred acres along a critical migratory bird corridor. The utility has planted native trees to restore important bottomland hardwood habitat and sequester approximately 275,000 tons of atmospheric carbon. Eventually the refuge will encompass fifty thousand acres and will offer public recreation opportunities such as fishing and hiking and educational exhibits.

Source: Lawrence A. Selzer, "Carbon Copy," *Energy User News*, November 8, 2002. See www.energyusernews.com.

THE ENVIRONMENTAL FUNCTIONS OF FORESTS, WETLANDS, AND OTHER OPEN SPACES

Green infrastructure networks provide many ecological benefits that most people take for granted. In addition to providing critical habitat for animal and plant species, trees purify the air we breathe: they remove nitrogen dioxide, sulfur dioxide, carbon monoxide, and ozone, and store or sequester carbon in wood. Once considered useless, wetlands—swamps, marshes, fens, and bogs—have been proven to be essential wildlife habitat, massive water filters, and natural basins that hold water when it rains. Wetlands act like sponges: they absorb precipitation and runoff and slowly release it into the ground or outlet streams.

> "Functioning natural ecosystems perform services that are the fundamental life-support systems upon which human civilization depends."
>
> ECOLOGICAL SOCIETY OF AMERICA

The environmental functions provided by wetlands include groundwater replenishment, shoreline stabilization and storm protection, sediment and nutrient retention, climate change mitigation, and water purification. Many wetland plants have the capacity to remove toxic substances that come from pesticides, industrial discharges, and mining activities. Wetlands can also be highly effective in dealing with high levels of nutrients. In Florida's cypress swamps, for example, 98 percent of all nitrogen and 97 percent of all phosphorous entering the wetlands from wastewater were removed before the water entered the groundwater. The destruction of wetlands or their conversion to agricultural use releases large quantities of carbon dioxide, the gas that accounts for at least 60 percent of global warming.

Trees also preserve watersheds and help improve the quality and quantity of drinking water. According to a study by the World Wildlife Fund, more than a third of the world's 105 biggest cities rely on fully or partly protected forests for much of their drinking water—a much less expensive option than building and maintaining water treatment plants (see Table 3.1).[4]

A study undertaken by American Rivers, the Natural Resources Defense Council, and Smart Growth America concluded that replacing natural areas with roads, parking lots, and buildings has a profound effect on water supply. Due to the increase in impervious surfaces, Atlanta lost an estimated 56.9 to 132.8 billion gallons of drinking water between 1982 and 1997—enough to supply the daily household needs of 1.5 to 3.6 million people per year.[5] More than one-third of the American population gets their drinking water directly from groundwater, and the remaining two-thirds who depend on surface water also are affected by changes in wetlands, as about half of a stream's volume comes from groundwater. As communities look for strategies to cope with water shortages, green infrastructure plans that provide adequate protection for watersheds and wetlands could provide a valuable answer.

Figure 3.3
Trees store nutrients from runoff and release water and oxygen into the atmosphere. Roots and vegetation encourage the infiltration of groundwater; contaminants and nutrients are filtered by plants and microbes. Credit: USDA National Agroforestry Center.

Table 3.1

They'll Drink to That

Big cities worldwide rely on protected areas to provide residents with clean drinking water. These lands offer a local, if unheralded and less controversial, alternative to piping in water from afar. Protecting land costs less than building filtration plants. Like giant sponges, forests soak up water and release it slowly, limiting floods when it rains and storing water when it does not. Watershed protection near cities is thus smart — both economically and ecologically.

	Population	Protected land (square miles)	
Rio de Janeiro, Brazil	6 million	1,249	14 protected areas supply 80 percent of the city's drinking water.
Johannesburg, South Africa	2 million	937	A significant part of the city's water comes from the Ukhlahlamba-Drakensberg World Heritage site.
Tokyo, Japan	8 million	1,013	A river fed by national parks provides 97 percent of the city's drinking water.
Melbourne, Australia	4 million	429	90 percent of its water supply is provided by protected mountain watersheds.
New York, New York	8 million	385	Catskill State Park protects watersheds that supply 90 percent of the city's drinking water.
Jakarta, Indonesia	9 million	212	Water that comes from watersheds in national parks is valued at $1.5 billion.

Source: Dan Parras, They'll Drink to That. *Audubon*, May 2004.

Flood Mitigation

Forests and wetlands also serve invaluable flood mitigation services. Forested areas help to reduce the amount of storm water runoff and its impact. On forest lands, some rainwater stays on the leaves of trees, giving it more time to evaporate directly to the air rather than adding to the water flowing over the ground. Leaves also reduce raindrop impact, which in turn reduces soil erosion. Tree roots absorb water from the soil, making the soil drier and able to store more rainwater, and hold the soil in place, reducing the movement of sediment that can shrink river channels downstream. Ground that is covered by vegetation also absorbs greater amounts of water than ground that is paved or has structures on it.

There are many examples around the world of what happens when we remove trees from the landscape. Deforestation releases sediments into rivers and streams,

Box 3.3

Natural Protection from Flooding

Scientists at the Centre for Ecology and Hydrology in Bangor, England, are looking at trees as a solution to the flooding that has plagued towns and communities in the region. They found that land with trees can hold vast amounts of water that would otherwise stream down hills and surge along rivers. "The extent of water absorption was entirely unexpected," said Dr. Zoe Carroll of the center.

Scientists at the centre have collaborated with farmers from Pontbren, in the North Powys hills to find more sustainable land use practices. The farmers cut back on grazing land, planted more trees to provide shelter for the animals, and made the land more ecologically friendly. When they noticed that during rainstorms their newly planted woodland seemed to absorb vast quantities of water while grazed land let the rain pour down the hillside, they invited scientists to study the land. Scientists found that the woodland was *60 times* more effective at absorbing water than soil on grazed land. "We expected to find a difference," said Carroll, "but not one of this magnitude."

Carroll and other scientists have suggested that planting trees in strategic areas could help mitigate against the risk of flooding. "Water will always move down a hill," said Carroll, "but this way we could stop it all arriving at the same time."

Source: Robin McKie, "Trees Hold Answer to Flood Menace," *The Observer*, Sunday, September 26, 2004.

shrinking channels and a river's ability to carry water without overflowing. Increased river channel sediments also impact stream ecology, reducing fish species and the natural productivity of aquatic species.

With deforestation, water tables fall, land once buffered by woodland becomes more prone to drought, and landslides and flash floods destroy roads, crops, and entire communities. Less than 1 percent of the land area on Haiti, once a lush tropical island, is forested. The lack of trees in this "desert of the Caribbean" has been blamed for the devastating mudslides and flash floods that have become almost commonplace, killing more than four thousand people in 2004 alone.

Analysts of the December 2004 tsunami that hit thirteen countries and killed more than three hundred thousand people suggest that the damage would have been far less if mangrove forests and reefs had been conserved. Mangroves have intertwined root systems that help to bind the shore together, effectively providing a shield against wind and waves. In Phuket, Thailand, for example, damage to the Marriott hotel, where strict environmental regulations led to the protection of the mangroves at the beachfront, was far less than in comparable areas. Experts also estimate that the tsunami's impact would have been far worse in the Maldives had the government not been diligent about protecting the network of coral reefs that shield the islands from the sea.

Unfortunately, many countries have stripped their coastlines of their natural protection. Experts say more than half of Indonesia's coastal mangrove forests have been destroyed in the past five decades to make way for commercial shrimp ponds, beachside resorts, and commercial development. Bangladesh has likewise destroyed its coastal mangroves, leaving it more vulnerable to flooding, especially during the annual monsoon season.

Wetlands also can play a particularly important role in preventing flooding in the watershed, storing water during heavy rains, slowing runoff into streams and reducing the overflow during peak floods. Converting wetlands sometimes requires major feats of engineering that can prove to be not only expensive but dangerous. Changes made to the river system to accommodate agriculture and urbanization were likely the principle cause of the great 1993 flood along the Mississippi and Missouri rivers. Levees and floodwalls constructed to control the path of the rivers increased the volume of water that could be held in the channel and thus the magnitude of the flooding when the levees broke. Moreover, approximately 80 percent of the wetlands that existed at mid-century had been drained. This not only reduced their ability to act as a natural storage reservoir for floodwaters it also enabled the water to run off more quickly.

Figure 3.4
Mangroves have intertwined root systems that help to bind the shore together and shield the land from wind and waves—natural protection from tropical storms and hurricanes that is much cheaper and more effective than man-made solutions. Credit: David Addison.

Box 3.4

The Danger of Building on Floodplains

The natural role of a floodplain is to carry excess water during periods of heavy runoff, but when the floodplain is walled off behind levees, the artificially narrow river must rise higher to compensate. And while levees protect farms and communities during minor floods, giant floods will still reclaim the floodplain, no matter how high the levees. This is what happened in 1993, when the Mississippi and Missouri rivers overflowed, causing major devastation to the communities in the floodplain.

Researcher David Galat is among those who believe that the most logical move is to get out of the line of fire—to move away from rivers that refuse to be tamed and to allow the floodplain to work as a natural damper on flood heights and a source of wildlife habitat. Since the 1993 flood, fifty thousand acres in Missouri alone have been returned to the floodplain by opening levees in areas like the Big National Muddy Fish and Wildlife Refuge.

Immediately following the 1993 flood, several towns were relocated above the Mississippi and Missouri floodplains, but the levees have been restored, and homes and malls are once again being built behind them. Galat and other scientists warn that these levees will eventually break again, if the water does not simply rise above them. Although scientists believe that little can be done to protect communities from 100-year floods, like the 1993 event, Galat argues that we should focus on what the effects of "messing with the river" are on the floods that occur every couple of years. The height of these floods is profoundly increased by building levees, wetland loss, deforestation, stream channelization, and changes in land use.

Galat argues that channelization and building reflect "the human attitude that technology will solve all your problems." The costly and futile struggle against floods reflects a mistaken assumption, Galat concludes. "A flood is not a disturbance of a river. The absence of a flood is a disturbance of a river."

Source: University of Wisconsin Disaster Management Center, Flood of Evidence, http://whyfiles.org/107flood/5.html, November 23, 2004.

The floods that occurred when the Mississippi and Missouri rivers overflowed killed fifty people, submerged 8 million acres of farmland, required the evacuation of twenty-six thousand people, and damaged over fifty-six thousand homes. Economic losses directly attributable to the flooding totaled $10 to 12 billion. Not surprisingly, the greatest economic losses occurred in cities located in the floodplain. In Des Moines, Iowa, located in the center of the flood region, the water treatment plant flooded, causing over 250,000 residents to go without drinking water for nineteen days. Water pipes, contaminated by floodwaters carrying sewage and agricultural chemicals, had to be flushed out before the municipal water supply was reconnected. The economic losses in Des Moines alone totaled approximately $716 million.

Urban Forestry

It is not only large rural forests that provide ecological benefits; in urban areas trees serve as what Frederick Law Olmsted called the "lungs of the city." For example, each year in Chicago, the urban tree canopy removes 15 metric tons of carbon monoxide, 84 metric tons of sulfur dioxide, 89 metric tons of nitrogen dioxide, 191 metric tons of ozone, and 212 metric tons of particulates. Meanwhile, the tree cover in New York City—consisting of more than 5 million trees covering nearly 17 percent of its land—helps remove enough airborne toxins to save taxpayers $10 million a year in pollution mitigation costs.[6]

Several cities have undertaken tree planting and preservation efforts to capitalize on these benefits. In Stuttgart, Germany, for example, urban forests are strategically maintained and managed at certain locations to intercept and purify predominant winds. In the 1990s, a public-private partnership planted more than two hundred thousand trees in the city of Sacramento, California. The Western Center for Urban Forest Research found that the resulting urban forest removes over two hundred thousand metric tons of carbon dioxide from the atmosphere each year, saving taxpayers as much as $3 million annually in pollution cleanup costs.[7]

Trees also help to cool our cities. Major shade trees can cool surface temperatures between nine and thirteen degrees.[8] Lower temperatures can be an important factor in stemming the production of hazardous air pollutants like ozone, which contributes to asthma and other respiratory diseases. And of course, trees provide important habitat for birds, squirrels, and a host of other animals that bring life to our urban neighborhoods.

Studies reveal that, to be environmentally healthy, the tree cover of an area should be at least 40 percent, a number that seems out of reach in many urban areas. Since 1973, the Atlanta metropolitan area has lost 25 percent of its tree cover. The 350,000 acres of land developed translates to a loss of nearly 50 acres of trees every day. Between 1973 and 1997, tree canopy in the Washington, D.C., metropolitan area was reduced by 64 percent.[9] These numbers are repeated wherever suburbanization is taking place. With the destruction of our forests, we lose the benefits they provide to people and nature. Strategic conservation through green infrastructure can help communities counteract the devastating effect by identifying and protecting places where trees and plants can flourish.

Box 3.5

Benefits of the Urban Forest

Research has shown that healthy city trees:
- Create cleaner, healthier, and more breathable air
- Cool parking lots and parked cars
- Mitigate the impacts of urban heat islands
- Shade homes and buildings, making them cooler and more energy efficient
- Block winter winds
- Retain rain on their leaf and branch surfaces, lessening the impact of storm runoff
- Increase real estate values
- Provide neighborhoods with a sense of place
- Attract more shoppers and more money to business districts
- Attract new business, homeowners, and tourism
- Reduce domestic violence and crime
- Improve children's performance in school
- Shorten hospital stays and reduce need for medication
- Lessen exposure to damaging solar radiation
- Provide restorative experiences that ease mental fatigue and stress

Source: *Urban Forestry News,* Spring 2004.

THE ECONOMIC VALUE OF NATURAL SYSTEMS

It is far less expensive to let Mother Nature's systems keep water and air clean than to craft technological solutions. In Massachusetts, for example, the 8,534 acres of freshwater marsh and wooded swamp in the Charles River Basin are estimated to provide more than $95 million in economic benefit annually, including $40 million in flood damage prevention, $31 million in recreation value from fishing and hunting, and $25 million in pollution reduction.

The nonprofit organization American Forests estimates that trees in the nation's metropolitan areas contribute $400 billion in storm water retention alone, by eliminating the need for expensive storm water retention facilities.[10] When lands are preserved for flood storage, national studies show an eight to one dollar savings ratio versus man-made flood-control structures.[11] The recent tree loss in the

Philadelphia metropolitan area has contributed a missed opportunity estimated at $105 million. In addition to the benefits gleaned by reducing stormwater runoff, the American Forestry Association estimates that a fifty-year-old urban tree saves seventy-five dollars a year in air conditioning, seventy-five dollars a year in stormwater and soil erosion control, seventy-five dollars a year in wildlife shelter, and fifty dollars a year in air pollution control. In the Delaware Valley, experts have quantified the benefits of trees: the area's urban forest removes 1.7 million pounds of air pollutants each year, a value estimated at $3.9 million annually; stores an estimated 26.8 million tons of carbon; and sequesters nearly 8,585 tons of carbon each year.[12]

A recent assessment estimated the average dollar value of the world's ecosystem services at $33 trillion per year.[13] The estimated cost of infrastructure improvements to provide safe drinking water nationwide amounts to over $138 billion. The city of Topeka is one of an increasing number of municipalities that are preserving or restoring natural landscapes rather than building man-made structures to direct the flow of water. One inch of rain in Topeka translates to 940 million gallons of stormwater. As the city became concerned about runoff, it looked to surrounding communities to find solutions. For example, rather than using expensive concrete channels and underground pipes, the Soldier Creek Watershed, a pilot project in North Topeka, is exploring the use of vegetated swales, constructed wetlands, and other practices to contain and treat storm water.

Faced with an order from the U.S. Environmental Protection Agency to build a filtration plant—a project estimated at $6 to $8 billion, New York City found a much less expensive option: protecting the 2,000-square-mile Catskill/Delaware Watershed in upstate New York from which it gets its water. New York City spent $1.5 billion on land acquisition, the construction of new storm sewers and septic systems, and programs to help farmers limit their pollution. The biggest expense for New York City was the purchase of property around the reservoirs, which created buffers of undeveloped land and let nature do its water-purifying work. In addition to the billions saved in construction costs for a new treatment plant, New York City has saved many billions more in maintenance and repair costs.

In the years since New York City initiated its watershed protection program, more than 140 cities have considered a similar approach. Boston enacted a comprehensive watershed program similar to New York's, including land acquisitions, wildlife control, and regulation of development along tributaries. In Ocean City, New Jersey, voters approved a property tax to provide nearly $4 million to buy land that would protect their water supply. Several countries beyond the United States have also begun to recognize the benefits of protecting watersheds. In 2001, the European Union included watershed protection in its water-quality protection requirements.

ECONOMIC BENEFITS

Studies indicate that people value natural ecosystems and are willing to pay for maintaining them. Although it is often difficult to translate people's love of open space or natural landscapes into a dollar amount, some studies have attempted to do so. A recent study of the Florida Everglades, for example, concluded that Florida residents are willing to pay an average of seventy dollars per household per year to protect Everglades wildlife—for what economists refer to as its "existence value"—and fifty-nine dollars per year to protect its water resources, which translates to $12 billion to protect the Everglades in perpetuity.[14]

A Boon for Tourism

An often overlooked benefit of green space and wetlands is their natural beauty and their attraction to tourists as sites for fishing, hunting, and wildlife watching. Many of the finest wetland sites are protected as national parks or wildlife refuges and generate considerable income from tourist and recreational uses. In fact, wildlife-related recreation is one of the most popular forms of recreation in the United States. In 2001, 82 million people participated in hunting, fishing, and wildlife watching, while about 89 million people attended a major league baseball or professional football game. Sport fishing alone boosted the nation's economy by $108.4 billion in 1996;[15] in 2001, the total direct expenditures by people engaged in viewing and photographing wildlife was $38.4 billion.[16] Setting aside new wildlife and birding trails as part of a green infrastructure network can help communities benefit economically from this growing nature-based industry.

In rural areas, the economy may be particularly vulnerable to a loss of open space. In West Virginia, for example, the hunting, fishing, and wildlife recreation industries represent a significant percentage of the state's economic receipts. Hunting alone generates over $243 million a year in retail sales and has a total impact statewide of almost $400 million. Roughly 6,246 jobs are supported by the hunting industry, which generates more than $108 million in workers' wages. The fishing industry generates another $304 million in retail sales, pumping over $300 million into local economies throughout the state. About 4,450 jobs are supported by the fishing industry, which generates over $71 million in wages. Other wildlife recreation activities, such as bird watching and camping, account for $115 million in retail sales, support 3,466 jobs, and provide $54 million in wages. Much of the economic gain is from out-of-state hunters and outdoor recreationists who travel to West Virginia from surrounding states, drawn by the vast amounts of land that remain undeveloped. The money generated by wildlife industries in rural communities tends to remain in local economies for a relatively long period of time, multiplying the boost to the economy. In West Virginia, as well as other rural states and regions, development that impacts hunting, fishing, and other outdoor recreation could have unintended impacts on economic stability.[17]

Ecotourism is the fastest growing segment of the tourism industry. A 1994 study found that 77 percent of North American consumers had taken a vacation involving nature, outdoor adventure, or learning about another culture. In a survey conducted by the 1987 National Commission on the Outdoors, natural beauty came out as the top reason for travel, followed by historic sites. As Americans become ever more environmentally conscious, the ecotourism industry is likely to grow. In 1998, the World Tourism Organization predicted that international travelers would remain "interested in visiting and maintaining environmentally sound destinations."[18] In a 2004 survey conducted by the University of Miami for the state of Florida, 92 percent of Florida's tourism leaders responded that they "agree" or "strongly agree" with the statement, "The conservation of Florida's natural and historic assets is necessary for the long-term success of my business."[19]

Recreational trails, which may be part of a green infrastructure plan, also serve to attract people and commercial enterprises that serve them. In 1996, Denver, Colorado, had 149 bicycle shops, compared to just 28 in Atlanta, Georgia, even though a million more people lived there. Denver's thriving market for bicycles is directly attributable to the availability of trails and pathways where people can ride.

The flow of tourists and recreational spending produce additional employment and opportunities for existing residents. Multiplier effects enhance the value of natural amenities. Additional incomes are generated from encouraging the people who service the tourist industry and retirees—from hotel workers, to hospital staff, to taxi and bus drivers—to spend their time and money within the community. "A community that expects to capture and maintain incomes from tourism and people with non-employment income must structure the economy to maintain the amenities that attract these people," conclude Clyde F. Kiker and Alan W. Hodges.[20] Although the goals of tourism-related developers and environmentalists are often perceived as being at odds with one another, the green infrastructure approach offers a means for simultaneously achieving the goals of both.

The elements of a green infrastructure network—whether hubs protecting vast tracts of open space (such as our national parks) or greenways in urban settings—often serve as a draw for new commercial activities. In the mid-1980s, community leaders in Augusta, Georgia, realized the potential for transforming the riverfront into a thriving business and tourist center. By converting an old levee on the Savannah River to a riverwalk, the town's investment of $8 million in the trail has attracted $198 million in new commercial investments. Today, Augusta's Riverwalk plays host to festivals, concerts, sporting events, and holiday celebrations, bringing in substantial revenues for area businesses and tax dollars for the town.

Increased Real Estate Values

Open space—parks, greenways, forests, and natural areas—also increases the value of real estate. In a recent poll of homebuyers, over three-quarters of respondents rated natural open space as "essential" or "very important"; walking and bicycling ranked third in the list of attributes homebuyers wanted. According to the National Association of Realtors, hiking and biking trails, *not* golf courses, are the top choice for open space amenities in a development.[21] In a survey of who uses public recreational facilities, 1 to 2 percent of respondents said they use golf courses; 5 to 6 percent use swimming pools; and 50 to 60 percent—*more than half*—use pathway systems. In another recent poll, the National Association of Realtors found that 57 percent of voters would be more likely to purchase a home close to green space, and 50 percent said they would be willing to pay 10 percent more for a home located near a park or other protected area. Other studies have shown that locating properties close to greenways increases land values by 10 to 30 percent, raising tax revenues without raising the tax rate. Considering that hiking and biking trails are far less expensive to construct than golf courses or swimming pools, this represents a considerable return on investment.[22]

A comparative study of developments in Amherst and Concord, Massachusetts, found that clustered housing with open space appreciated at a higher rate than homes in more conventional subdivisions without open space. This translated into a difference in average selling price of $17,100 between the two developments. In Salem, Oregon, land adjacent to a greenbelt was found to be worth about $1,200 an acre more than land only a thousand feet away; in Oakland, California, a three-mile greenbelt around Lake Merritt was found to add $41 million to surrounding property values; a developer who donated a forty-foot-wide, seven-mile-long easement along a popular trail in Front Royal, Virginia, sold all fifty parcels bordering the trail in just four months—these statistics prove that an approach that jointly takes into account both conservation and development is economically advantageous.[23]

A Better Place for Business and Retirement

Many businesses report that access to outdoor recreation and a clean environment are among the most important determining factors when selecting a location. In a survey undertaken in the mid-1990s, corporate CEOs cited quality of life for employees as the third most important factor in locating a business, behind access to domestic markets and availability of skilled labor.[24] In another study, owners of small companies ranked recreation/parks/open space as the highest priority in choosing a new location for their business.[25] As cell phones, computers, the Internet, and other advances in technology make it easier for businesses to locate away from commercial hubs and transportation links, such quality-of-life factors will be even more critical to location decisions.

Retirees also are looking for communities with aesthetic appeal and open-space amenities. According to data of the American Association of Retired People, access to outdoor activities is among the most important priorities for new retirees.[26] As increasing numbers of baby boomers retire, providing places that they want to live and recreate will prove to be an economically sage move.

Protecting natural amenities as the community grows is critical, however. If the natural environment deteriorates, the community will become less attractive to tourists, retirees, and other new residents.

Protecting the Prosperity of Working Lands

A critical component of many green infrastructure networks are the farms, ranches, and forests that serve as the backbone of the local economy. In addition to their ecological, recreational, and aesthetic benefits, working lands also provide direct benefits to the economy. Agricultural lands produced $200 billion in commodities nationwide in 2002, translating into more than $1 trillion in total value added of food and fiber products generated by the production of livestock and crops. Private forestlands produced more than $25 billion in forestry products. Agriculture provided direct employment to about 795,000 people in 2002; forest, conservation, and logging workers held about 81,000 jobs.[27]

Not only do working lands support many local economies, they also have been shown to cost communities less in service delivery. Studies show that farming and forestry generate more revenue than they require in public services (schools, road maintenance, water and wastewater, etc.), while residential development has the opposite effect: residential lands typically demand more in service costs. (See chapter 9 for further discussion of the costs of various land uses.)

HEALTH BENEFITS

Green infrastructure also directly benefits people. Many green infrastructure networks provide trails, waterways, and other natural sites for outdoor recreation and nature-based education. Forests, meadows, and stream corridors not only provide natural filtration functions, they also enhance the aesthetics of a community. By protecting what a community holds dear, green infrastructure can enhance community pride and quality of life.

Connections to the landscape are critical to a person's sense of history, continuity, and stability. Yet, the places that are dearest to our hearts are often among those destined for development. Each year sees further erosion of the country's historic resources through demolition, neglect, increasing sprawl, highway construction, inefficient use of existing infrastructure, and development occurring in areas increasingly distant from urban centers. Moreover, the conversion of

Figure 3.5
Farms and other working lands are an important component of many green infrastructure networks. In addition to providing ecological, recreational, and aesthetic benefits, in many communities, working lands are an integral aspect of the local culture and a vital part of the economy. Credit: Ed McMahon.

farms and other working lands makes it difficult for the businesses that once supported them to survive, resulting in a decline in the local economy and a rapid erosion of the traditional way of life. The green infrastructure approach incorporates community values into the criteria used to prioritize what lands are to be protected, thereby ensuring that our most cherished places remain free from the threat of development.

Studies have found that simply experiencing nature and the outdoors are good for one's mental health. For many people, forests, lakes, parks, and other open space elements are havens of tranquility, recreation, and inspiration. Studies undertaken by the University of Illinois at Urbana-Champaign have documented less stress and lower crime rates in tree-lined neighborhoods.[28] Another recent study showed that people living near parks and other natural areas live healthier lives with fewer hospital visits.[29]

There is also evidence that contact with nature enhances emotional, cognitive, and values-related development in children.[30] Teens in green communities have fewer symptoms of attention deficit disorder than those who live in places without trees. Natural environments elicit positive feelings, reduce fear, and even help block stressful thoughts. Programs that engage youths in working in nature have been successful as therapeutic intervention, helping young people who are in trouble to realign their lives and gain greater clarity about who they are. Other studies cite that the physical benefits of outdoor-based programs for young people extend beyond fitness to cognitive gains, the ability to cope with new challenges, and improved self-esteem.

People also benefit from increased exercise in communities with open space and trail systems. Even modest physical activities, such as walking, can reduce the risk of coronary heart disease, high blood pressure, diabetes, and some types of cancer. Regular physical activity also relieves symptoms of depression and anxiety and generally improves mood. A study conducted by Brown University concluded that

Figure 3.6
Green infrastructure networks can include waterways for kayaking, canoeing, and other types of outdoor recreation, providing mental and physical benefits for the people using them. Studies show that outdoor recreation reduces stress, enhances cognitive reasoning, and builds self-esteem of children and teens. Credit: Mountains to Sound Greenway Trust.

the nation could save $20 billion per year if every sedentary American walked just an hour a day.[31] With obesity a national epidemic, protecting interconnected green space systems that enable people to get around safely without an automobile is an ever more valuable amenity.

WHY UNDERTAKE GREEN INFRASTRUCTURE?

A green infrastructure approach also provides communities with a wide range of benefits. First, green infrastructure initiatives help communities forge consensus about their futures and create a vision that sparks the imagination and enthusiasm of citizens. A green infrastructure plan can help communities determine where to develop and prioritize their conservation and protection needs and desires.

As communities grow, the economic value of their natural lands also grows. But this occurs only if the viability of the land's natural ecological and hydrologic systems is maintained. When lands deteriorate their value diminishes, affecting the economic viability of communities dependent on farming, ranching, forestry, fishing, tourism, or other resource-dependent industries.

By protecting key landscapes and natural systems, green infrastructure helps to reduce the cost of providing community services and building water retention, filtration, and drainage systems that are needed when natural systems cannot perform their natural functions. The cost savings realized are multiplied by the tax revenues brought about by an increase in the value of homes and the desirability of the community as a site for new commercial enterprises. Perhaps most important of all, the enhanced quality of life that green infrastructure offers communities benefits all who live there.

GREEN INFRASTRUCTURE IN ACTION: THE METRO GREENWAYS PROGRAM, TWIN CITIES, MINNESOTA

The Twin Cities metropolis has a long history of conserving land for its amenity values. In the 1890s, landscape architect Horace W. S. Cleveland designed urban park systems for both Minneapolis and St. Paul. Each included an interlinking network of lakes and parks connected by scenic drives and river boulevards that preserved the natural features of the land adjacent to the city's lakes and rivers. Since Cleveland's time, a variety of agencies, governmental units, organizations, and individuals have worked to enhance the plan and protect green space within and beyond urban boundaries.

Despite the area's legacy of land protection, rapid growth and development in the 1980s and 1990s converted natural and agricultural lands at an unprecedented rate. Alarmed by this trend, the (then) Metro Region of Minnesota's Department of

"Look forward for a century, to the time when the city
has a population of a million, and think what will be
their wants. They will have wealth enough to purchase
all that money can buy, but all their wealth cannot purchase
a lost opportunity, or restore natural features of grandeur
and beauty, which would then possess priceless value."

HORACE W. S. CLEVELAND, 1883

Natural Resources (MN-DNR) convened a group of local experts to assess the natural habitats that remained or might be restored in the region. This group used natural resource and recreation maps to identify valued habitat patches and potential corridors. When digitized, this information created a "regional greenways opportunities" map and sent a strong visual message that it was possible to reweave the region's tattered natural fabric. In response, the state legislature provided the MN-DNR with a $50,000 grant to investigate the possibility of a regional green space network.

To carry out its responsibilities under this grant, the state created the Greenways and Natural Areas Collaborative, which was comprised of representatives from twenty-seven metro area organizations. The Collaborative created a regional greenways vision, goals, and objectives. The group's final recommendations, contained in MN-DNR's *Metro Greenprint*, included the establishment of a formal greenways program and funding for program administration, community technical assistance, and land protection.

Supported by the Collaborative and a powerful legislative champion, the 1998 Minnesota legislature appropriated $4.34 million to the MN-DNR Metro Region. Approximately $340,000 was used annually for program operations and to establish a greenways planning grant program. About $4 million in bonds was used for land protection and restoration activities. The state pledged to work with local units of government and nongovernmental organizations to accomplish the goals identified by the Collaborative. In 2003, an eleven-member citizen advisory committee was formed to build community support and credibility.

Accomplishments

Conducting an inventory of existing natural resources and mapping them is the first step in developing sound protection and stewardship plans. As a combined result of many planning grants and independent local actions, detailed land cover

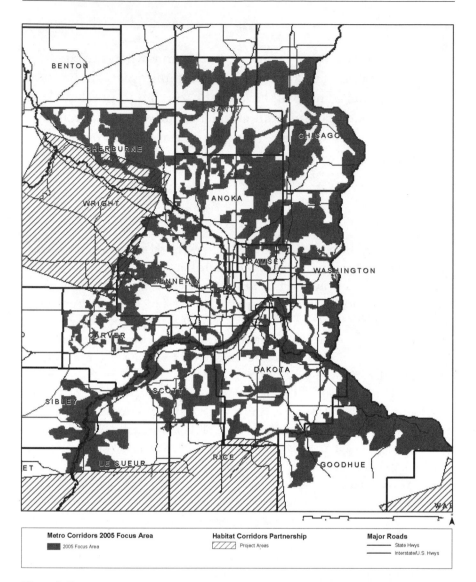

Figure 3.7
The Minnesota Department of Natural Resources worked with several nonprofit
organizations to map wildlife corridors in the Twin Cities region. Using findings from
an ecological assessment, the partners identified twelve focus areas for protection and
restoration efforts. These areas include parks and the surrounding landscapes that
buffer, connect, and protect the natural resources in regional parks. Credit: Metro
Greenways, Minnesota Department of Natural Resources.

data for the Twin Cities metropolitan region has been generated. As of September
2004, land cover analysis was complete for 67 percent (1.28 million acres) of the
region. In addition, Metro Greenways has awarded nearly $1 million in matching
grants to communities to help them undertake such resource inventories and
develop local plans for preserving and managing their natural infrastructure.

Metro Greenways helps local units of government and citizens more effectively incorporate nature into their communities. By coordinating funding sources, providing technical assistance and grants, and identifying significant natural features, the program empowers communities to preserve the resources that are important to them in a way that earns local support. At the same time, its seven-county scope assures that individual projects contribute to a larger network of green spaces and a healthier environment for all metro residents.

The program also has committed $8.2 million to protect some of the region's best remaining natural areas and open spaces by means of Metro Greenways Protection and Restoration Cost-Sharing Funds. This money has leveraged an additional $11 million in other funds. Nineteen projects involving thirty-two parcels of land totaling nearly 1,500 acres have been approved for protection though acquisition and conservation easements.

Ultimately, the Metro Greenways partnership has led to a more holistic approach to land conservation. In 2003, the MN-DNR, six nonprofit partners, and two special local projects received $4.85 million from the state's Environmental Trust Fund for a new program called Metro Wildlife Corridors. Using the findings from science-based regional ecological assessment, the project partners identified twelve focus areas for their protection and restoration efforts. The Metro Wildlife Corridors focus areas include parts of the regional park system and the surrounding landscapes that buffer, connect, and protect the natural resources in regional parks. Under this new approach, groups that request planning or land protection funding need to work within the boundaries of one of these focus areas. The partnership also has gained two more nonprofit partners and has expanded into seven additional counties adjacent to the initial target area.

The Benefits of Metro Greenways

The efforts of the Metro Greenways Program have directly and indirectly benefited the Twin Cities region in myriad ways. More than 2,500 acres of natural habitat and open space, from the urban core to the developing rural fringe, have been protected. The identification and prioritization of needs has helped to facilitate the restoration of 606 acres, covering a variety of habitat types, and the reconnection of a few selected landscapes, including the St. Croix River Greenway.

Metro Greenways also has fostered a new level of trust and cooperation among the state and local governments and nonprofit organizations. Citizens have a new awareness of the importance of land conservation and stewardship. The visibility of the Metro Greenways Program and its citizen education component has helped to generate local support, resulting in bond referenda for land conservation that total $23.5 million.

The Regional Greenways Collaborative's work group on economic benefits is working with the University of Minnesota to investigate the benefits that citizens reap from the protection of open space. These benefits include increased property values, aesthetic appeal, improved water quality, and overall higher quality of life.

Fueled by the beauty of the Big Woods deciduous forest, tall-grass prairies, and mighty rivers, outdoor-based recreation and tourism are important elements of the region's economy, generating several million dollars annually. Tourists from all over the world are drawn to the banks of the Mississippi, the North Shore, the Boundary Waters Canoe Area, and the many fields and forests in between. These unique natural places make up a large percentage of Minnesota's $9 billion tourism industry.

• *For more information, about The Metro Greenways Program, visit www.dnr.state. mn.us/greenways/index.html.*

Notes

1. Wildlands Network, The Ecological Effects of Roads. See www.wildlandscpr.org/resourcelibrary/reports/ecoleffectsroads.html.

2. U.S. Environmental Protection Agency, Our Built and Natural Environment: A Technical Review of the Interactions Between Land Use, Transportation, and Environmental Quality, 2000. See www.smartgrowth.org.

3. National Wildlife Federation, "Paving Paradise: Sprawl's Impact on Wildlife and Wild Places in California," February 2001.

4. World Wildlife Fund, *Running Pure* (Washington, D.C.: WWF, 2003).

5. American Rivers, NRDC, and Smart Growth America, *Paving Our Way to Water Shortages: How Sprawl Aggravates the Effects of Drought* (Washington, D.C.: American Rivers, NRDC, and Smart Growth America, 2002), 1–2, 8.

6. The data in this paragraph is from David Nowak, project leader of the U.S. Forest Service's Urban Forest Ecosystem Research Unit, as quoted in *Earth Talk: Questions and Answers about Our Environment,* "Do Urban Trees Really Help Reduce Pollution and Clean the Air?," by John Alderman, August 22, 2004. Available at http://environment.about.com/library/weekly/bldearearthtalk08-22-04.htm.

7. Ibid.

8. "Executive Directions," *Casey Trees News,* June 2004, 3.

9. Statistics from "Fen Montaigne, There Goes the Neighborhood," *Audubon* (March–April 2000), and Southern Environmental Law Center, 2002. Additional cost estimates and data regarding the financial benefits of trees and forests can be obtained from American Forests, which conducts a variety of ecosystem analyses.

10. Steve Lerner and William Poole, *The Economic Benefits of Parks and Open Space: How Land Conservation Helps Communities Grow Smart and Protect the Bottom Line* (San Francisco: Trust for Public Land, 1999).

11. Community Open Space Partnership, *Paint the Town Green: Green Infrastructure for Tomorrow* (Madison, WI: Community Open Space Partnership, 2003).

12. Statistics in this paragraph are from *Urban Forestry News* 10, 2 (Autumn 2003):7;

American Forests, *Urban Ecosystem Analysis, Delaware Valley Region: Calculating the Value of Nature* (Washington, D.C.: American Forests, March 2003), 3.

13. Taken from Costanza et al., "The Value of the World's Ecosystem Services and Natural Capital," *Nature* 387 (May 15, 1997):253–260.

14. Clyde F. Kiker and Alan W. Hodges, *Economic Benefits of Natural Land Conservation: Case Study of Northern Florida* (Washington, D.C.: Defenders of Wildlife, 2002), 47.

15. *The Economic Benefits of Parks and Open Space* (San Francisco: Trust for Public Land, 1999), 26.

16. U.S. Department of Interior Fish and Wildlife Service, *2001 National and State Economic Impacts of Wildlife Watching* (Washington, D.C.). Available at library.fws.gov/nat_survey2001_economics.pdf.

17. The statistics in this paragraph are from Edward Marshall, "Wildlife Gaming Scores High Marks," *The Journal* (March 20, 2005), Vision 2005 section, 3.

18. Quoted in Martha S. Honey, "Treading Lightly? Ecotourism's Impact on the Environment," *Environment* (June 1999).

19. Defenders of Wildlife, *Investing in Nature: The Economic Benefits of Conserving Natural Areas in Northeast Florida* (Washington, D.C.: Defenders of Wildlife, 2004).

20. Clyde F. Kiker and Alan W. Hodges, *Economic Benefits of Natural Land Conservation: Case Study of Northern Florida* (Washington, D.C.: Defenders of Wildlife, 2002), 24.

21. Golf courses are not always antithetical to green infrastructure. The ArborLinks program promoted by the National Arbor Day Foundation is among the organizations committed to making golf courses part of a healthy functioning landscape in places where people want golf courses instead of nature areas.

22. Statistics in this paragraph are from the National Association of Realtors, *On Common Ground: Realtors and Smart Growth*, Summer 2001. Conducted by Public Opinion Strategies for the National Association of Realtors. Available at www.realtor.org/SG3.nsf/pages/mngrtpresssurvey?opendocument; Stanly Hamilton and Moura Quayle, "Corridors of Green and Gold: Impact of Riparian Suburban Greenways on Property Values," *Journal of Business Administration and Policy Analysis* (January 1, 1999); and National Park Service, Rivers, Trails, and Conservation Assistance Program, *Economic Impacts of Protecting Rivers, Trails, and Greenway Corridors* (Washington, D.C.: National Park Service, 1995).

23. Lerner and Poole, *The Economic Benefits of Parks and Open Space*, 13.

24. National Park Service, Rivers, Trails, and Conservation Assistance Program, *Economic Impacts of Protecting Rivers, Trails, and Greenway Corridors*, chapter 7.

25. John L. Crompton, Lisa L. Love, and Thomas A. More, "An Empirical Study of the Role of Recreation, Parks, and Open Space in Companies Location Decisions," *Journal of Park and Recreation Administration* (1997):37–58.

26. National Park Service, Rivers, Trails, and Conservation Assistance Program, *Economic Impacts of Protecting Rivers, Trails, and Greenway Corridors*.

27. Statistics in this paragraph are from the U.S. Bureau of the Census, *Census of Agriculture* (Washington, D.C.: Government Printing Office, 2004–05 edition), available at www.nass.usda.gov/census/; and U.S. Department of Labor Bureau of Labor Statistics, *Occupational Outlook Handbook* (Washington, D.C.: Government Printing Office), available at stats.bls.gov/oco/home.htm.

28. "Green Streets, Not Mean Streets: Vegetation May Cut Crime in the Inner City," *Urban Forestry News* 12, 1 (Spring 2004); Research undertaken by Dr. Frances Kuo at the University of Illinois at Urbana–Champaign has documented less stress and lower crime rates in tree-lined neighborhoods.

29. Howard Frumkin, "Beyond Toxicity: Human Health and the Natural Environment," *American Journal of Preventive Medicine* 20, 3 (2001):234–240; quoted in Reid Ewing and John Kostyack, *Endangered by Sprawl: How Runaway Development Threatens America's Wildlife* (Washington, D.C.: National Wildlife Foundation, Smart Growth America and NatureServe, 2005), 5.

30. Howard Frumkin, "Healthy Places: Exploring the Evidence," *American Journal of Public Health* 93, 9 (September, 2003). For other research, see R. S. Ulrich, "Biophilia, Biophobia, and Natural Landscapes," in S. R. Kellert and E. O. Wilson, eds., *The Biophilia Hypothesis* (Washington, D.C.: Island Press, 1993), 73–137; G. P. Nabhan and S. Trimble, *The Geography of Childhood: Why Children Need Wild Places* (Boston: Beacon, 1994); and Andrea Faber Taylor, Frances E. Kuo, and William C. Sullivan, "Coping with ADD: The Surprising Connection to Green Play Settings," *Environment and Behavior* 33, no. 1 (January 2001). Additional studies showing the benefits of green space on children and neighborhoods can be found at the Web site for Human-Environment Research Laboratory at www.herl.uiuc.edu.

31. Ohio Parks and Recreation Association, The Benefits Are Endless, 1999. See www.opraonline.org.

chapter four

Where Do We Begin?

T here is no single blueprint for green infrastructure network planning and design. Green infrastructure programs are as different as the regions, states, counties, municipalities, and landscapes in which they occur. Almost all successful efforts share some common planning approaches: they bring together stakeholders, establish a mechanism for making decisions, develop a clear vision and mission, and engage the public throughout the process. When a community chooses to begin planning for green infrastructure, these steps can help to ensure success.

GREEN INFRASTRUCTURE STAKEHOLDERS

The leaders of the green infrastructure initiative should be careful to reach out to stakeholders *before* the green infrastructure planning process begins. Stakeholders include public entities and private individuals who own or manage land that may fall within or adjacent to the green infrastructure network, as well as anyone else who has an investment in the future of the community. Even though a green infrastructure initiative may begin as a government-led effort, the most successful results are achieved when the greater community is brought into the process at the outset. In addition to representatives from conservation and recreation organizations, a broad effort that engages longtime and newer landowners and residents, the tourism and travel industry, developers and the real estate sector, and other influential members of the community will likely have wider appeal and meet with less resistance. Although it can be more difficult to get off the ground, an effort that engages a wide range of perspectives is typically better able to accomplish ambitious goals.

Green infrastructure initiatives benefit from the involvement of people with a wide range of knowledge, experience, and resources, including experts in conservation science, landscape architecture, GIS, and related areas; community leaders and others who have political power or influence within and beyond the community; organizations with GIS modeling and mapping capabilities, as well as knowledge and data regarding the study area; and financial resources or the ability to tap funding sources.

Box 4.1

Green Infrastructure Keys to Success

Drawing on work under way in states, regions, and communities of various sizes across the country, a number of strategies emerge that are critical to successful green infrastructure initiatives. A wide range of organizations and partners have used these strategies to implement green infrastructure and other strategic conservation efforts. In essence, these are steps that can be taken to build a green infrastructure program, regardless of the size, resources, or experience of those taking the lead. Chapter 4 discusses the creation of a leadership group; subsequent keys to success are discussed in the chapters that follow.

- Create a leadership group to guide the green infrastructure initiative.
- Design a green infrastructure network to link green space components across scales and political boundaries.
- Develop an implementation plan to make the network design a reality.
- Prepare a management and stewardship plan that meets the restoration and maintenance needs of all green infrastructure network components.
- Inform and seek input from the public on the green infrastructure network design and plan.
- Integrate green infrastructure into the planning processes of local, state, and federal agencies and other community and regional planning efforts.
- Sell the public on the benefits of green infrastructure and the need for a green infrastructure network design.
- Build partnerships with the people and organizations that can help support and sustain the green infrastructure initiative.

Figure 4.1
Involving a wide range of stakeholders in reviewing resource data, identifying potential
hubs, links, and sites for a green infrastructure network, and reviewing preliminary
maps can help ensure that the green infrastructure network accomplishes its intended
goals. Credit: Mark Benedict.

Although green infrastructure initiatives often grow out of a publicly mandated
land-use planning process, they can also emerge as an initiative of a local land trust,
chamber of commerce, or another nonprofit or community-based board or committee. Sometimes a coalition of several smaller groups in a community takes ownership of a green infrastructure initiative. In some communities, civic groups and
neighborhood associations may play a powerful role; in others, the local chapter of a
national or regional conservation organization may take on leadership responsibility.
In some cases, a university or other academic institution is brought on board to
provide expertise, GIS capability, and/or other resources. The key is to tap into the
groups within a specific community that have an interest in identifying and protecting green infrastructure and the influence to carry such an initiative forward. (Forging
partnerships for action is discussed in detail in chapter 9.)

LEADING THE EFFORT

One key to success is having a well-defined and ongoing forum for people to come
together, build connections, and reach consensus on what is to be accomplished
and the strategies to be used. If the initiative is government-led, this could be done

Box 4.2

Green Infrastructure Stakeholders

Potential participants in a green infrastructure initiative include:
- Elected officials at state, county, and local levels
- Members of appointed boards engaged in zoning or land-use planning, parks and recreation, environmental management, etc.
- State or local government agency personnel in planning, natural resources, parks and recreation, transportation, agriculture, forestry, water management, economic development, etc.
- Councils of government or other regional organizations
- Nonprofit organizations focused on conservation or outdoor recreation
- Farmland protection or historic preservation organizations
- Corporate landowners
- Land trusts
- Forestry councils and Farm Bureaus
- Real estate developers
- Neighborhood or homeowner associations
- Civic groups
- Tourism boards
- Chambers of Commerce
- University professors and graduate students in landscape architecture, urban and regional planning, ecology, conservation biology, etc.
- Private landowners and residents
- Teachers, school board members, and staff
- Other interested citizens who live, work, or play in the community.

through a commission appointed by the governor, mayor, county executive, or other elected leader; a coordinating council given power by the legislature; a citizen task force charged with completing a specific task in a given time period; or some other type of collaborative group. If it is a nonprofit-led initiative, the group is more likely to be a self-appointed coalition of interested parties.

Some communities have tapped existing coalitions to spearhead a green infrastructure initiative, adding representatives from groups that are underrepresented. There are obvious advantages to having an existing organization take the lead, but there are some obstacles to be considered. The biggest challenge with using an already active group is engaging new organizations and interests in a way that ensures their equal status. Once a group has formed, it can be difficult to change its habits and routines. A group may be unprepared to start anew and may never view newcomers as equal partners. On the other hand, new group members may feel intimidated, unprepared, or unmotivated to participate fully in work that has already begun. If an existing organization is tapped to take the lead, the best approach might be to engage others through an advisory council charged with giving input and making recommendations.

Many green infrastructure initiatives have begun with the inauguration of a new group charged exclusively with planning and implementing a green infrastructure system. In this approach, care should be taken to avoid duplicating or undermining existing leadership and activities, but rather to use the green infrastructure effort to build bridges among organizations and programs. This requires taking inventory of the public and private organizations already involved in conservation activities, as well as the recommendations they have put forth for conservation action.

In local communities, green infrastructure initiatives are often charged to a task force with broad community representation. In the Tampa, Florida, metro area the Hillsborough River Greenways Task Force has brought together representatives from the public and private sectors to review land and water conservation issues and offer recommendations to minimize increasing developmental threats to the natural resources of the Upper Hillsborough River.

Citizen advisory committees are another way to engage the public in planning for open space. Douglas County, Colorado, grew by 191 percent in the 1990s, making it the fastest-growing county in the nation. At the heart of the county's efforts to combat the effects of such rapid growth by protecting open space is a broad-based citizen advisory committee charged with making recommendations regarding disbursement of public funds and the lands to be protected. Land is evaluated based on specific criteria within areas targeted for protection; criteria include the protection of buffers, the creation of linkages, and the level of development threat.

These conservation efforts in Douglas County incorporate many aspects of green infrastructure, particularly because they focus on interconnected systems. More than seventy-five public and private agencies, organizations, and businesses have joined the effort to conserve an interconnected system of open space for wildlife and people surrounding the Chatfield Reservoir; and fifteen local, state, and federal entities are working together to fund the Cherry Creek Greenprint, a plan that links parkland along the thirty-five-mile creek that connects rural, suburban, and urban landscapes.

Structure and Support

Regardless of how the leadership group is brought into being or who takes the lead, it should include representatives from diverse interests, sectors (public, private, and nonprofit), and disciplines. The leadership group should not be viewed

Box 4.3

Tips for Success

Regardless of the scope or origins of the green infrastructure initiative, a successful leadership group:

- **Represents all interests of the community or affected area.** The commitment of key groups is essential to success.
- **Is a manageable size.** The group must be large enough to represent all stakeholders but small enough so that everyone can play a role. The ideal size is typically twenty to thirty people.
- **Has clear expectations.** Clarifying expectations at the outset will help air differences between people's priorities and perspectives. A written vision and/or mission statement and work plan are essential to keeping the group on track.
- **Meets regularly.** This enables a leadership group to keep up momentum and establishes checkpoints for assessing progress, reevaluating strategies, and changing plans or priorities as needed.
- **Is motivated.** Participants need to be committed to achieving the mission and vision. Celebrating milestones and accomplishments along the way can help continue momentum.

simply as a government body with a government mandate. One way to help bring a sense of inclusiveness is to have equal numbers of government and nongovernment (private/nonprofit) members and to have a co-chair or vice chair that represents the private/nonprofit sector.

Particular care must be taken to ensure that the group's make-up and leadership matches the multisector and multiscale characteristics of successful green infrastructure-based strategic conservation efforts. A group that is perceived as multifaceted and representational of all the various interests within a given area will be in a better position to explain its vision and mission and to engage a wide range of citizens in planning and implementing the vision.

A chairperson should be selected at the first meeting of the leadership group. The chair is responsible for running group meetings and for working closely with staff and subcommittee chairs to accomplish tasks between group meetings, including preparing the agenda and sending reminders for upcoming meetings. Since most participants are usually volunteers, it is important to task one organization with taking the lead in managing the group's activities and providing staff support.

Within the leadership group, working committees should be established to take on the various activities required for planning and implementing green infrastructure. Subcommittees can meet and undertake activities between group meetings and report periodically on progress or findings before the entire group. The group as a whole or its leaders will need to determine what subcommittee structure will work best to achieve results, but it is important that all subcommittees share the representative and inclusive nature of the leadership group. The working committees could help to obtain broader input by encouraging the involvement of other interested parties in the committee's work.

It is critical that members of the leadership group understand that they are making a firm commitment over a specific period of time. The leadership group should have a specific written charge, so that everyone understands what the group is—and is not—expected to accomplish. Although deadlines need not be set in stone at the outset, the group should have some idea of the timeline under which it will operate and the deadlines for key tasks. In addition, the group should determine how often, when, and where meetings will take place. The group will need to meet more frequently at the beginning of the effort to build momentum and decide what needs

---

Box 4.4

Florida Greenways Commission Working Committees

At its September 1993 meeting, the Florida Greenways Commission created four working committees and gave each specific assignments related to the charges in the governor's executive order:

- **The Greenways Identification and Mapping Committee** was charged with answering the question "What is a greenway?" and with creating a statewide map of existing and proposed greenway connections. This committee also was charged with developing greenway definitions and a classification system, and discovering where greenways already exist and where there were missing connections.
- **The Program Integration Committee** was charged with putting together the pieces of the program puzzle, focusing on how the state's existing conservation and recreation programs and private projects fit into the greenways initiative.
- **The Community Action Committee** was charged with figuring out how the state could help communities create greenways and surveying communities to learn about local greenways projects and what made local projects successful.
- **The Partners, Awareness and Involvement Committee** was charged with identifying groups and individuals interested in working on greenways projects. The committee's work included creating materials to publicize the greenways initiative, planning a statewide greenways celebration for Florida's 150th anniversary, and preparing a Florida Greenways Marketing Plan.

to be done. Over time, the frequency of meetings may change depending on the group's charge, its structure, deliverables or end products, and timetable.

The group will also need to determine how it will make decisions. Consensus decision-making is usually the operational framework of choice for multisector and multidisciplinary groups. The consensus process does not require voting on individual issues; in fact, the only voting takes place at the end of the process when the group is ready to finalize its recommendations and findings. Some groups prefer following *Robert's Rules of Order*, which provides a more structured way for bringing topics to the attention of the whole and making decisions.

Coming to consensus is often difficult, particularly when members come from vastly different backgrounds and have different perspectives and objectives. A professional facilitator can play a key role in helping the group air differences of opinion and come to consensus on key issues. An outside facilitator may be particularly valuable at the outset of the project, when the difficult work of defining a vision and mission statement is done.

THE LEADERSHIP GROUP'S PLANNING PROCESS

Once a leadership group has been formed, it will need to clarify and communicate its mission and how it plans to undertake the work it has been charged with. Most groups begin by defining a shared vision that can be used to engage others and then use this vision to develop a mission statement that will be used to guide decisions and action planning. Throughout this process, it is important to be as open and inclusive as possible, by holding meetings that are open to the public, engaging stakeholders in establishing a broad vision, and maintaining ongoing communication within and beyond the leadership group.

> "Our plans miscarry because they have no aim.
> When a man does not know what harbor he is making for,
> no wind is the right wind."
>
> SENECA (4 B.C.–A.D.65)

The Vision

In his book, *The 7 Habits of Highly Effective People*, author Stephen Covey says one of the key habits is to "begin with the end in mind."[1] Seeing something in the mind's eye is often the first step to actually achieving it. Olympic athletes imagine their course down the ski slopes or their routine on the balance beam before they step onto the world stage. A recent study showed that simply imagining the golf ball going into the hole improved putting among golfers by 60 percent. Making progress in any collaborative effort also involves first envisioning what you want to accomplish and describing this vision through words and/or pictures.

Visioning plays an essential role in collaborative planning. It not only helps a group identify what it wants the future to look like, it also helps to identify the steps needed to make its dream a reality. Planning, guided by visioning, provides collaborative groups with the power to act. The visioning process also provides groups with a unique opportunity to come to consensus on shared values, breaking down barriers among different constituencies and enhancing the level of trust and understanding among them.

A green infrastructure vision fits well into a broader community visioning effort. In some cases, green infrastructure has grown out of community visioning; in others, visioning has been seen as the first step of the green infrastructure effort. Chicago Wilderness, a coalition of over a hundred organizations in the Chicago metro area, crafted a vision that includes "a network of protected lands and waters that will preserve habitat for a complete spectrum of the region's natural communities. . . . A critical mass of sites will be large enough to maintain a sustainable complex of interdependent species and natural communities. Carefully monitored habitat corridors will connect sites, both small and large, opening paths for ancient patterns of migration and dispersal."[2] In West Michigan, the vision statement stems from the need to protect open space: "West Michigan's natural environment is essential to our quality of life and plays an important role in defining our region. Rapid population growth and development have placed our natural environment in jeopardy. We must identify, prioritize, and protect these precious environmental assets before they are lost to further development."[3]

A vision statement, like those above, describes what a given group—preferably with representative membership—wants the community (or state or region) to look like in the future. An effective vision statement focuses on the ideal future of the community; it does not include information about how to achieve the desired future, but instead describes an ideal state of affairs.

It is important to emphasize that developing a vision should not take place in a vacuum. Visioning should incorporate the assumptions, frustrations, and dreams of people with a wide range of perspectives. Effective visioning requires extensive outreach to citizens; only a vision statement that has been developed by the community will have the buy-in needed to drive the planning process.

In addition to drafting a vision statement, it is often useful to reach consensus on a vision schematic. Used in conjunction with the vision statement, this map or diagram can help clarify what the vision means for the affected region or community. When completed, the vision schematic can serve as a powerful tool for engaging the general public in the green infrastructure initiative.

Box 4.5

Reaching Agreement

Many communities find themselves grappling with the very real need to involve citizens against the backdrop of mistrust. In some cases, mistrust stems from a long history of antagonism between conservationists and developers, between citizens and their government, or between different constituencies, neighborhoods, or ethnic groups. A green infrastructure effort can help resolve these issues and find common ground between people who tend to be on opposing sides of any given issue.

When people are brought into a consensus-building process, they must believe that the process will be open and fair and that their input will be valued. A skilled facilitator can help ensure that the ground rules are obeyed, move the discussion to ensure that everyone has a voice, and change the tone of interaction from negative to positive.

In the bestselling book *Getting to Yes*, Robert Fisher and William Ury describe a system for reaching wise and fair agreements based on the following guidelines:

- **Separate the people from the problem.** Because discussions involve people, egos and emotions can sidetrack otherwise good agreements. Success means concentrating on the common purpose, attacking the problem and not each other. Relationships are built separately, based on accurate perceptions, clear communication, appropriate emotion, and a forward-looking, purposeful outlook.

- **Focus on interests, not positions.** Positions typically represent people's underlying interests: the desires and concerns that motivate them. Compatible interests are often behind conflicting positions. Identifying interests involves asking "Why?" and "Why not?" When people can discuss interests in specific, concrete terms, they can work toward agreement that reconciles those interests.

- **Invent options for mutual gain.** Before trying to reach agreement, identify choices that advance shared interests and creatively reconcile differing interests. Mutual gain often means the same option must offer different benefits to different people. Brainstorming can generate possibilities for consideration.

- **Insist that any agreement be based on some objective standard.** Objective criteria can facilitate agreement by providing a framework for decision making. A standard based on fairness and efficiency may mean a group decides to first define all the roles in a project before anyone can decide who fills what role. This ensures that each participant has an incentive to design an equitable and efficient project. Try to jointly define objective criteria for each issue.

Source: Roger Fisher and William L. Ury, *Getting to Yes: Negotiating Agreements without Giving In.* New York: Penguin Books, 1991.

Like the vision statement, the vision schematic can be a valuable tool not only in communicating the end goal, but also in helping to elicit opinions of group members. Various members of the group may have different opinions about how to represent their vision graphically. Differences could arise about the amount of detail that should be included in the schematic. The vision schematic might also bring to light differences in opinion about the appropriate project scale and boundaries. Will the green infrastructure network design focus on a watershed, on a community or communities defined by jurisdictional boundaries, or some other type of geographic entity? By surfacing such issues early on, the process of developing the vision schematic can help the group fine-tune the focus of its green infrastructure initiative.

The Mission Statement

The vision statement describes the ideal future; the mission statement describes how the group will go about achieving that future. The mission statement is a statement of what the green infrastructure leadership group wants and expects to accomplish. It answers the questions: Why are we here? What is our purpose? What specifically do we expect to accomplish?

The mission statement should be short, concise, and easy to remember. The statement can be used as a tool to describe on short notice what the group is doing when asked at a cocktail party or by a reporter on camera. The mission statement of the Yellowstone to Yukon Conservation Initiative clearly describes its purpose and intent: "Combining science and stewardship, we seek to ensure that the world-renowned wilderness, wildlife, native plants, and natural processes of the Yellowstone to Yukon region continue to function as an interconnected web of life, capable of supporting all of the natural and human communities that reside within it, for now and for future generations."[4]

Some organizations choose to keep the mission statement concise enough to include on their letterhead or put on the back of the business cards used by staff and partners. The mission statement for The Conservancy of Southwest Florida, a nonprofit formed forty years ago by a group of residents concerned about the loss of the area's natural resources, is "Preserving Southwest Florida's natural environment . . . now and forever." Where a coalition of organizations is involved, the mission statement may be followed by a list of the participating organizations.

The simplicity of the mission statement belies the difficulty involved in creating it. Crafting a mission statement is sometimes a time-consuming and even painful process, but—as with the vision statement—the resulting interchange of ideas helps group members find common ground on which subsequent activities can be built.

The Work Plan

The mission statement serves as the foundation for the work plan. The work plan should answer these questions: What must be done? By when must it be done? Who is responsible for getting it done? An effective work plan includes a clear statement of the specific goals and the order in which they are to be accomplished, a step-by-step description of the tasks that must be taken, a schedule, a list of the resources needed, and a description of how progress or results will be measured.

Because different organizations use different approaches to developing a work plan, it may be useful for the leadership group to come to consensus on what the various elements (such as goals, objectives, and tasks) of the work plan are, how they differ from one another, and how they will be used to define what is to be accomplished.

The main differentiating feature between goals, objectives, and tasks is the time frame in which they are used. A goal can be thought of as a specific statement of project intent—what is to be done. Goals should be flexible, realistic, and easy to understand. Some goals might take several months to accomplish; others may be relatively easy to achieve. Defining explicit goals helps to focus the attention of the leadership group or other work group and can help those outside the group—elected officials, funders, the general public, and so on—understand what the group is doing.

It is important when developing the work plan to consider the order in which goals are to be completed. This not only helps prioritize work and target resources to the priorities, it also helps clarify how the lack of progress toward one goal would affect the group's ability to accomplish other goals.

Usually each goal in the work plan has several objectives. While a goal identifies what the team would like to attain, objectives quantify the goal and, where possible, establish deadlines for completion.

Finally, for each objective, the work plan will include one or more tasks or activities that must be undertaken to accomplish the objective. Often, each task will need to be broken into several subtasks that further define what is to be done. The work plan should specify who (what person, organization, and/or subcommittee) is responsible for undertaking each task, as well as when and how it is to be completed. As with goals, the work needs to be prioritized when developing objectives, tasks, and subtasks. The resulting work plan is a critical tool for helping the group to focus its time and schedule its resources.

The final step is to include information about how results will be monitored. The work plan should include goals, objectives, and tasks for evaluating progress so that midcourse corrections can be made. It is difficult—if not impossible—to predict all of the challenges that will present themselves during the planning and implementation of a complex project like designing a green infrastructure network; allowing adequate flexibility in the work plan and revisiting and updating it regularly are the only ways to make sure it remains a viable and valuable planning tool.

Box 4.6

Florida Greenways Commission Goals and Objectives (from Governor Lawton Chiles's Executive Order)

Goal:
To promote the creation of a linked network of greenways and greenspaces across Florida that will benefit the state's citizens, native wildlife, and environment.

Objectives:
a. To assess the current status of greenway activities within federal, state, regional, and local governmental and private entities;
b. To develop a state agency framework to support community greenway initiatives and further interagency greenway activities;
c. To identify statewide greenway issues and goals and draft recommended actions and alternatives for meeting key issues and goals;
d. To hold workshops at selected locations across the state to obtain the input of local citizens and elected officials while formulating shared visions for community greenway and greenspace networks; and
e. To develop further initiatives and plans for the achievement of the commission agenda as directed by the Governor.

To help advance this statewide network, and to emphasize the diverse public and private initiatives necessary to make it a reality, the governor and the commission shall initiate formal recognition of 150 state, regional, or local greenways by the state's 150th birthday in 1995.

Further Direction:
The Commission shall provide a report to the Governor containing items (a) through (e) with particular attention to the following:
1. Current activities by state and federal agencies and by private and nonprofit organizations associated with greenways;
2. Greenway partnerships between local and state governments, private interests, nonprofit organizations, and citizens;
3. Local government efforts in the development and implementation of local government comprehensive plans associated with greenways; and
4. A plan with recommendations to the Florida Legislature and Executive Branch for accomplishing these requirements and objectives.

Box 4.7

Florida Greenways Commission Work Plan/ Meeting Schedule

The Florida Greenways Commission held a total of ten meetings during 1993 and 1994 in association with the preparation of its Report to the Governor. During the early meetings, Commission members learned about greenways in Florida and around the country, developed a mission and vision, and put together a process for developing recommendations for the Governor. Later meetings were devoted to going over the work produced by the Commission's working committees, discussing and refining the group's report, and developing additional materials on greenways.

Educational/Organizational Phase, May–July 1993

May: Organizational meeting of Commission gave an opportunity for members to introduce themselves and discuss their interests and talents as well as Commission issue areas, partners' roles, and organizational considerations.

June: Commission met to hear presentation of national greenway/greenway system cases studies, and to discuss the Commission's vision, mission, schedule, work plan objectives and products, and participants' roles.

July: Commission met to hear presentation of Florida case studies and discussed mission and vision statements as well as working committee structure.

Assessment/Issue Analysis Phase, September–December 1993

September: Commission met to adopt mission statement and discuss draft vision statement, work plan and schedule, as well as working committee structure, charges, activities, and products. Each committee held an organizational meeting and reported back its work plan for approval by the Commission.

October–November: Each working committee met independently to assess their committee charge (e.g. greenway network components, programs, community actions, partners); analyze selected priority issues; and prepare preliminary assessment and issue analysis findings.

December: Commission met to adopt vision statement and 1994 meeting schedule, hear reports and provide feedback on each working committee's findings and discuss the public forums.

Florida Greenways Objectives and Recommendations Formulation Phase, January–April 1994

January–March: Each working committee met independently to complete assessment and issue analysis, finalize assessment and issue analysis findings, and formulate preliminary strategies and recommendations for presentation to full Commission.

April: Commission met to discuss the format and schedule for its report to the Governor and to hear committee reports and provide feedback on each committee's progress.

Florida Greenways Committee Report Preparation Phase, May–August 1994

May–June: Each working committee met independently to finalize draft strategies and recommendations and draft committee report.

July: Commission met to hear and discuss each working committee's draft strategies and associated recommendations, to review plans for the public forums and discuss Florida Greenways public awareness activities.

August: Each working committee met as necessary to finish strategies/recommendations and committee report.

Final Commission Report Preparation Phase and Public Forums, September–December 1994

September: Commission met to preview the Florida Greenways video, finalize plans for public forums, hear reports from the working committees, and discuss the 150 Greenways Recognition and Small Grants programs as well as 1995 greenways celebration activities.

September: Five public forums were held across Florida to educate participants about greenways, provide a forum for input on key recommendation topics, and to generate excitement for the 1995 greenways celebration.

November: Commission met to hear a summary report on the public forums and to review in detail and provide input on the draft chapters and data/maps to be included in the Report to the Governor.

December: Commission met to review and adopt the Report to the Governor and to discuss the proposed 1995 working committee structure and associated priority activities.

Source: Florida Greenways Commission, *Report to the Governor,* 107–112.

MAKING LINKS TO RELATED EFFORTS

No successful effort exists in a vacuum. Just as ecosystems and landscapes are interconnected, so must be our efforts to conserve them. Effective green infrastructure efforts build on related initiatives within and beyond the project area.

The first step is to learn about what projects are already underway that can help advance the green infrastructure vision and mission. These may be in the areas of environmental protection, natural resource protection, green space planning, or smart growth. It is important to know also about any community visioning efforts and the plans that have resulted. Environmental impact studies, demographic and development trends and projections, water management assessments, and a wealth of other information can help inform a green infrastructure effort.

Green infrastructure advocates need to fully understand the parameters in which they are working. It is important to be familiar with existing land-use plans (such as transportation plans or brownfield redevelopment plans), zoning ordinances, and federal and state laws that may affect land-use options or preferences. Project leaders should obtain related reports and recommendations related to open space planning in their project area (or area of focus). If green infrastructure is being planned for a state or other large area, leaders will need to meet with people from various communities within the project area to learn more about land-use planning and issues that might affect the green infrastructure initiative.

A complementary approach to obtaining written reports and plans is to hold one or more forums to share information about conservation-related projects. Invite representatives of public, nonprofit, and private organizations involved in open space planning and stewardship, and ask each representative to provide a brief overview of his or her organization's current conservation initiatives and plans. Using maps to illustrate where these efforts are taking place can help demonstrate the diversity of activities and reinforce the need to connect them.

Keep in mind when planning such gatherings that you do not have to restrict the participation to those who are involved in current conservation initiatives. People working on related projects could contribute to a green infrastructure initiative that has diverse goals. Bring together representatives from conservation agencies, local land trusts, water management agencies, and recreation and parks programs to learn what they are planning and how their efforts could dovetail into an approach that benefits both people and nature.

GREEN INFRASTRUCTURE IN ACTION: SONORAN DESERT CONSERVATION PLAN

Who says green infrastructure always has to be green? In Pima County, Arizona, the green infrastructure approach has been used to help protect desert ecosystems and maintain the quality of life in this rapidly growing region of the American Southwest.

Pima County lies at the intersection of four ecological regions—the Sonoran and Chihuahuan deserts and the Rocky and Sierra Madre mountains—which makes the area home to a great diversity of wildlife and plants. The lush, undeveloped mountains also provide an important north-south migratory pathway for mammals and birds. The Sonoran Desert, rich in biodiversity, has been identified by The Nature Conservancy as one of the most sensitive eco-regions worldwide, deserving of special conservation attention.

The Tucson area has been one of the fastest growing regions of the country since World War II. In 2000 and 2001, an average of almost 1,800 new residents moved to Pima County each month. Each year, new construction consumes an estimated ten square miles of desert. At the turn of the twenty-first century, five decades of steady population growth had outpaced the county's ability to establish and implement effective regional land-use and conservation planning, and the rapid development threatened many native plants and animals as well as the open space that makes the area special.

The need to address growth issues intensified in 1997 with the addition of the cactus ferruginous pygmy owl to the endangered species list. Pima County wanted not just to meet the requirements of the Endangered Species Act, but also to comply with the spirit and intent of that law. The county wanted to address the problems that led to the owl's listing in the first place and reverse the decline of a host of other vulnerable species. The community also recognized that its economic viability depended in part on protecting its natural assets and preserving its cultural identity—those things that made Pima County an attractive place to live and to visit. The county set about formulating a conservation plan that would also accommodate and address the unique pressures the county faced and protect community assets.

The result is the Sonoran Desert Conservation Plan (SDCP). The SDCP covers 5.9 million acres in Pima County, which includes the Tucson metropolitan area, and encompasses two major eco-regions: Sky Islands and the Sonoran Desert. The SDCP extends protection to a range of species by conserving and restoring large-scale natural systems and addresses other resource protection needs in the county.

From Meeting ESA Requirements to Broader Planning Efforts

When the U.S. Fish and Wildlife Service listed the cactus ferruginous pygmy owl as an endangered species in 1997, Pima County had to comply with new federal requirements for managing land use to protect the owl population. Pima County enlisted a volunteer Science Technical Advisory Team, which after studying the issue suggested that protecting the habitat of other rare species at the same time as the owl's would help the county save money by keeping ahead of future endangered species issues.

Figure 4.2
The need to protect the cactus ferruginous pygmy owl, on the federal endangered species list, prompted Pima County, Arizona, to formulate a comprehensive conservation plan that would not only protect sensitive native species but would also preserve the area's cultural identity and unique assets in the face of growth pressures. Credit: U.S. Fish and Wildlife Service.

The county decided to take the advisory team's advice to develop a multispecies conservation plan. Without an approved habitat conservation plan, the county would have to stop all development in areas where the owl occurs or require a separate plan for each new proposed development in the owl's habitat area. County administrators saw the owl as an opportunity to conduct comprehensive land-use planning that could help direct development and protect the natural and cultural resources that enhanced quality of life.

The goal of the resulting multispecies conservation plan is to "ensure the long-term survival of the full spectrum of plants and animals that are indigenous to Pima County through maintaining or improving the habitat conditions and ecosystem functions necessary for their survival."[5] The multispecies conservation plan describes how Pima County will meet the requirements of the Endangered Species Act by focusing development on the least environmentally important lands, thereby protecting critical habitat.

County officials recognized that while the multispecies conservation plan would help identify critical habitat that should be protected, it would not protect the full range of natural and cultural resources that residents valued. The SDCP was developed to address this need. The initial elements of the plan to be studied were critical habitat and biological corridors (from the multispecies conservation plan), riparian protection, mountain parks, cultural resources, and ranch conservation.[6] The strong interconnections of all these elements are critical to a viable land management plan that ensures continuing biodiversity for Pima County. When fully implemented, the plan will help to define urban form, slow sprawl, and protect the lands with the highest quality resources. Together, the planning components represent a far-reaching and groundbreaking approach to strategic conservation planning.

The SDCP intended to meet three areas of need: a science-based conservation plan, an update of the comprehensive land use plan, and compliance with federal regulations that protection of endangered species be addressed through a multi-species conservation plan. By turning attention to the biological and scientific concepts behind land-use planning and conservation, the Pima County Board of Supervisors helped to diffuse the opposition and to depart from the traditional mindset that placed political considerations at the forefront of land-use decision making.

> "The work on the biological corridors and critical habitat element of the Sonoran Desert Conservation Plan revealed that biology is the basis for all other elements."
>
> S D C P   W E B   S I T E

Inclusive Leadership

From its inception, the Pima County Board of Supervisors fully recognized that the success of the Sonoran Desert Conservation Plan required the support and approval of citizens and made broad participation a top priority. The planning process brought together divergent interest groups to create a balanced and fair approach to planning and decision making. Hundreds of agencies, citizens, and organizations contributed thousands of hours to meetings and workshops. The effort included planners, scientists, and resource experts from Pima County and local governments, the University of Arizona, U.S. Fish and Wildlife Service, Bureau of Land Management, USDA's Natural Resources Conservation Service, and The Nature Conservancy.

In 1999, a citizens' steering committee was formed of over eighty members representing diverse constituencies of the community, including developers, ranchers, realtors, neighborhood group leaders, conservationists, off-road enthusiasts, business owners, property rights advocates, representatives of mining interests, and others. The committee hired a professional facilitator for its meetings and spent a lot of time deciding on process issues, such as how they would vote and what constituted a consensus. Initially, members were reluctant to elect committee leaders because representatives worried that they would lose control to other interests. The committee members were committed to working out their differences, however, in part because they feared that if left to the county, the recommendations might fail to address their concerns. The steering committee met steadily for four years, and over time, the members grew to trust each other. Once antagonistic groups found common ground and forged new relationships, which proved critical to the ultimate success of the committee's efforts.

The steering committee also played a critical role in educating the public. The first year, it held a series of educational lectures on topics such as the science of the cactus ferruginous pygmy owl, the content of a habitat conservation plan, and historic land-use patterns in the county. The public education and outreach included a component to educate young people about the importance of land and resource conservation and the steps the county was taking. Pima County created Sonoran Desert Kids, which used education, recreation, communication, and action to engage children in the issues and to educate them about the Sonoran Desert Conservation Plan. The Sonoran Desert Kids Web site (www.co.pima.az.us/cmo/sdcp/kids) continues to provide information, games, and activities to engage children in conservation action.

Local jurisdictions and state and federal agencies also were involved from the outset. Elected and appointed officials from all levels of government participated in meetings, on committees, and as members of the Science Technical Advisory Team and a government working group. All of the meetings of the steering committee and the technical advisory team were open to the public and included time for public comment. Pima County also held open houses about once a month at area libraries, where county staff and scientists were available with maps to answer questions.

A twelve-member subcommittee of the citizens' steering committee put forward recommendations for the content of the multispecies conservation plan and persuaded the whole committee to endorse them. The "Preferred Alternative" specified the committee's recommendation for the multispecies conservation plan, including priority areas to be protected, what methods should be used to protect land, and how the plan should be financed. These recommendations weighed heavily in the plan the county produced for citizen review.

The Role of Science

The Science Technical Advisory Team played a critical role in the development of the multispecies conservation plan. Pima County assembled the team with input from William Shaw, a professor of wildlife and fisheries resources at the University

Figure 4.3
The Sonoran Desert habitat, as seen through the eyes of a child. The artwork was
an activity for six to twelve year olds in conjunction with Sonoran Desert Kids.
Credit: Pima County Graphic Services.

of Arizona, who chaired the team. The advisory team consisted entirely of people
with expertise in biology and included representatives of most of the major land
management agencies in the area. That they were all volunteers lent credibility to
their work.

To support the science-based nature of the planning process, the county administrators helped to buffer the advisory team from political issues, such as the effect of
various land acquisition efforts, so that the team could stay focused on the science of
habitat protection. The team's decision-making process was well documented, their
meetings were open to the public, and all the information that was used to make
decisions was made readily available. The county's focus on protecting a number of
species allowed the Science Technical Advisory Team to take more of an ecosystem-
oriented approach than is typically used for a multispecies conservation plan under
the Endangered Species Act.

Pima County's environmental consulting firm for the plan, RECON, worked
extensively with the Science Technical Advisory Team to conduct detailed analyses
and GIS mapping of priority species' habitat distribution. The county used GIS to
map the most biologically important categories of land so citizens could see and
comment on the system. Together, the advisory team and RECON developed a

plan for an interconnected system of conservation lands to provide long-term protection for more than fifty of the most sensitive plant and wildlife species in southern Arizona.

In addition, twelve advisory and technical teams were brought in at various stages of the planning effort and about 150 different experts offered recommendations on various aspects of the work of the Science Technical Advisory Team. Reed Noss, a prominent voice in landscape-scale conservation planning, and Laura Hood Watchman, the director of habitat conservation planning for Defenders of Wildlife, reviewed the broader process to ensure that the methods used and the assumptions made were valid. Noss and Watchman praised the county government's staunch protection of the Science Technical Advisory Team from political issues and described the SDCP as "a credible, science-based process designed to achieve clear and laudable goals for the long term conservation of biodiversity in Pima County."[7]

Results

When Pima County's effort began in 1998, the community did not have a list of priority vulnerable species of concern, a set of biological standards, or even a vegetation map that could serve as the starting point for determining the locations in need of protection for the species that are in decline. After an intensive research effort, much has been achieved. Today, a list of potentially covered species has been identified, the best available vegetation maps are now assembled, and scientists have identified the critical habitat and connecting corridors that will establish an effective and lasting biological reserve.

The county went beyond the Endangered Species Act's requirements, recommending the conservation of biological corridors and critical habitat, mountainous and riparian areas as well as ranches, historic, and cultural sites. Early results of the SDCP include the creation of two new national preserves—Ironwood Forest National Monument and Las Cienegas National Conservation Area, both managed by the Bureau of Land Management. The county also updated its com-

"The SDCP has taken conservation planning
to the next level by integrating ecosystems, economic growth,
cultural resources, and development. This is an excellent
model of creative planning that shows growing communities
how to balance our built and natural environments."

BRUCE KNIGHT
AMERICAN INSTITUTE OF CERTIFIED PLANNERS

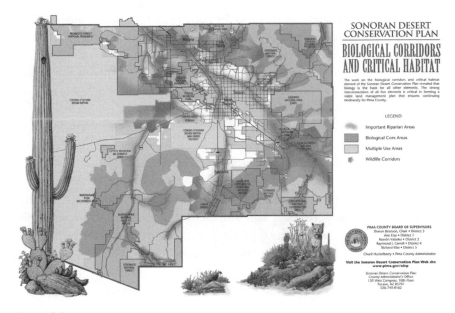

Figure 4.4
Pima County used GIS to map the most biologically important lands and develop an
interconnected system of conservation lands that would provide long-term protection
for sensitive plant and wildlife species in southern Arizona. Credit: Pima County
Graphic Services.

prehensive land-use plan to incorporate the Science Technical Advisory Team's
map of habitat to be protected (known as the Conservation Lands System). The
Conservation Lands System gives extra protection to hillsides and riparian areas
for their habitat value and uses relative habitat value to determine how much land
should be left in its natural state when a parcel is developed. In a groundbreaking
display of green infrastructure-based strategic conservation planning, in 2001
Pima County adopted the Conservation Lands System map as the basis for its
updated comprehensive land-use plan.

County officials emphasize that this, the SDCP, and other land-use planning
efforts are not about stopping development but about fostering responsible growth
while preserving the landscapes that make the area special. County officials
realized the county would save money if they could redirect growth to areas where
infrastructure such as roads and sewer lines already exist and used this advantage
to sell the community on the idea of strategically planning for growth. Having a
countywide strategy enables developers to plan further into the future because
there is less uncertainty about which land uses will be permissible where.

Tremendous public participation and volunteer work enabled the effort to succeed. All interested parties were invited to join the citizens' steering committee,
giving voice to the many constituencies involved in land-use issues in the county.
The sheer number of members and the wide diversity of interests sometimes

threatened to overwhelm the process, but committee members recognized that they could gain more by working through issues than by allowing someone else to make decisions. The use of a professional facilitator and giving the committee time to air concerns and come to agreement helped to build trust among the various interests and overcome the polarization that typifies land-use decision making. The result is an innovative plan for conservation and growth.

Beginning as a plan for a specific species, the SDCP has become increasingly inclusive and comprehensive over time. The process has helped to increase citizen awareness of and local support for the SDCP and other related conservation efforts. The county emphasizes that the SDCP is not about whether Pima County continues to grow; it is about where the county will grow. By designing a plan for the urban environment that will work within a natural and cultural resource protection framework, Pima County is fostering an environmental ethic that will protect the community's most valuable assets and contribute to a sustainable economy for many years to come.

• *For more information about the Sonoran Desert Conservation Plan, visit www.co.pima.az.us/cmo/sdcp.*

Notes

1. Stephen R. Covey, *The 7 Habits of Highly Effective People* (New York: Simon and Schuster, 1989).

2. Chicago Wilderness Coalition, Biodiversity Recovery Plan. See www.chiwild.org.

3. West Michigan Strategic Alliance, The Common Framework. Available at www.wm-alliance.org/Brix?pageID=26.

4. Yellowstone to Yukon's mission statement is found on many project materials and at its Web site, www.y2y.net.

5. See the Pima County Multi-Species Conservation Plan at www.pima.gov/cmo/sdcp/reports.html.

6. As the SDCP evolved, historical preservation was added to the cultural preservation component and a new conservation reserve and development reserve component was also added.

7. Tony Davis, "Desert Conservation Plan Credible," *Arizona Daily Star* (October 27, 2001). Noss and Watchman praised the fact that the plan's scientists were insulated from politics and that the conservation plan was linked with the county's proposed conservation plan. They also praised the county for providing enough money and staffing for planning and for consulting with 150 experts on various species.

chapter five

The Basics of Network Design

Once there is a shared vision and a mission statement that clarifies your goals, you are ready to design a green infrastructure network—a blueprint or map of how green infrastructure will look on the ground. Essentially, the green infrastructure network design is a spatial vision of a desired future. The network design is the "output" of the leadership group and reflects the desires of constituents and the particular characteristics of the project area.

The process used to develop the green infrastructure network design will differ from one community to another, depending on the level of conservation action, future land-use plans, ecological and geographic characteristics of the landscape, and community priorities. Green infrastructure thus represents the unique conservation and quality-of-life goals of each community, whether a state, region, or neighborhood.

The green infrastructure network design can be completed by the leadership group, but many groups choose instead to contract with a natural resource agency, university, or consultant to do this work. Regardless, it is important to work closely with those leading the effort and the stakeholders who will be affected by the design.

NETWORK DESIGN GUIDANCE

Fundamental to any conservation initiative is selecting the focus of land conservation and/or restoration actions. For many years, researchers, conservation activists, land-use planners, land managers, and others have considered how to prioritize conservation needs and target resources—time and funding—to the top priorities. At the turn of the century, George Wright, Victor Shelford, and other scientists researched how to best protect wildlife in America's national parks and forests. Later research efforts, such as UNESCO's Man and the Biosphere Program, addressed how conservation planning and design could balance natural resource values with sustainable development and community economics. In recent years, conservation biologists, landscape ecologists, geographic information specialists, and others have studied reserves and reserve networks throughout the world as part of an effort to learn what works and what does not.[1]

"The process of reserve selection and design, although largely empirical and reasonably objective, is still as much an art as a science. It is a science in that scientific theories, models, methods, and data form the basis of all analyses. It is an art in that the process of combining, weighing, and evaluating various criteria and data layers requires human judgment and the 'intuition' of experienced ecologists."

REED F. NOSS
WILDLANDS PROJECT

Although the focus of these research efforts differed greatly, there is a surprising amount of congruence among their findings. The work on island biogeography is perhaps the most relevant to green infrastructure network design. Conservation biologists used their understanding of island biogeography and related research findings to develop principles for the design of nature reserves.[2] Later incorporated into the 1980 IUCN World Conservation Strategy, these principles state that, if all else is equal, large reserves are better than small reserves; a single large reserve is better than several small ones of equivalent total area; reserves close together are better than reserves that are far apart; rounded reserves are better than long, thin ones; reserves clustered compactly are better than reserves in a line; and reserves that are connected by corridors are better than unconnected reserves.

Although some scientists have debated these principles, they are generally accepted as guidelines for designing and evaluating reserve networks. For example, in *Saving Nature's Legacy*, Reed Noss and Allen Cooperrider base their findings about reserve design on five similar reserve design concepts described in the conservation strategy

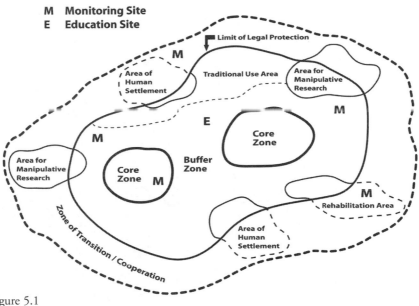

Figure 5.1
The layout for an ideal biosphere reserve. UNESCO's Man and the Biosphere Program addresses how conservation planning and design could balance natural resource values with sustainable development and community economics. Adapted from Noss and Cooperrider (1994).

for the northern owl, adding a sixth "that applies to species that are especially sensitive to human disturbance and, therefore, greatly in need of protection."[3] Noss and Cooperrider found that species that are well distributed across their native range are less susceptible to extinction than species confined to small portions of their range, large habitat blocks containing large populations of a target species are superior to small blocks of habitat containing small populations, blocks of habitat close together are better than blocks far apart, habitat in contiguous blocks is better than fragmented habitat, interconnected blocks of habitat are better than isolated blocks, and dispersing individuals travel more easily through habitat resembling that preferred by the species in question. The authors further advised that nature and people are not always a good fit, so that blocks of habitat that are roadless or otherwise inaccessible to humans are better than more accessible habitat blocks.

Historically, people have focused on protecting large areas of wildlife habitat and other natural features with little attention paid to connectivity. Yet, research demonstrates that the connectivity of natural systems is an important aspect of landscape health. Much of the scientific literature has focused on connectivity as a measure of how connected or continuous a corridor is, usually narrowing in on habitat and/or the role of a corridor as a conduit or migration route for one or more species. In green infrastructure network design, connectivity is more than just corridors. Connectivity also refers to the landscape matrix as a whole. It can be thought of as the opposite of fragmentation—the more fragmented a landscape, the less connected

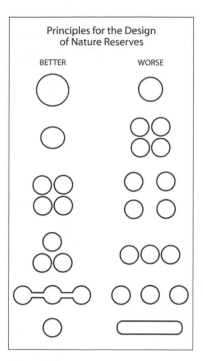

Figure 5.2
Principles for the design of nature
reserves. Adapted from Noss and
Cooperrider (1994).

it is and the more susceptible it is to loss or impairment of the ecosystem function due to natural and human disturbances, including exotic or edge species.

Community green infrastructure proponents can find guidance on green infrastructure network design by reviewing the recent literature relating to designing conservation networks and green space systems. In the past twenty or thirty years, a variety of books and articles have put forth design ideas based on the theories and practices of conservation biology, landscape ecology, conservation geographic information systems (GIS), urban and regional planning, and landscape architecture. Although they focus on different aspects and/or goals of conservation or reserve or network design, taken in their entirety, they offer a wealth of information that can be tailored to any individual geographic area and any set of priorities.[4]

GREEN INFRASTRUCTURE NETWORK DESIGN

The green infrastructure mapping process discussed here is but one approach that has been used successfully to identify networks of conservation areas. Another is SITES. Developed by The Nature Conservancy, the SITES process can be used to determine where conservation network elements should be located and how large the elements and the overall network should be. The Nature Conservancy has used the SITES model to develop ecoregional plans for nine different ecoregions of the United States. The Wildlands Project has used a similar approach to conservation planning in the Rocky Mountains along the "spine" of the continent and elsewhere in the United States. (The Wildlands Project in the Southern Rockies is discussed in the "Green Infrastructure in Action" section at the end of this chapter.)

In the 1990s, both Florida and Maryland developed similar GIS-based models to design statewide green infrastructure networks. These models have since been applied in different geographies and at different scales. The Southeastern Ecological Framework and the Chesapeake Bay Watershed Resource Lands Assessment are examples of how the modeling approach has been applied at the multistate level; the Delmarva Conservation Corridors at the substate level; the Saginaw Greenways Collaborative at the multicounty level; and the Anne Arundel Greenways Master Plan at the county level.

The first step in network design is to develop or adapt a network design model that is suited for the scale, size, and geographic diversity of the project area, the available spatial data, and the funds and time that are available. In some cases, green infrastructure advocates might feel that one model accommodates the needs of the program completely; in others, a combination of approaches might be appropriate.

NETWORK DESIGN: THE FLORIDA/MARYLAND APPROACH

The remainder of this chapter focuses on the green infrastructure network design models developed by Florida and Maryland. Both models use five basic steps to design the network: (1) develop network design goals and identify desired features, (2) gather and process data on landscape types, (3) identify and connect network elements, (4) set priorities for conservation action, and (5) seek review and input. These steps are rarely as sequential or as clearly defined as outlined here. Several steps may overlap; others may be completed several times as the network design is refined. Step 5, in particular, is not a sequential element; it is important to seek public input and participation throughout the design process.

Step 1: Develop Network Design Goals and Identify Desired Features

The first step of green infrastructure network design involves developing network design goals and selecting the natural and man-made features that should be included within the network. Drafting clear goals and objectives that represent desired outcomes is critical. If the primary focus of the team's work is the protection and restoration of water resources, for example, the goal and associated objectives will need to be tailored to this end. If, on the other hand, the community wants to use green infrastructure to help preserve its rural character, the design goals and objectives would be far different.

The goal for Maryland's statewide green infrastructure assessment was "To identify those areas of greatest statewide ecological importance, and provide a consistent approach to evaluating land conservation and restoration opportunities in Maryland. Specifically, to recognize: (1) a variety of natural resource values (as opposed to a single species of wildlife, for example), (2) how a given place fits into a larger system, (3) the ecological importance of open space in rural and developed areas, (4) the importance of coordinating local, state, and even interstate planning, and (5) the need for a regional or landscape-level view for wildlife conservation."[5] Lands providing silvicultural, agricultural, or health and recreation benefits were not included in Maryland's assessment, primarily because several statewide programs already addressed those needs. Working lands were addressed in terms of protecting natural ecosystems from high-intensity disturbances associated with urban development. A buffer of low-intensity land use was defined around the entire green infrastructure network. This compatible use buffer was defined as existing natural land, silviculture, agriculture, or lawns up to one mile from hubs, corridors, or the nearest major road.

Network design goals are needed to guide the many decisions that will have to be made during the design process. The goals also help to show others—including those who may disagree with the results—that there is an objective rationale for design decisions. For this reason, it is important to have goals and objectives that are aligned with the vision, mission, and network design focus that have been developed in conjunction with the greater community.

At this point in the process, it is important to identify the features or attributes that will be incorporated into the green infrastructure network. As shown in Table 5.1, possible attributes include resources that support or protect water, wildlife, recreation, and so forth. One way to think about such attributes is by the benefits they provide: whether these are associated primarily with natural ecosystem values and functions or with benefits to people. As shown in the table, attributes characteristic of natural ecosystem values and functions include ecological communities and other natural attributes, fish and wildlife resources, watersheds and water resources, and working landscapes with ecological values. Attributes with benefits to human populations include recreation and health resources, cultural resources, growth pattern and community character, water resources, and working lands with economic values.[6]

As an example, if better protection of water quality and quantity is a desired outcome of your strategic conservation effort, you would want to include watershed and water resource features as elements of the green infrastructure network. Water

Box 5.1

Ecological Design Goals and Objectives: Florida's Statewide Greenways System

The formulation of design goals and objectives was fundamental to the University of Florida's design for Florida's Statewide Greenways System. The following is the university's ecological design goal, which was endorsed by the Florida Greenways Commission and the Florida Greenways Coordinating Council.

Use a regional landscape approach to design an ecologically functional Statewide Greenways System that:

- Conserves critical elements of the state's native ecosystems and landscapes;
- Restores and maintains connectivity among native ecological systems and processes;
- Facilitates the ability of these ecosystems and landscapes to function as dynamic systems;
- Maintains the evolutionary potential of the elements of these ecosystems to adapt to future environmental changes.

The university's ecological design objectives included:

- Protect ecosystems, landscapes and processes native to Florida across their natural range of distribution and variation, including coastal, riverine, and upland landscapes, while giving special consideration to those inadequately protected by existing conservation programs;
- Protect the full range of Florida's biodiversity including viable populations of native plant and animal species that are endangered, threatened, rare, or otherwise imperiled;
- Conserve Florida's surface and ground water resources for the benefit of the state's native ecosystems, landscapes, residents, and visitors;
- Incorporate ecologically compatible working landscapes that minimize the impact of natural disturbances such as fire on the human-built environment and/or minimize the impact of human-built environments on native ecosystems and landscapes;
- Incorporate degraded lands through restoration that will enhance the ecological function of the Statewide Greenways System;
- Incorporate functional ecological linkages, including river floodplains, ridgelines, and other native landscape attributes that will enhance the ecological viability and manageability of presently isolated biological reserves;
- Design the ecological elements to absorb and dissipate the effects of naturally

occurring events, such as hurricanes, fire and flood across the landscape when management so dictates;

- Maintain ecological and evolutionary processes, such as disturbance regimes, nutrient cycles, biotic interactions, and range shifts, by protecting functional landscape gradients of aquatic, wetland, and upland ecosystems.

Source: University of Florida, Statewide Greenways System Planning Process Report. PDF available at www.geoplan.ufl.edu, under Greenways Projects.

resource attributes could include coastal and interior wetlands and shorelines, riparian corridors, floodplains, lakes, and ponds, as well as groundwater recharge areas, reservoirs, and other sources of drinking water. In considering water resource attributes, you should also think about the general watershed characteristics of your project area (e.g., level of imperviousness) and areas of known water quality or quantity problems (e.g., waterways not supporting their "designated uses"). Several other areas might be considered integral, such as areas of high aquifer recharge, areas with high densities of forested, first-order stream reaches or rivers (or stretches of rivers) that do not have dams. If the goal is to conserve and restore the natural ecological systems, the network should include ecological features that would help enrich biodiversity, support native plant and animal communities, and maintain natural landscape-scale ecological processes such as flooding and fire.

Working landscapes and resource-based industries, such as agriculture, forestry, recreation, and ecotourism, can also be important parts of green infrastructure networks. Because it is unlikely that an entire green infrastructure network can or should be purchased for nature preservation, lands that are compatible with green infrastructure goals can be important features to include. Working landscapes that provide habitat for fish and wildlife resources, help protect water resources (for example as aquifer recharge areas) or connect or buffer other network elements are particularly important. The economic value of working lands should also be considered. This means including lands that are important to soil productivity, actively farmed areas, and designated agricultural districts. Factors affecting the economic importance of working forests include forest type, timber stand characteristics including the age and size class of timber, and proximity to forest processing facilities.

Tourism, particularly ecotourism, and outdoor recreation may be important attributes. In selecting sites, consider factors such as access to passive and active recreational areas, trails and trailheads, public water access, and hunting and fishing opportunities. Also of potential importance are the identification and protection of major scenic vistas, overlooks, important travel corridors, scenic rivers and waterways, and other viewsheds. Viewsheds can be identified by examining relief

Figure 5.3
Watershed and water resource attributes could include coastal and interior wetlands and shorelines, rivers, streams, floodplains, lakes, and ponds, as well as groundwater recharge areas, reservoirs, and other sources of drinking water. Credit: Mark Benedict.

on U.S. Geological Survey topographic maps or calculated with the use of GIS from digital elevation data.

Although not ecologically significant, cultural and historic resources that have implications for ecosystem conservation and restoration should be documented. Cultural resources include national and state registered historic sites, historic districts, battlefields, cemeteries, and archeological resources.

Recreational and cultural resources, scenic viewsheds, and the like are often important attributes of green infrastructure networks. They not only provide broader benefits to the community, but also can help to gain the support of residents. The size, use, location, and other characteristics of these features should be determined based on the quality and characteristics of underlying ecological framework in order to ensure compatible uses and minimize activities that would degrade key ecological attributes. Building a recreational trail through sensitive habitat for rare plant or animal species, for example, undermines the fundamental goals of a green infrastructure network.

The desired attributes and the relative importance given to each should be carefully considered, as these decisions will have a profound affect on what the resulting

Table 5.1

Attributes that Could Be Part
of a Green Infrastructure Network

Natural ecosystem values and functions (biodiversity, ecological processes, and ecological services)		
Attributes	**Examples of places**	**Examples of functions provided**
Ecological communities and other natural attributes	Public, private, and nonprofit parks, preserves and reserves at state, regional, and local levels; lands in native habitat, waterfalls, gorges, canyons	Protect and restore native plant and animal communities, enrich biodiversity, maintain/restore natural landscape attributes
Fish and wildlife resources	Wildlife refuges, game reserves, landscape linkages/wildlife corridors, ecobelts, streams and lakes	Provide habitat for wildlife, support animal migration, maintain population health
Watersheds/water resources	Riparian and associated nonriparian lands, wetlands, floodplains, groundwater recharge areas	Protect and restore water quality and quantity, provide habitat for aquatic and wetland organisms
Working landscapes with ecological values	Forestlands, rangelands, and farmlands with native habitats and natural attributes; working landscapes with potential for restoring ecological values	Habitat for fish and wildlife species, protection of water resource values (floodplains, wetlands), connecting and/or buffering network components, protecting soils

Associated benefits to human populations (ecological services, societal values, and economics)		
Attributes	**Examples of places**	**Examples of functions provided**
Recreation and health resources	Parks, greenways, blueways, trails	Encourage exercise and active lifestyles, provide space for outdoor activities, create places of solitude and respite, connect people with nature, connect communities, provide alternative transportation
Cultural resources	Historic/archaeological sites, interpretative/educational sites/facilities, town/county open spaces/commons	Preserve link to natural and/or cultural heritage, foster education and involvement through "nature's classroom," encourage resource stewardship, protection of cultural site context/integrity
Growth pattern and community character	Greenbelts, scenic vistas/viewsheds, community open spaces/commons, greenways, river corridors, developing lands in proximity to ecological resources lands	Guide patterns of growth, create appealing visual landscapes, enhance character of development, foster community identity and pride, attract and retain businesses, residents, visitors
Water resources	Watersheds, wetlands, floodplains, groundwater recharge areas	Protect water quality and quantity, manage storm water, provide sites for regional wetland mitigation banks
Working lands with economic values	Farms, orchards, ranches, managed forests	Protect working lands as a business as well as a place, maintain rural character and traditions, support sectors of the economy

Figure 5.4
Cultural and historic resources, such as the Civil War battlefield at Antietam,
Maryland, have implications for ecosystem conservation and restoration and
can be part of a green infrastructure network. Credit: Ed McMahon.

network will look like and the benefits it will provide. The list of desired attributes
should reflect the vision and mission that have been developed, as well as the green
infrastructure network design goals and objectives. The features identified now will
guide the remaining network design steps, from identifying the landscapes that will
be modeled and the attributes on which data will be collected, to identifying and
linking the network's elements, to evaluating and prioritizing the different parts of
the network for conservation action.

Many green infrastructure initiatives incorporate as many attributes as possible;
others take a more targeted approach. By definition, however, green infrastructure
networks identify, protect, restore, and manage natural ecosystem values and functions. A system that focuses only on the benefits to people is a greenway system,
not a green infrastructure network. Green infrastructure networks should give
priority to natural ecosystem attributes.

Step 2: Gather and Process Data on Landscape Types

The next step in the network design process is to identify the landscape types
in the study area and gather and process data on the attributes that characterize
those landscapes. The identification of the landscapes provides the rationale for
determining what resource attributes to include and connect within the green
infrastructure network.

Box 5.2

Criteria for Identification of Potential Green Infrastructure Sites

The following criteria should be considered when determining conservation values:

- **Size:** Importance to nature conservation increases with size; bigger is better.
- **Diversity:** Variety (e.g., range of species and habitats) is better.
- **Naturalness:** Less modification is better.
- **Representation:** Natural communities that are not well represented in existing protected areas should be priorities.
- **Rarity:** Sites that contain rare elements are better.
- **Fragility:** Fragile communities are more valuable and deserving of protection.
- **Typicalness:** Maintaining good examples of common species is important.
- **Recorded history:** Selecting well-researched and documented sites with known presence of species and habitats is better than suppositions.
- **Landscape position:** Particularly important in green infrastructure, the contiguity a site maintains with surrounding landscape elements is an important consideration (connectivity of habitat).
- **Potential value:** Sites with diminished value but with restoration or enhancement potential are important.
- **Intrinsic appeal:** The protection of certain conspicuous species may be appealing to society and may result in a greater overall appreciation for nature conservation.

Source: Derek A. Ratcliffe, *A Nature Conservation Review*, Cambridge, UK: Cambridge University Press, 1977; and Tony Kendle and Stephen Forbes, *Urban Nature Conservation*, London: Spon, 1997.

So what are landscapes and how do you categorize them for your study area? Richard Forman defines a landscape as "a mosaic of ecosystems or land uses that possess common attributes that are repeated across a large area."[7] Landscapes can be categorized in different ways, depending on the geographic extent of the project area, the scale at which the team is working, and the desired outcomes. Because the Florida green infrastructure effort focused on protecting natural systems as well as the human attributes that could benefit them, the state's landscapes were grouped into two categories: native landscapes and human-dominated landscapes. Native landscapes encompass the juxtaposition and interaction of ecosystems and their associated processes. These include riverine landscapes, coastal landscapes, and upland landscapes. Human-dominated landscapes encompass areas that have been significantly altered by the activities of people. These include residential, commercial, industrial, and working lands (farmlands, ranchlands, tree plantations, mining lands, etc.).

Maryland's green infrastructure assessment, on the other hand, emphasized areas of statewide ecological significance and based its analysis on native upland, wetland, and aquatic ecosystems. Maryland's statewide network design included a number of attributes associated with these native ecosystems, such as presence of large or unique unmodified wetlands, large blocks of contiguous interior forest, healthy streams and their riparian zones, presence of rare, threatened or endangered (RTE) species, colonial waterbird nesting sites, waterfowl concentration areas, natural heritage areas, habitat protection areas, and existing protected lands.

Once the landscapes and attributes that will be used to design a green infrastructure network have been identified, the next step is to collect information on these landscape attributes. It can be expensive and time-consuming to generate new data; fortunately, it is also increasingly unnecessary. Many websites allow users to download data directly or to use the data to create maps. Electronic databases enable more flexibility than traditional, hard-copy data: users can create complex overlays, change scales, weigh values, and perform and replicate analyses. Print databases are less flexible than Web-based data, but they usually are also less expensive. Previously published data may be a better option for project teams that lack expertise in data analysis as they require neither sophisticated analysis nor GIS capability.

Ideally, all data should cover the entire project area. Holes in the data complicate the decision-making and priority-setting process. If data are not available for the entire study area, the green infrastructure design team may need to compile data from several smaller areas and integrate them into one hybrid data set. If the green infrastructure network is being designed for a watershed, for example, project planners may need to incorporate the land-use or zoning data generated by several different jurisdictions. Conversely, a state or large county may need to incorporate data on natural functions from several smaller watersheds. Of course, data layers for geographic areas that are larger than the project can be used; the data that cover the specific area of focus can be cut out from a data set covering a larger area. It is important to note, however, that since one of the main goals of a green infrastructure network is to maintain or enhance landscape connectivity, the network design and data should consider areas and connections just beyond the boundaries of the study area.

Data should be collected at a scale and resolution suitable for the project type and scale of analysis. If you are designing a multistate regional network, for example, parcel-specific data will provide more detail than is needed and add unnecessary computation time.

With the exception of soils information, data should be as current as possible. Since some information might be outdated, incomplete, or even inaccurate, fieldwork or some other form of ground-truthing may be required. For instance, Maryland developed a field assessment protocol to precede conservation or

Box 5.3

California Legacy Project

The California Legacy Project is a new initiative that involves a broad range of government agencies and citizen organizations in developing new tools and maps to guide decision-makers in conserving and protecting California's landscapes. The Legacy Project will provide better information in easy-to-use formats and a more timely understanding of pending threats to natural resources. The project's analytical tools will help to identify a long-range strategy to conserve the most important natural resources and will show how individual conservation investments, whether by acquisition or stewardship, fit into the regional and statewide context.

The project will assemble a statewide digital atlas, including maps of key resources, and existing and future stressors on the health of resources. Through this statewide atlas, the California Legacy Project will be able to highlight important resources that either lack a strong local constituency or are critical to inter-bioregional linkages.

The California Digital Conservation Atlas is California's comprehensive public Web site for conservation information. It is designed to provide easy-to-use map views of California's natural resources and working landscapes for people who may not be familiar with specialized geographic software.

restoration decisions. Information about when the data were collected, the collection process that was used, and who undertook the collection can help facilitate the fact-checking and quality assurance process.

This is not say that older data or data that is not of the desired spatial resolution should be ignored. In reality, network designers use data from a variety of sources with various levels of documentation (known as metadata) and of various levels of quality. One way to compensate for discrepancies is to weigh the data sets differently within the network design approach by weighting newer or better quality data heavier than older, grosser resolution or suspect data.

In some cases, the available data will not meet a project's design or analysis needs, so new data will need to be derived from one or more of the data sources. For instance, slope can be derived from topography data, erosion risk from slope data, roadless area and road density data from road data, habitat maps for focal species using land cover data, and so forth. Although hard-copy data can be compiled by hand, it is much easier to create secondary data from digital data sources using GIS analysis tools.

CATEGORIZING LANDSCAPE ATTRIBUTES

After collecting data on landscape attributes, both ecological and human-dominated resources can be categorized according to their significance and compatibility with network design goals and objectives. Since green infrastructure networks cannot contain all of the ecological landscape attributes in the project area, the design process necessitates establishing criteria that will be used to prioritize the attributes for inclusion within network hubs and links. These criteria can be based on a number of different considerations, including the attribute's contributions to the region's natural life support system (both its ecosystem elements and ecological processes) and its need for protection (including its vulnerability to development). Three classifications or rankings are usually sufficient for the purposes of prioritizing what should be included. Distinguishing between more rankings once they are graphically displayed could prove to be difficult.

In addition to data on ecological attributes, data on attributes of human-dominated landscapes should be categorized with respect to the degree to which those attributes help address or detract from network design goals and objectives. For example, agricultural land can buffer conservation areas from the effects of more intensive urban land uses. Lands used for less obtrusive forms of silviculture or ranching might serve as hubs. Large tracts of agriculture and other working lands, when effectively managed, can contribute habitat values, especially for species that need large landscapes. Conversely, other human-made attributes can adversely affect the network and therefore need to be identified as areas to avoid.

The result of these activities is a series of data layers or maps that reflect the location of ecological and human-dominated landscape attributes in the project area and the categories that will be used to make network design decisions.

Step 3: Identify and Connect Network Elements

Once the data on landscape attributes have been collected and categorized, the next step is to identify and connect the elements of the green infrastructure network. This is done by selecting the largest and highest quality areas as hubs—the large areas that will anchor the network—and then linking those hubs across the landscape. Green infrastructure networks can be designed using GIS technology or by hand using a base map and transparent data overlays. The best results are generated from weaving together both approaches, utilizing GIS capabilities to maximize the use of available spatial data and using hard-copy maps to obtain input from diverse stakeholders, thereby ensuring their buy-in to the process and the resulting network design.

Put simply, a GIS combines layers of information about a place to enable a better understanding of that place. The information layers used depends on the purpose—

Box 5.4

Categorization of Landscape Attributes: Florida Statewide Greenways Project

NATURAL RESOURCE ATTRIBUTES

The University of Florida's greenways planning team classified the natural resource attributes used in the design process into the following special area categories:

- **Priority Ecological Areas:** Ecological landscape attributes and conservation designations that reflect national and statewide importance are given the highest priority for inclusion and physical linkage as primary building blocks for the Statewide Greenways System. Selection criteria for Priority Ecological Areas include existing conservation lands, the highest ranked natural areas, and wildlife sites statewide, as identified by the Florida Game and Fresh Water Fish Commission and the Florida Natural Areas Inventory, and areas important to hydrological resources and processes.

- **Significant Ecological Areas:** Other ecological landscape attributes and conservation designations of statewide, or regional significance considered for inclusion as other potential locations for hubs and linkages. Selection criteria for Significant Ecological Areas include large water bodies and moderately ranked Florida Natural Areas Inventory and Florida Game and Fresh Water Fish Commission sites.

- **Other Ecological Landscape Attributes:** Lower priority ecological attributes that may be used to fill in or expand ecological elements within the Statewide Greenways System because of their potential to contribute to meeting the System's ecological conservation goals and objectives.

The design team then categorized all collected ecological landscape attribute data according to these three categories using selection criteria related to their relative importance.

Examples of Selection Criteria

Special Area Category	
Priority Ecological Area	Highly Ranked Florida Game and Fresh Water Fish Commission Habitat Types, Hot Spots and Priority Wetlands, and Strategic Habitat Conservation Areas
Priority Ecological Area	Florida Natural Areas Inventory S2 Global/State Rankings and Areas of Conservation Interest Categories A & B

Special Area Category	
Priority Ecological Area	Existing Conservation Lands, including Federal Wilderness Areas, Proposed CARL & SOR Conservation Lands, Aquatic Preserves, Outstanding Florida Waters, National Estuarine Research Reserves, Wild & Scenic Rivers
Priority Ecological Area	Roadless Areas of Native Habitat or Category I Lands that are 100,000 acres or larger for FDOT Roads or 5,000 acres or larger for TIGER roads
Significant Ecological Areas	Moderately Ranked Florida Game and Fresh Water Areas Fish Commission Hot Spots and Priority Wetlands, Florida Natural Areas Inventory Area of Conservation Interest Category C and National Marine Sanctuary Program Lands
Significant Ecological Areas	Roadless Areas of Native Habitat or Category I Areas Lands that are 50,000 to less than 100,000 acres for FDOT Roads or 1,000 to less than 5,000 acres for TIGER roads
Other Ecological Landscape Areas	Other Areas of Native Habitat as Defined by the Florida Game and Fresh Water Fish Commission. Open Water, Estuaries, Bays, Lakes, and Rivers, Excluding All Man-made (i.e., artificial) Water Attributes.

HUMAN-MADE RESOURCE ATTRIBUTES

The University of Florida's greenways planning team classified the human-made resource attributes into the following three categories:

- **Potentially Compatible Non-Native Landscape Attributes:** Non-native landscape attributes that may be selected for inclusion in the Statewide Greenways System because they are potentially compatible with the ecological conservation goals and objectives. Potentially compatible non-native landscape attributes fall into two categories of land use/land cover:
  - **Category I Lands:** Non-native land use/land cover types with moderate ecological value and high restoration potential, such as silviculture lands, pine plantations, ranch lands, and restored mining lands.
  - **Category II Lands:** Non-native land use/land cover types with low ecological value and moderate restoration potential, such as improved pastures, croplands, horse farms, and golf courses.
- **Incompatible Non-Native Landscape Attributes:** Non-native landscape attributes that are excluded from the Statewide Greenways System because they are incompatible with the System's Ecological Conservation Goals and Objectives. Incompatible non-native landscape attributes fall into a

category of land use/land cover called Category III. These include residential, commercial, and industrial development.

The design team identified Category I, II, and III lands using the Florida Land Use Classification System and land use/land cover data available through the state's water management district.

Examples of Associated Land Use/Land Cover Types

Category	
Category I Lands	Rangeland, Unimproved and Woodland Pastures, Tree Plantations, Reclaimed Lands, Fallow Land, Other Open Land
Category II Lands	Row and Field Crops, Tree Crops (e.g. Citrus), Improved Pasture, Nurseries/Vineyards, Other Agriculture, Golf Courses, Undeveloped Urban Land
Category III Lands	Residential, Commercial, and Industrial Land Uses; Transportation, Utilities, Communication

Source: University of Florida, Statewide Greenways System Planning Process Report. PDF available at www.geoplan.ufl.edu, under Greenways Projects.

identifying land conservation priorities, finding the best location for a transportation hub, analyzing environmental damage, or assessing the pattern of development. GIS allows for a meaningful generalization or simplification of a given area's geography. An increasing number of state and local governments use GIS to identify development patterns, plan gray infrastructure, and detect trends. GIS data also can be used to assess the current status of potential or existing elements of a green infrastructure network, the interrelationships of elements, and changes over time. GIS greatly enhances the ability to do complex modeling, but, as discussed in chapter 8, network design can also be done by hand, using a base map and overlays with different types of data.

HUBS

Depending on network goals and objectives, hubs might accomplish a variety of goals, including providing habitat for native animals and plants, allowing ecological processes to function undisturbed, or providing an origin and destination for wildlife and people moving through the system. Green infrastructure hubs include the highest-quality, largest, and least fragmented ecological landscape attributes. Wilderness areas, national parks, and other federal and state reserves can serve as the building blocks for an ecologically based network.

It is important to ensure that the lands selected as hubs are suitable for the conservation of native plant and animal populations and the maintenance of natural ecological processes. In Florida's model, unsuitable lands—those with incompatible land uses, a high density of roads, or negative edge effects—were removed. Maryland's green infrastructure initiative similarly rejected as hubs agricultural, developed, and cleared land.

Hubs need to be large enough to serve as suitable ecological building blocks for the network. This size will vary according to the size and scale of the focus area. A 5,000-acre minimum was selected for modeling Florida's green infrastructure network based on a review of the literature and an analysis of existing conservation lands. A much smaller size may be appropriate in smaller states, regions, and communities, particularly if there is little open space remaining. Maryland, a small state in which much of the land is already developed and the remaining rural landscapes are fragmented by farms, used a minimum size of 250 acres for most hubs. This criterion was reduced to 100 acres if there was the presence of RTE species or a unique natural community. (Even with this minimum, Maryland's model resulted in an average hub of 2,000 acres.) Once a minimum size is determined, it can be used to filter the identified attributes, and areas that do not meet the minimum size can be dropped from consideration.

To function optimally as ecological building blocks, hubs should be a complete unit with a relatively smooth border. In Florida's modeling work, internal gaps were filled and irregular borders were smoothed when native habitat and compatible nonnative lands with moderate ecological value and high restoration potential were contiguous. In Maryland, adjacent forests and wetlands were added to the model, and edges were smoothed. It is important to note that hubs will contain "gaps," or pockets of disturbed or human-dominated land cover. These areas represent excellent opportunities for restoration activities. (Restoration is discussed further in chapter 7.)

The final step in identifying the network's ecological hubs is to categorize them according to their landscape types (e.g., coastal, riverine, and upland landscapes in Florida's modeling work). This enables the network to be designed in a way that will replicate the area's natural ecological patterns and will provide appropriate starting and ending points for landscape linkages.

LINKS

Comprehensive landscape planning optimizes connectivity by linking hubs with appropriate land uses into an integrated conservation system. These are the connections that tie the green infrastructure system together.

For green infrastructure, it is important to consider the scientific basis for and ecological principles of linkages rather than merely connecting the dots between two hubs. Hubs or other core areas that are vastly different in terms of plants, animals, or hydrology usually should not be connected. If connecting upland forests to wetlands is the only option, design teams will need to consider whether this is worth the time and effort. Will it accomplish network goals? Design teams also should carefully consider the potential effects of connecting smaller, relatively degraded hubs with little or no interior habitat or species to larger, more pristine hubs. Making these links could facilitate the migration of unwanted plants and animals into the more pristine area and cause degradation over time. New linkages also might facilitate the movement of species that once thrived in an unconnected pristine area into smaller, degraded areas that become ecological traps. In an ideal world, design teams would have the option of avoiding these pitfalls, but degraded areas are often all that is left, leaving their restoration as the only option for creating a viable green infrastructure network. In such situations, the network design team needs to carefully weigh the pros and cons of creating new linkages.

Selecting an appropriate link between two hubs requires the design team to identify those lands that contain ecological attributes and processes suitable for linkage. Topography, distribution of natural vegetation, habitat quality, and characteristics of the species of interest may all play a role in selecting appropriate linkages. Corridors may link hubs of the same landscape type (e.g., riverine-to-riverine hubs), hubs of landscapes that are connected in nature (e.g., riverine-to-coastal hubs), and/or other hub linkages that meet the needs of specific species or have some other ecological purpose (e.g., cross-basin connections between selected ecological hubs). A suitability surface, which identifies areas as appropriate for a linkage (ranking them from most to least appropriate) or inappropriate, can be used to help find the best location for network links. The most suitable path is the corridor that uses the most appropriate lands to connect two hubs.

In Maryland, landscapes were grouped into three functional categories: upland, wetland, and aquatic. The landscape between hubs was assessed for its linkage potential, identifying conduits and barriers to movement (see Table 5.2). For each landscape type, a unique "corridor suitability" layer was created, based on habitat, road, slope, urban proximity, and land management impedance to animal and seed movement. (Impedance measures the degree to which the landscape parameter inhibits wildlife use and movement.) Analysts then used a most suitable path analysis (which Maryland called least-cost path analysis) to model the best ecological connections between core areas or hubs of similar types. Pathways that crossed major roads or urban areas were deleted, as were redundant pathways that were marginal.

One question often asked is how wide the links between hubs should be. While there is no magic formula, generally the wider the corridor the better. In addition, the longer the corridor is, the wider it should be. If the area around the corridor is disturbed, it is particularly important to expand the width by adding suitable contiguous native and nonnative land covers while avoiding any land identified as unsuitable. River corridors should be bordered on both sides by upland habitats that are wide enough to mitigate the impacts of runoff, provide a conduit for upland for interior species, offer suitable habitat for floodplain species displaced by flooding or lateral channel migration, and provide area for storing and attenuating floodwaters. Where unbroken corridors are impossible, *stepping stones*—small, closely spaced patches of habitat—may provide for the movement of interior species between patches.

In determining the widths of their linkages, Maryland used a minimum of 1,100 feet, which was based on the needs of interior, forest-dwelling species, or the width of the FEMA floodplain, whichever was greater. The 1,100-foot width was based on the desire to provide linkages with interior forest conditions of at least 500 feet wide, with an additional 300 feet of transition to edge on either side of the interior forest. Where the link followed a stream, the model also included the floodplain and adjacent steep slopes, as well as adjacent forest and wetlands. In both riparian and nonriparian linkages, corridor width was extended to account for compatible landscape features, such as adjacent forest or wetlands. Florida let the model "run out" away from the most suitable path, adding appropriate lands to the corridor until it ran into land types that were not suitable for the type of linkage being modeled. Smoothing the edges then followed.

Table 5.2

Maryland's Green Infrastructure Corridor Parameters and Weights

Parameter	Weight
Corridor links most important ecological hubs	2
Ecological ranking of hubs connected by corridor	4
Variety of ecotypes connected (terrestrial, aquatic, wetland)	2
Segment area (indirect measure of length)	1
Node area along corridor segment	2
Number of corridor breaks	4
Number of primary road crossings	4
Number of secondary road crossings	2
Number of county road crossings	1
Number of railroad crossings	1
Proportion of gap area in corridor segment	4
Percent of gap area in corridor segment	4
Buffer suitability within 300 feet of corridor	2

Because most areas have been modified by human activities, it is unlikely that you will be able to identify continuous paths between all network hubs. Even where continuous paths can be identified, they might be too narrow to support the ecological viability of the network. It is therefore important to identify areas where the restoration of native landscapes may be able to close gaps within links and/or to enhance the links that have been identified. Keep an eye out for potential opportunities to address these limitations to connectivity by restoring altered lands to native landscapes. If these opportunities are not available, the less-than-viable corridors should be deleted to maintain network integrity.

For the green infrastructure network to function as intended, linkages are every bit as important as hubs; in fact, the connectivity of natural systems is an important indicator of landscape health. Research has shown that a small patch or node connected to a network of corridors is likely to have more species and a lower rate of local extinction than a patch of the same size that is separated from the network. Alternative or redundant routes or loops in a network reduce the negative effects of gaps, disturbances, predators, and hunters within corridors, thus increasing the efficiency of movement. Multiple corridors can be highly beneficial. For example, Maryland's green infrastructure network was interrupted by development in twenty-eight areas between 1997 and 2000. However, alternative pathways could be identified for twenty-four of the twenty-eight broken routes, demonstrating the value of redundancy in conservation networks.[8]

ADDITIONAL HUBS AND LINKS

While some green infrastructure networks focus primarily on the natural processes of landscapes and their ecological benefits, others also include lands that benefit people, such as parks, trails, recreation areas, viewsheds, working lands, and so forth. In Florida, the University of Florida first modeled the ecological network and then added a recreational/cultural network to the statewide system. The recreational/cultural network used the same basic GIS methodology, identifying hubs that would serve as trailheads and links that could serve as trails connecting them to urban areas and cultural sites. Modeling the ecological network first enabled the design team to consider the underlying characteristics of the land when determining the suitability of recreational hubs and links that might cross ecologically important lands.

The Virginia Land Conservation Needs Assessment also focused first on ecological features, but the Virginia Department of Conservation and Recreation has made it clear that it plans to work with partners to include additional modeling layers representing other desired green infrastructure features, including sustainable forests, agricultural lands, and trails. The three-county green infrastructure network design undertaken by the Saginaw Bay Greenways Collaborative includes trails and other people-centered uses, as well as ecological hubs and links.

Box 5.5

Ten Principles for Ecological Corridors

1. Corridors not only provide habitat but also enhance the movements of wildlife.
2. A corridor should be designed to lead animals to suitable habitats without directing them into areas with a high risk of mortality.
3. The ecology and biology of species potentially using the corridor should always be considered in the design and establishment of wildlife corridors.
4. Newly established corridors should be designed to minimize edges, minimize disturbances from surrounding land-use practices, strive to establish and maintain complex vegetation structure in the corridor, and aim to mimic the original vegetation species composition and structure.
5. Wider corridors are better than narrow corridors.
6. Corridors must be viewed as subcomponents of much larger ecosystems and other conservation issues need to be addressed concurrently to be successful.
7. A logical, sensible, and sequential process should be constructed for identifying, developing, and conserving corridor networks in the region.
8. Consideration should be given to conducting an ongoing program to manage and protect corridors, as well as to monitor the use of corridors by wildlife once they are established.
9. Consider ways to mitigate the potential disadvantages of corridors.
10. We cannot wait to have all the "answers" and scientific information— we must accept that we need more knowledge but cannot wait to establish networks of corridors.

Source: Richard A. Fischer, *Wild-Link, Connecting Fragmented Habitats with Ecological Corridors in Northern Michigan.* Traverse City, MI: Conservation Resource Alliance, 2001.

Step 4: Set Priorities for Conservation Action

At this stage in the process, the design team needs to undertake an ecological assessment of the network design to make sure that it meets its goals. Ecological value should be considered for the network as a whole, as well as between and within individual elements. In addition, a risk assessment can help determine the areas that are most vulnerable to development, degradation, or fragmentation.

These two assessment components can be carried out concurrently, enabling the design team to set priorities for action.

In reviewing the design as a whole, consider issues of scale. For instance, protecting examples of fifty habitat types in a region will require much less area than protecting examples of five hundred habitat types in the same region. Different network designs will need to take into account different issues, including wildlife viability issues. The goal is to include examples of all communities, habitats, or land classes in a reserve network and, by so doing, to assure that species associated with these habitats are also represented. Rare species and habitats are of particular concern. In Florida, for example, the network design assessment considered the movement of the Florida panther by comparing the panther's actual movement with the hubs and links that were identified for the green infrastructure network. In Maryland's assessment, the only species-specific habitats considered were for native brook trout and the endangered Delmarva fox squirrel.

Green infrastructure assessments should also consider existing institutional arrangements that affect land use and land management within the network. For example, the distribution of land ownership is a fundamental consideration for implementing conservation and restoration strategies. Other considerations relating to existing institutional opportunities and constraints include lands that buffer existing public lands or that provide a transition zone between potentially incompatible uses (e.g. between residential areas and wilderness), inholdings surrounded by public lands, properties that are key to connecting existing protected or dedicated open space, properties providing public access to recreational attractions, and lands zoned or otherwise designated for open space, agriculture, or conservation purposes.

It is also important to identify the parcels that are most likely to be developed and to consider the geographic distribution of these threats within the network. This requires understanding the factors that contribute to land conversion, such as proximity to population centers, particularly those undergoing rapid growth; proximity to infrastructure (roads, water, and sewer); proximity to the coast or large bodies of water; proximity to protected open space; and property ownership factors. A risk and vulnerability analysis should also take into account the laws that affect development and conservation, such as those addressing wetlands, steep slopes, or RTE species habitats, as well as local comprehensive plans, zoning ordinances, and subdivision ordinances. In Maryland, a study found that proximity to previous development, market land value, population growth, and presence of wetlands were the most significant predictors of forest loss to development between 1997 and 2000.[9] Table 5.3 summarizes the parameters and weights Maryland used to evaluate development risk.

Florida also set priorities for protection. The University of Florida developed a GIS methodology to rank lands within the network for their relative value to statewide connectivity based on ecological criteria and the level of development

Table 5.3

Development Risk Score: Maryland

Maryland parameters and weights for ranking overall development risk for hubs and corridors within physiographic regions

Level of current protection from development	4
Percent of hub managed primarily for natural values (GAP Management Status 1 or 2)	2
Mean development pressure, as calculated by Maryland Department of Planning	2
Proximity to commercial, industrial, or institutional land use	1
Mean distance to DC beltway	1
Cost of land (at county scale)	1
Mean distance to nearest interstate, primary state, secondary state, or county road	1

threat. This prioritization was done first separately and then together through the application of a matrix. The result was the compilation of a list of twenty-four candidate areas. Assessment of the degree to which an area was critical to completion of the statewide network and nearby linkages, the likelihood of conversion of an area to an incompatible use in the near future, and the analysis of land ownership

Figure 5.5
Critical linkages identified for Florida's Statewide Ecological Network. Credit:
Executive Summary, The Florida Statewide Greenways System Planning Project, 1999.

Box 5.6

Interior Forests Benefit Birds

Studies reveal that interior forests provide critical habitat for a wide range of species. In the summer of 2003, the Maryland Department of Natural Resources studied bird and vegetation data at 136 interior forest sites on Maryland's Eastern Shore. These sites were both inside and outside of green infrastructure hubs, in many types of forest, and on both public and private land. The study revealed that both the condition of a forest and its landscape context were important to the bird communities. Forest interior dwelling birds preferred forest within green infrastructure hubs and preferred undisturbed, broadleaf forests.

Of the sixteen forest interior dwelling birds observed, thirteen were neotropical migrants—species that breed in temperate and boreal regions of the Western Hemisphere and over winter in the Western tropics. Populations of many neotropical migratory birds are declining in the state of Maryland and through-out the United States. In Maryland's study, neotropical migrants preferred forests inside green infrastructure hubs, especially in the top 10 percent of ecological rankings, and were found more often in regions that had higher percentages of forest cover.

These results underscore the importance of retaining large blocks of forest, especially mature broadleaf forest containing streams and wetlands. Protecting such areas will help more area-sensitive species than will protecting isolated woodlots and allowing further fragmentation of the surrounding landscape.

patterns to assess the feasibility of purchase were used to winnow this list down to ten critical linkages encompassing about 2.7 million acres, of which about 17 percent is existing conservation land, 30 percent is proposed conservation land, and over 50 percent is private land. Purchase options are being pursued for many of these properties through Florida Forever and other land conservation programs.

Establishing green infrastructure priorities requires combining and weighing seemingly unrelated factors to arrive at a composite conservation or restoration "score." The weights assigned to each parameter should reflect its overall importance in achieving network design goals. If one of your goals is to provide viable habitat for species requiring large blocks of contiguous forest, for example, parameters that directly pertain to this goal should be assigned a higher weight than other parameters. Another important objective is to consider the possible relationships between or among the factors you have selected to rank network elements. Try to avoid criteria that may be redundant or overlapping. Incorporating the productivity of both agricultural and woodland soils into the same ranking protocol, for example, could result in overemphasizing the importance of soils. On the other hand, if sustainability of resource-based industries was among the network design goals, and within that goal designers wanted to emphasize forest-dependent industries, then woodland soil productivity would be weighted higher than agricultural soil productivity in the assessment.

One of the main advantages of this process is its flexibility. As new data become available, new parameters can be added to the ranking scheme. In addition the assigned weights can be adjusted without changing the underlying data, enabling analysts to change the preferred characteristics of the network to reflect different design goals.

Step 5: Seek Review and Input

Of all the steps in the process, this step is perhaps most critical to success—and the least likely to be undertaken in sequential order. A green infrastructure network might affect people who are not involved in the design process, so the design team should seek input throughout the design process. In fact, in some cases, review will take place after each of the first four steps—or even during them. In Florida, for example, the design team came up with a list of goals and objectives for the green infrastructure network, but sought review and approval from the Florida Greenways Coordinating Council before proceeding with the process.

The design team and leadership group will need to determine who should be involved at various stages of the design process. Some factors to consider include the characteristics of the study area, the political context in which the process is taking place, and available resources. Regardless of these factors, it is critical to have appropriate people review the preliminary network design to ensure that it meets desired goals and that the information is accurate and up to date.

In cases in which the leadership group does not create the network design, its members should nevertheless play a role in the design process. As representatives of the community and the leaders in the process, their input is essential to the successful implementation of the network design. Not only should this group be involved in reviewing the design to ensure that it meets the desired goals and objectives, the leadership group should also play a key role in public hearings at which the design is reviewed.

In addition to the leadership group, reviewers should include private landowners and other stakeholders, people knowledgeable about various aspects of green infrastructure design and implementation, those with specific knowledge of the landscapes and other elements of the green infrastructure network, and experts in the content areas involved. Local public agencies (planning and zoning, public works, parks and recreation departments), land trusts, realtors, recreation interests, and the public-at-large can all be involved in corroborating the results and giving feedback. These individuals and groups provide an important reality check. For instance, they might have knowledge of proposed roads or developments that will influence the network design. Private landowners, particularly those with large holdings, are a particularly critical group; some green infrastructure programs provide one or more separate review opportunities for landowners.

Methods for gathering input vary. Supplementary maps, including aerial photography or satellite imagery, are typically used to delineate how the network design will accomplish specific goals and objectives. Field data can help to describe how the network design includes appropriate sites and landscapes.

In Maryland, after having the assessment methodology reviewed by local and national experts, staff from the Department of Natural Resources (MD-DNR) held meetings with each county in Maryland and the city of Baltimore to discuss the resulting green infrastructure network maps. The staff used a modeling exercise to explain what had been done and asked the local officials whether the maps that were generated from the network design model reflected reality. In some cases, local officials identified sites within the green infrastructure network that had been developed and were no longer appropriate. MD-DNR staff used this information to produce an updated *Atlas of Greenways, Water Trails, and Green Infrastructure*.[10]

Maryland's review process demonstrates how input by county and state agencies can positively influence the network design. In reviewing the preliminary network design, county planning departments and parks and recreation departments recommended several dozen areas for inclusion as hubs or corridors. In most cases, these were county parks or other public lands missed by the model. Counties also identified several areas for deletion, mostly areas that had been developed since the model's data was acquired. In a few cases, proposed corridors were too heavily parceled for feasible implementation, and reviewers identified alternative linkages. Finally, ecologically significant areas digitized by the Maryland Department of Natural Resources' Natural Heritage Program were added if they were adjacent to the hubs or corridors in the model. Revised maps were then mailed to the planning departments of each county for further review. The revised green infrastructure network was 43,604 acres (1.65 percent) larger than the preliminary design.

Florida's multiphase review process focused on obtaining input from a wide variety of sources. The first phase involved the review of the goals, objectives, assumptions, and data used for the design of the ecological network. The review was conducted by national and state experts, Florida Greenways Coordinating Council (FGCC) staff and representatives from regional and statewide stakeholder groups. During the next phase of the review process, ten workshops were held at locations across the state. Participants heard about the concepts of the statewide system and the procedures being used to design it and then were given an opportunity to identify hubs and linkages on a base map that depicted conservation lands and trails within their region. Each workshop was held twice: in the afternoon, the workshop was geared to agency and local government participants; in the evening, to the general public.

The coordinating council appointed six regional task forces for the third review phase. The task forces served as regional advisory committees to the statewide leadership group; their key purpose was to review the statewide design and planning effort to ensure that it met local needs and aspirations. Following a detailed briefing on the process used to develop the preliminary network design for their region, each regional task force held a number of working sessions to review and provide input on the network design. A public workshop was held in conjunction with the final meeting of each of the regional task forces to broaden the opportunity for public input. The regional task forces provided the most widespread and comprehensive forum for participation by local and regional interests in the statewide effort. This approach is particularly useful when the green infrastructure network covers a large geographic area.

In the final phase, the members of the FGCC reviewed the University of Florida's preliminary network design as well as the recommendations from the six regional task forces. The FGCC also held a public workshop where participants reviewed maps of the network design and provided verbal and/or written comments.

A cornerstone of Florida's effort was the assumption that private lands were critical to the implementation of the statewide greenways system, but that participation of landowners should be voluntary. Florida took particular care to ensure the involvement of private landowners in the network design process. Individuals representing landowner interests were appointed to the statewide leadership group. Landowner representatives were invited to review the network design approach and comment on how to address private property concerns, and they participated in the regional task force and coordinating council public workshops. At the request of landowners, some private parcels were deleted from the network design.

THE RESULTS OF THE MODELING PROCESS

The model used by Florida and Maryland succeeded in identifying ecologically significant natural resources features statewide—features that should be priorities for protection. The GIS-based network design model allowed objective, goal-driven analysis of the ecological value of various pieces of land. Land acquisition activities could then be prioritized on the basis of this analysis.

Florida's Ecological Network includes hubs, which are large regionally important protected areas or entry points, and sites, which are smaller or more locally important areas. Because it cuts across county, local, and watershed divisions, the network facilitates cooperative land-use planning and management. This helps people to see that natural ecosystems rarely align with jurisdictional boundaries and therefore require joint action.

The preliminary design for the Ecological Network included approximately 57 percent (22.8 million acres) of the state's land and open water. Open freshwater, coastal waters, existing public conservation lands, and private preserves composed 53 percent of the Ecological Network (the five largest hubs were national parks and wildlife refuges, national and state forests, and U.S. Air Force land), and proposed public conservation lands composed 10 percent. Other private lands made up the remaining 37 percent of the network, approximately one-third of which were wetlands or within the hundred-year floodplain.

In Florida, the groups that spearheaded the modeling process were not charged with developing land acquisition strategies; however, by identifying priority lands for protection, the green infrastructure plan has increased the effectiveness of land protection and acquisition activities in the state. Florida Forever, the state's leading land acquisition program, has targeted the ten critical linkages that were identified in the network design. In addition, being within the Ecological Network is one of the criteria used to evaluate lands proposed for purchase under Florida Forever. Florida also established an official voluntary greenways designation process under which over 700,000 acres and nearly 1,500 miles of land and water trails have been designated. As Florida's population continues to grow, the Ecological Network will provide the state with a framework for conservation that protects and enhances its natural assets.

Maryland's process similarly resulted in the vision for an interconnected network of ecologically valuable hubs and corridors that, if protected, will help preserve the natural ecosystem functions on which life depends. The assessment also resulted in the identification of those lands in the network that are most ecologically valuable, most vulnerable to development, and most highly ranked for restoration activities. This in turn led to the establishment of GreenPrint, a new funding program designed to acquire lands identified as part of the assessment.

Maryland's Green Infrastructure Assessment identified 33 percent of Maryland's total land area as providing important green infrastructure benefits, including 63 percent of all forest in the state; 90 percent of the state's interior forest; 87 percent of the state's remaining unmodified wetlands; 91 percent of Maryland's streams within interior forests; 99.7 percent of the state's Natural Heritage Areas; 88 percent of the known occurrences of RTE species in the state; 90 percent of areas identified as important breeding habitat for forest-dependent birds; and 89 percent of Maryland's steep slopes. The diversity of land types in Maryland's model demonstrates the strength of the approach taken. The high correspondence between lands identified in the Green Infrastructure Assessment and lands previously identified as having conservation value indicates that the evaluation method used provides a good representation of the many different types of ecosystems that should be part of a comprehensive conservation approach.

Maryland GIS data sets were also used to identify those areas that would benefit most from restoration—that is, where the greatest ecological benefit would result from applying limited restoration dollars because the land is connected to or part of the green infrastructure network. The idea is to link restoration projects with the green infrastructure assessment to fill network gaps. The emphasis in restoration projects has been on wetlands, streams, riparian forest buffers, and forestation.

GREEN INFRASTRUCTURE IN ACTION: SOUTHERN ROCKIES WILDLANDS NETWORK

Southern Rockies eco-region habitats range from alpine tundra to ponderosa pine forests to sagebrush grassland. These diverse ecological communities support over 500 vertebrate species and a rich variety of plants and invertebrate species. This abundant biodiversity exists in the Southern Rockies partially because of its continuous stretches of wild, remote, and undeveloped lands.

Even in remote areas, however, human expansion and development are threatening the diversity of life in the Rockies. Native species have been extirpated, old-growth forests logged, wild and powerful rivers dammed and polluted, and land degraded. The Southern Rockies Ecosystem Project (SREP) is among the organizations actively working to mitigate these effects.

Founded in 1992, SREP is a nonprofit conservation biology organization working to protect and restore large, continuous networks of land in the Southern Rockies eco-region of Colorado, Wyoming, and New Mexico. SREP is working to realize its vision for a healthy eco-region by connecting networks of people in order to connect networks of land.

As part of its efforts to address the threats to the Southern Rockies, SREP, in conjunction with the Wildlands Project and the Denver Zoo, produced the Southern Rockies Wildlands Network Vision. The Vision uses conservation science principles and GIS-mapping technology to identify and protect wildlands critical to the preservation of native biodiversity in the Southern Rockies. The mission of the Vision is to protect and "rewild" the regional landscape. Rewilding emphasizes large core wild areas, functional connectivity across the landscape, and the vital role of keystone species and processes, especially large carnivores.[11]

The Southern Rockies Wildlands Network Design is a critical component of the Vision. This is a landscape-based conservation map that designates areas as core protected, wildlife movement and riparian linkages, or compatible-use areas. The Southern Rockies Wildlands Network Design is one of several such designs prepared for the Rocky Mountain region. Wildlands network designs are based on site-specific proposals for cores, linkages, and compatible-use areas that stretch across a landscape. The boundaries of the landscape are defined for each plan, and the network of protection is mapped in detail within those boundaries. These networks also include varying levels of protection, from core wilderness to responsibly managed compatible-use areas with wildlife corridors that link them all across the ecoregion.

Figure 5.6
To protect the rich diversity of life and the natural beauty of the Rocky Mountains, the Southern Rockies Ecosystem Project, the Wildlands Project, and the Denver Zoo teamed up to utilize a green infrastructure-like approach to identify and protect ecologically valuable lands and to "rewild" the regional landscape. Credit: Doug Shinneman, Southern Rockies Ecosystem Project.

Vision of the Southern Rockies Ecosystem Project

We envision a Southern Rockies ecoregion that is whole—a vast, connected landscape where native species thrive and natural ecological processes maintain a healthy balance. Such a holistic vision transcends political and human-made boundaries and addresses large landscapes on the ecosystem and ecoregional level.

We must start healing the wounds that degrade the health of the ecoregion by restoring critical species and ecological processes to the land by rewilding the Southern Rockies. Rewilding emphasizes large core wild areas and functional connectivity across the landscape; the importance of top-down regulation to healthy ecosystems, which includes the crucial role of large carnivores and keystone species; and the importance of natural processes such as wildfire and predation that are critical to sustaining functioning ecosystems.

To heal the Southern Rockies, we must establish a network of connected wildlands that facilitate the flow of life across the landscape. This wildlands network will include varying levels of protection, from core wilderness, to responsibly managed compatible-use areas, with wildlife corridors that link them all across the ecoregion.

Source: Wildlands Network Homepage, www.restoretherockies.org/vision.html.

Goals of the Southern Rockies Wildlands Network Vision

1. Protect and recover native species.
2. Protect and restore native habitats.
3. Protect, restore, and maintain ecological and evolutionary processes.
4. Protect and restore landscape connectivity.
5. Control and remove exotic species.
6. Reduce pollution and restore areas degraded by pollution.

The Southern Rockies Wildlands Network Design

To determine the location and size of cores, connections, and compatible use lands, SREP used the three-track approach advocated by Reed Noss: one track embraces representation of habitats and vegetation types within a network of core areas; a second track identifies and protects special elements such as the locations of threatened species, biodiversity hotspots, and important places such as roadless areas; and the third track identifies and protects key habitat for focal species that indicate healthy, functioning systems.[12]

> "The Southern Rockies are a critical link in a potential 4,000 mile network of public and private lands that constitute the spine of the continent megalinkage—a grand-scale wildlife corridor."
>
> REED F. NOSS
> WILDLANDS PROJECT

The Southern Rockies Wildlands Network Design used SITES computer modeling, least cost path analysis, and expert opinion to craft a design that includes the best available data and best meets the overarching goals of rewilding and ensuring persistence of native biodiversity in the ecoregion.

The SITES model is a computer-based tool for regional conservation analysis that explicitly incorporates spatial design criteria into the site selection process. SITES 1.0 is a customized ArcView project that facilitates designing and analyzing alternative portfolios. The software used to select regionally representative systems of nature reserves for the conservation of biodiversity is called the Site Selection Module (SSM). It is a streamlined derivative of SPEXAN 3.0 (Spatially Explicit Annealing) that was developed by Ian Ball and Hugh Possingham. SPEXAN was originally developed as a stand-alone program with no GIS interface for displaying portfolios and ancillary spatial data.

The Southern Rockies eco-region was used to determine the specific boundaries of the Southern Rockies Wildlands Network Design. The Southern Rockies Wildlands Network Vision overlaps the New Mexico Highlands Vision to the south and the Heart of the West Vision to the northwest. This overlap ensures a relatively seamless transition between regions.

The initial steps in running the SITES model involve selecting a set of target elements (species and communities), identifying levels of representation for each target, and then identifying a set of sites (the "conservation portfolio") from among a larger set of "planning units" within an ecoregion. This portfolio provides a systematic basis for site planning and acquisition. The overall objective of

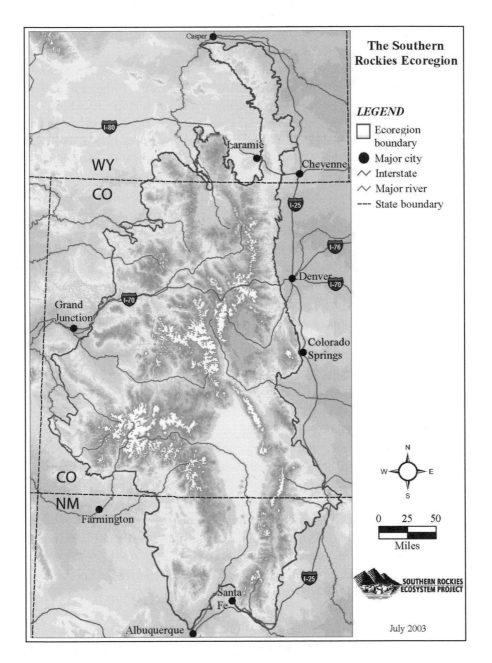

Figure 5.7
The Southern Rockies Ecosystem Project uses natural ecosystem boundaries, rather than jurisdictional boundaries, to identify areas in which to work, encouraging an intergovernmental, cross-jurisdictional, holistic approach to conservation and development. Credit: Southern Rockies Ecosystem Project.

the portfolio selection process is to ensure that all conservation goals for representation and spatial configuration have been met.

The SITES model attempts to minimize the cost of a conservation network while maximizing attainment of conservation goals, usually in a compact set of core areas. The use of the SITES model determines what the costs are, which can include the actual cost of acquiring and protecting lands for conservation or the relative cost of restoring these areas back to wild land. An additional cost, called the penalty cost, is assessed for failing to meet stated target goals. The weighted boundary length is the cost of the spatial dispersion of the selected sites (the "cost" or ecological consequence of sites being too far apart). In other words, the total portfolio cost equals the cost of selected sites, plus the penalty cost for not meeting the stated conservation goals for each element, plus the cost of spatial dispersion of the selected sites as measured by the total boundary length of the portfolio.

SITES is best suited to situations where an ecoregion has been divided into "planning units" that completely fill the region and are of roughly the same size and shape. Planning units could be regular grids, watersheds, landscapes, or any other geographic features that make sense from data compilation and conservation planning perspectives. Since planning units serve as the basic building blocks for assembling a portfolio, their delineation should be made carefully. For the Southern Rockies Wildlands Network, 1,000-hectare hexagonal areas were used as the individual planning units.

The SITES algorithm uses a process called "simulated annealing."[13] This algorithm evaluates the complete alternative portfolio at each step, and compares a very large number of alternative portfolios to identify a good solution. The procedure begins with a random set and then swaps planning units in and out of that set and measures the change in cost. If the change tends to improve the set, the new set is carried forward to the next iteration.

Because the simulated annealing does not necessarily find the "perfect" solution each time, but instead returns a near optimal solution, several runs of the model are recommended. The Southern Rockies Ecosystem Project ran the model in sets of ten runs, each with one million iterations. SITES then selected the run that best met the target goals with the least cost as the "best" run for that set of ten. SITES also created a summary file indicating the number of times that a particular planning unit was included in the final set of planning units. Planning units that are selected in multiple runs of the set, even though they do not necessarily appear in the "best" solution, may highlight potential linkages between core wild areas and/or areas with more intrinsic value to the overall design.

Preliminary drafts of the SITES analysis were reviewed during three expert workshops, with participation from the scientific, academic, and conservation communities. Feedback was evaluated and incorporated in a second run of the SITES model. These data were then made available again for further review. The results formed the basis of the Southern Rockies Wildlands Network Design.

Results

The resulting Southern Rockies Wildlands Network connects to other wildlands networks along the spine of the North American continent, creating a megalinkage that enables the movement of large carnivores and keystone species through the region.

The scope of the Southern Rockies Wildlands Network Design is monumental; its vision ambitious. It covers 25,772,037 acres—or about 62 percent of the Southern Rockies ecoregion. In comparison, currently protected areas—national wilderness areas, National Park Service lands, and other congressionally protected areas—only cover about 10 percent of the ecoregion.

> "The Southern Rockies Wildlands Network Vision is bold, yet practical. Ambitious, yet achievable—scientifically credible, and hopeful. Together, these characteristics create an outstanding opportunity to produce real change in the Southern Rockies ecoregion."
>
> BRIAN MILLER AND MONIQUE DIGIORGIO
> *SOUTHERN ROCKIES WILDLANDS NETWORK VISION*, JULY 2003

The Southern Rockies Wildlands Network Vision is viewed as a launching pad for on-the-ground action. Implementation with government agencies, land trusts, and local conservation groups has begun. SREP is working with local conservation groups like High Country Citizens Alliance and the Central Colorado Wilderness Coalition to provide newly released data on important wildlife areas in the Southern Rockies.

Recognizing the importance of working at the local level, SREP is meeting with local groups, land trusts, and public agencies to provide GIS assistance through map-making, analysis, and data availability and to apply the Network Design at the local level. SREP provides scientific information and assistance to the twenty-six member groups of the Southern Rockies Conservation Alliance (SRCA), which in turn assist local efforts. SREP also provides assistance for local conservation plans and projects that fall within the Vision boundaries, helps guide priority setting for new projects, and assists groups in campaigns and protection for priority lands identified in the Vision.

The Network Design has informed local planning efforts. For example, the Upper Arkansas and South Platte Project applied the regional SITES data to a local plan (The Upper Arkansas and South Platte Inventory). The SITES output matched very well with the local inventory that was based on field work and expert opinion. The SITES analysis covered the federally protected wilderness areas, the areas proposed for wilderness protection, and potential connections for animal movement. It also identified several areas of biological importance that were not initially included in the Inventory.

SREP also is translating its work into on-the-ground action, working with the Central Colorado Wilderness Coalition and the Upper Arkansas South Platte Project to support the designation of new wilderness areas in this region and to refine the Wild Connections Conservation Plan for the Pike and San Isabel National Forests. SREP also is involved in Mountains to Mesas, a collaborative project, providing Vision data as the basis for developing sound scientific management recommendations for critical wildlife linkages, wilderness areas, and compatible-use areas. In the Linking Colorado's Landscape project, SREP is working with the Colorado Department of Transportation to identify the most important wildlife linkages across highways in the state of Colorado and has initiated a public awareness campaign to educate citizens about places where animals tend to cross the highways and to encourage motorists to be on the lookout. At least five wildlife crossings have been constructed in Colorado, and underpasses and deer-proof fencing have been used on Interstate 70 to protect mule deer.

These efforts are successful in part because they combine scientific models with local expert opinion to produce a plan of action. The Southern Rockies Wildlands Network Design provides a visual depiction of biologically critical landscapes and corridors throughout the region, while the Vision serves as an ambitious yet realistic approach to maintaining and restoring viable populations of native species. The project's vision provides a blueprint for conservation work and a context for wildlands that is scientifically credible and practically achievable. By bringing together networks of people to work toward a future in which networks of wildlands fit into a civilized human community, the Southern Rockies Wildlands Network Vision offers the promise that humans and nature can live in harmony.

• *For more information about the Southern Rockies Ecosystem Project, visit www.restoretherockies.org/vision_doc.html.*

Notes

1. For further information about the evolution of reserve design and guidance on designing a green space network, see Reed F. Noss and Allen Y. Cooperrider, *Saving Nature's Legacy: Protecting and Restoring Biodiversity* (Washington, D.C.: Island Press, 1994), chapter 5; Craig R. Groves, *Drafting a Conservation Blueprint* (Washington, D.C.: Island Press, 2003), chapter 8; Dave Foreman, *Rewilding North America: A Vision for Conservation in the 21st Century* (Washington, D.C.: Island Press, 2004), chapter 10; and Craig L. Shafer, *Nature Reserves: Island Theory and Conservation Practice* (Washington, D.C.: Smithsonian Institution Press, 1990), part 12.

2. For example, see J. M. Diamond, "The Island Dilemma: Lessons of Modern Biogeographic Studies for the Design of Nature Reserves," *Biological Conservation* 7 (1975):129–146; E. O. Wilson and E. O. Willis, "Applied Biogeography," pages 522–534 in M. L. Cody and J. M. Diamond *Ecology and Evolution of Communities* (Cambridge, MA: Belknap Press at Harvard University Press, 1975); J. M. Diamond and R. M. May, "Island Biogeography and the Design of Natural Reserves," pages 163–186 in R. M. May,

ed., *Theoretical Ecology: Principles and Applications* (Philadelphia: W. B. Saunders, 1976); J. Terbourgh, "Preservation of Natural Diversity: The Problem of Extinction Prone Species," *BioScience* 24 (1974):715–722.

3. See Noss and Cooperrider, *Saving Nature's Legacy.*

4. As an example, see Wenche E. Dramstad, James D. Olson, and Richard T. T. Forman, *Landscape Ecology Principles in Landscape Architecture and Land-Use Planning* (Washington, D.C.: Island Press, 1996).

5. Ted Weber, *Maryland's Green Infrastructure Assessment: A Comprehensive Strategy for Land Conservation and Restoration* (Annapolis, MD: Maryland Department of Natural Resources, May 2003), 5.

6. It is important to note that all of these attributes benefit people. While the second list is more direct, the attributes that benefit natural systems are, in the long run, critical to human survival.

7. Richard T. T. Forman, *Land Mosaics: The Ecology of Landscapes and Regions* (Cambridge, UK: Cambridge University Press, 1995).

8. Ted Weber and R. Aviram, *Forest and Green Infrastructure Loss in Maryland, 1997–2000, and Implications for the Future* (Annapolis, MD: Maryland Department of Natural Resources, 2002), 10.

9. From Ted Weber, *Risk of Forest Loss in Maryland's Green Infrastructure, Based on 1997–2000 Patterns of Development* (Annapolis, MD: Maryland Department of Natural Resources, 2004), 11.

10. This atlas, which included maps of the proposed statewide green infrastructure network, was published in 2000.

11. Southern Rockies Ecosystem Project, The Denver Zoological Foundation and The Wildlands Project, *Southern Rockies Wildlands Network Vision* (Golden, CO: Colorado Mountain Club, 2003).

12. See Noss and Cooperrider, *Saving Nature's Legacy.*

13. S. J. Andelman, et al. *SITES V 1.0: An Analytical Toolbox for Designing Ecosystem Conservation Portfolios, Report for The Nature Conservancy* (Arlington, VA: The Nature Conservancy, 1999).

chapter six

The Implementation Quilt: Matching Available Resources to Network Needs

A green infrastructure network design is a spatial vision of a desired future. But as difficult as developing this vision might be, it can be even more challenging to make the vision a reality and to translate a community's vision and desires into concrete actions with the resources and tools readily available. A key to successful implementation is moving seamlessly from planning to on-the-ground results. This means taking the first step to implement the project on the very first day it is envisioned. In some cases, opposition to implementation can dampen enthusiasm and create obstacles. Solutions to any large, complex problem necessitate change, and people whose interests are negatively affected can easily delay or completely halt a project.

When people think of implementing a land conservation project, such as a green infrastructure plan or network design, they often assume that it will be done by the government with public funding. This can be a dangerous assumption. There has never been—and will never be—enough public funding to fully implement a green infrastructure plan. Rather, there are many ways to accomplish conservation goals; successful efforts select the strategies that work best for the goals at hand and make the best use of available resources.

Grants and other types of funding are available for almost every possible land management practice, including land conservation. Broadly describing the activities within the overall initiative expands the potential funding sources for green infrastructure projects. Funding categories that might be applied to a green infrastructure network include wetland protection, forestation, creation of forest buffers, source water protection, stormwater control, endangered species habitat conservation, rural assistance, farm preservation, and so forth.

Identifying the actions that are needed for a green infrastructure network to become reality and matching these with the available financial resources is vital to the successful implementation of green infrastructure efforts. By knitting together land conservation initiatives, restoration and long-term management efforts, technical assistance programs, and innovative financing techniques, communities can identify and implement the broad-based solutions needed for green infrastructure.

WHAT IS AN IMPLEMENTATION QUILT?

A green infrastructure network is by necessity complex. Typically, the network consists of both public and private lands. Hubs may be of various sizes and include different types of landscapes. Some of the land identified as part of a green infrastructure network may need to be acquired, but other parcels may not. There also could be a host of restoration needs. Linkages may be incomplete, insufficient, or broken.

At the same time, in any community, there may be a host of projects already underway that can become part of a more holistic effort to implement the green infrastructure design. Conservation organizations may be working to protect a rare species or to preserve land along a river or stream, for example. Community volunteers may be involved in stewardship activities, cleaning up local riverways or parks. Local, state, or federal agencies may have grants or other types of funding available for programs that could be used to meet green infrastructure goals. Successful projects find ways to integrate complementary activities into the green infrastructure initiative, even if they have different goals and objectives.

What is needed is a way to match the available resources—tools, programs, funding, and people—to the needs of the green infrastructure network. The term *implementation quilt* implies that projects weave together these various components.[1] The idea of a quilt also implies that green infrastructure uses a patchwork approach—green infrastructure, like a quilt, will not be cut from the same piece of cloth, but will instead include a variety of landscapes and protection methods. The metaphor of a quilt captures the idea of having many pieces of different sizes, shapes, and types stitched into one comprehensive whole with a unified purpose. Just as swatches of cloth are sewn together to make a quilt, landscapes are joined together to create a functional green infrastructure network.

Moreover, every green infrastructure initiative, like every quilt, is unique. They have different geographies, systems, and functions. The political, social, and economic context could differ greatly. As a result, different green infrastructure networks have different goals, and the people who are implementing the network may have very different values. Depending on the state in which the network is planned and the nature of its laws and programs, green infrastructure advocates will have different tools at their disposal. Different green infrastructure networks also may have different restoration needs; a network planned in a relatively pristine area may need fewer resources devoted to filling in gaps or "rewilding" than a network in a developed area. Conversely, in areas where people do not feel the imminent threat of losing natural areas to development, there might be a need for more resources devoted to public awareness and civic engagement or nature-based economic development (e.g., trails and facilities for outdoor recreation).

The metaphor also applies to the process of bringing people together to complete the work; just as people from different backgrounds came together for quilting bees, various sectors of the community come together to plan and complete a green infrastructure implementation quilt. The green infrastructure approach serves as a catalyst to nurture existing relationships and forge new partnerships. One benefit of the green infrastructure approach is that it provides a tangible, real-life goal that people with diverse interests can work toward together.

As with a quilt stitched from cloth, the key to a green infrastructure implementation quilt is finding the right materials and organizing them in a way that enhances the design. This requires identifying the available tools, programs, and funding and matching each to the component of the green infrastructure network for which it is most appropriate. The final step of this process is to match the component and implementation tool with an agency, organization, and/or individual who can make the concept a reality—the people who will bring the resources and stitch the quilt.

The end result is an implementation plan that, for each element in the network, identifies *what* tool(s) will be most appropriate, *who* will use them, *when* the activity will be undertaken, and *how* it will be financed. This requires having a sound understanding of the tools and the organizations that can or will be involved.

IMPLEMENTATION TOOLS

The objective of green infrastructure planning is to identify, protect, and provide long-term management for a network of interconnected green spaces that support natural functions while providing associated human benefits. There are many tools that can help a community—or neighborhood, state, region, or country—identify, prioritize, and protect important areas for conservation. This becomes part of an overall approach to land use in which growth is encouraged in appropriate areas and discouraged on lands with high conservation values or high natural hazards.

First, however, those implementing a green infrastructure project must identify available tools. There are three basic ways to protect land: through acquisition, regulation, or incentives. Since there will never be sufficient funds to purchase all priority lands in a green infrastructure network, regulatory mechanisms and incentives are important to complete the quilt. Regulatory tools also may be better suited to protect sensitive areas, control land-use development patterns, and address problems with pollution or other human-use activities, but they require constant public monitoring and the commitment of elected officials. In some communities, there is significant opposition to land-use regulations from people who believe they undermine individual property rights.

Voluntary conservation techniques are generally better received by citizens. Providing incentives to encourage landowners to undertake a desired conservation action can be more effective than regulatory approaches. Moreover, it is often easier to get volunteers to help with restoration and management activities in a green infrastructure network than it is to get the needed support for funding such activities. Acquisition of priority conservation lands has an additional major advantage over regulatory approaches: it is a permanent solution. Regulations are temporary and can be reversed by a future county board of supervisors or other decision-making entity.

Just which techniques should be used depends on many factors, including the availability of federal and state funding, local enabling options, and the level of citizen support. Making decisions about which approaches will work best requires a sound understanding of community preferences, perspectives, and perceived benefits. Tools that are acceptable in one community may bring stalwart opposition in another. One way to facilitate community support is to reach *early adopters*—highly respected community members who are open to new and innovative ideas. Early adopters talk to others and facilitate the acceptance of new ideas in otherwise conservative communities.

As seen in Table 6.1, these tools can be divided into four general categories: land acquisition, regulation, incentives, and overall funding. In reality, however, there is significant overlap among these categories; one program may provide a means of land acquisition, funding, and voluntary incentives.

Land Acquisition

Land acquisition is an important tool for any strategic conservation initiative. Private land or property rights can be purchased outright, can be obtained through donation, or can be swapped for other land of value to the landowner. Acquisitions

Table 6.1

Potential Tools for Green Infrastructure Implementation

	Local	State	Federal[1]	Private
Land acquisition	• Fee-simple acquisition • Conservation and/or agricultural easements • Purchase of development rights • Transfer of development rights	• Conservation easements • Fee-simple acquisition • Forest-legacy program • Historic preservation easement • Smart growth initiatives	• Land and water conservation fund • Fee-simple acquisition • Conservation easements • Farmland Protection Policy Act • Community development block grants	• Conservation easements • Conservation and wetlands banking • Fee-simple purchase • Local corporations • Local land trusts • National land trusts • Riparian easement
Regulation	• Buffer or landscaping ordinances • Building permitting • Comprehensive plans • Conservation banks • Development impact fees • Environmental impact regulations • Mitigation banking • Special assessment districts • Storm water regulations • Subdivision ordinances • Zoning, including downzoning, cluster or open space zoning, and performance zoning	• Scenic highway or byway legislation • Scenic rivers legislation • Conservation and/or mitigation banking • Wetland, river setback and shoreline permitting programs • Rare and endangered species permitting programs • Water management and water resource permitting	• Clean Air Act • Clean Water Act • Endangered Species Act • National Environmental Protection Act • National Historic Landmarks • National Natural Landmarks • National Oceanic and Atmospheric Administration • National Register of Historic Places • Safe Drinking Water Act • Wild and Scenic Rivers Act	• Privately owned mitigation banks • Private/NGO remediation programs to address permit violations
Incentives	• Management agreements • Notification and education recognition and rewards • Tax incentives; estate management strategies • Technical assistance and local government support	• Best management practices • Smart growth initiatives • Tax benefits	• Agricultural best management practices • Conservation Reserve Enhancement Program (Farm Bill) • Environmental Quality Incentives Program • FEMA Flood Insurance Program • Landowners Incentive Program • Partners for Wildlife • Reforestation Tax Credit, Federal Water Bank Program • Wetlands Reserve Program • Tax benefits	• Conservation and wetlands banking • Environmental trading • Landowner recognition

	Local	**State**	**Federal**[1]	**Private**
Funding	• Developer fees • Environmental impact fees • Environmental mini-bonds • Open space protection bonds • Special assessment fees • Transfer tax	• Transfer tax • Transportation equity funds • Transportation enhancement funds	• Clean Air Act • Clean Water Act • Cooperative Endangered Species Fund • Environmental Quality Incentives • Farmland Protection and Policy Act • Landowners Incentive Program • Migratory Bird Conservation Fund • North American Wetlands Conservation Act • Partners for Wildlife • State revolving fund • Transportation Equity Act (TEA-21)	• The Conservation Fund • The Nature Conservancy • The Trust for Public Land • Local, regional and statewide land trusts

[1] For a summary of federal conservation initiatives, go to www.biodiversitypartners.org/incentives/programfed.shtml.

can be made at fair market value, at assessed value, or at a reduced rate. Landowners may accrue tax benefits for bargain sales or land donations.

FEE-SIMPLE ACQUISITION

Purchasing high-priority conservation land may be the fastest way to ensure its immediate protection and long-term preservation. Governments often acquire land in green infrastructure networks, using bonds or other capital financing mechanisms. Land may also be purchased by a local land trust or a national conservation organization such as The Conservation Fund, The Nature Conservancy, or the Trust for Public Land. Acquisition can include outright purchase (known as *fee-simple acquisition*) or the acquisition of undivided interests, which involves the purchase of a percentage ownership in a property and allows for a legal interest in its management.

Some land acquisition programs are funded through earmarked taxes or fees. In Monroe County, Florida, for example, a tourist impact tax of 1 percent on hotel and motel rooms is used to finance land acquisition. (The county is the gateway to the Florida Keys and home to four national wildlife refuges.) Half of the revenue goes to the county general fund as compensation for the loss of property-tax revenue from publicly owned land. The other half supports the Monroe County Land Authority, a local agency that has bought over one thousand acres of wetlands, wildlife habitat, recreation areas, and sites for affordable housing.

Some land acquisition programs include rights of first refusal. This guarantees an organization the opportunity to purchase important property, but does not obligate its purchase. By granting a right of first refusal, a property owner agrees to notify an organization that the property has been offered for sale and invites the organization to match an offer. This allows an organization to identify prospective buyers and negotiate an agreement to protect the property with the potential new owner. This right may be donated to an organization or sold for a nominal fee. Similarly, an option to purchase involves paying the landowner for the guarantee that he or she will reserve a property at an agreed upon price for a set period of time (typically six months to one year).

The Guilford Land Trust in Connecticut used the right-of-first-refusal concept as part of its strategy for protecting a major wetland. When the land trust approached the owner of a fifty-four-acre parcel about selling, he was not interested, but the land trust persuaded him to sign letter of intent to sell the property to the organization if and when he decided to dispose of it. Although a letter of intent is not enforceable (as a record of right of first refusal is), the land trust was confident that continued contact with the owners would remind them of this agreement. Eight years later, the owner decided to donate the wetland portion of the property to the land trust and sell the high ground to a developer. The land trust was then able to persuade the owner to donate the entire property rather than sell any of it.

LIMITATIONS OF FEE-SIMPLE ACQUISITION

Purchasing all the parcels in a green infrastructure network can be a complicated and time-consuming task requiring legal and financial expertise. In some cases, conserving the hubs and links given highest priority might require combining parcels of land; in others, dividing the land might be required. It sometimes takes years to obtain the desired acreage.

By their very nature, governments are not usually well positioned to conduct land transactions or compete in the real estate market. At the mercy of political pressures and administrative changes, funding for land acquisition is often put on the back burner just when it is needed most. Appropriated funds for the purpose of land conservation may not be available when a parcel comes on the market. Moreover, distrust of government among landowners and a strong sense of private property rights can hamper negotiations. For these reasons, land trusts are often far better equipped to handle complex transactions and might be better able to piece together several parcels in a manner that accommodates the needs of both the government and the private landowner.

Acquisition is usually the most expensive way to protect land. The successful implementation of green infrastructure networks requires taking advantage of the many free or less expensive tools that are compatible with network goals. Floodplain protection, for example, can discourage or prevent development in

Box 6.1

Open Space Preservation in Boulder, Colorado

Boulder has one of the oldest open space preservation programs in the United States, dating back to 1898. Its current program began in 1967 when Boulder became the first city to pass a sales tax of 0.40 percent for the acquisition and management of open space lands. An additional 0.33 percent was approved by the voters in 1989. Since the program's inception, over 28,000 acres of land have been preserved and protected. Funding for the purchases has come from sales tax revenues, bond issues, private donations, and development dedications. To date, nearly $100 million have been spent on the acquisition of open space. Acquisitions are approved by the City's Open Space Board of Trustees and City Council, with extensive opportunity for public input.

riparian or coastal wetlands without the need to purchase them. Only by making use of the full range of regulatory and voluntary tools can you target the limited funds for acquiring those parcels that are the most valuable, the most threatened, and/or the least suitable for other protection methods.

Groups implementing a green infrastructure plan often assume that buying up all the land in the network is the best solution, but it is unrealistic to assume that all the hubs, links, and sites in a green infrastructure network can be acquired. Nor would this necessarily be the best approach even if there were sufficient money. This is because acquisition does not ensure long-term land management or the viability of the system to provide its intended benefits. Where land use is compatible with network goals, it may be preferable to find nonacquisition solutions that will enable the land to continue to function as before and that engage landowners in helping to protect the resources. This is not only a more realistic approach to meeting green infrastructure goals, it may be more successful in the long run.

Strategic conservation seeks to protect important natural areas without diminishing a community's economic base or limiting its revenues. But land acquisition, particularly if the alternatives are not carefully considered, can sometimes have an adverse effect on the local economy. If a nonprofit conservation organization or a government agency were to purchase all the land in a green infrastructure network currently used for forestry, agriculture, hunting, or other resource-based activities, it could hurt local businesses. Any large-scale acquisition project therefore should consider the economic effects of changing the land use. In some cases, putting an easement on working lands may be preferable to fee-simple acquisition.

CONSERVATION EASEMENTS

A *conservation easement* is a legal agreement that restricts the use of private property in order to protect its conservation value. Landowners agree to give up specific rights regarding how the land will be used but can otherwise continue to use and enjoy the property as before.

To illustrate the concept, consider land ownership as a bundle of sticks. Each stick represents a landowner's right to do something with the property: to develop a subdivision, build a house, farm, ranch, extract minerals, cut timber, and so on. With a conservation easement, a landowner sells or gives away some or all of these rights while still maintaining ownership of the land.[2]

One of the main benefits of easements is their flexibility. A conservation easement might prohibit industrial and commercial use on the property, restrict the number of residential units, or prohibit the construction of new roads. Or the easement might allow for limited development by specifying parts of the land that cannot be developed or setting a maximum number of acres allowable for development. Conservation easements also tend to be less expensive than fee-simple acquisition and allow lands to remain on the tax rolls.

The most common type of easement is the agricultural easement, by which landowners are compensated for keeping their land in agricultural production. Most conservation easements are permanent and "run with the land" even if it is sold. This ensures permanent protection of the land's identified resource values while allowing private ownership and traditional uses.

Purchase of development rights (PDR) programs are another related land conservation tool. PDR programs pay landowners for placing a deed restriction on their land that limits its future development. Because PDR programs are voluntary, they are an attractive option for landowners who want to keep their land and have access to new capital. They also allow local governments to protect land at relatively low cost because the primary management responsibility is maintained by the landowner.

Virginia Beach, Virginia, has a nationally recognized agricultural PDR program that enables the city to purchase conservation easements from farm and forestland owners. Established in 1995, this voluntary, market-based program is funded at $3.5 million per year from a dedicated property tax increase, a new cellular phone tax, and the payment in lieu of taxes made by Back Bay National Wildlife Refuge. Under the voluntary program, farmland owners can sell development rights to the city in exchange for working capital that they can reinvest in the farm.

PDR programs can help communities to direct development away from important natural or cultural resources. Madera, California, is among the many towns that have used the purchase of development rights as a conservation and growth management tool. Here, PDRs are being used to create a four-mile-wide "farmland security perimeter" intended to protect eight square miles of grape, alfalfa, and dairy farms from development.

Box 6.2

Using Easements to Protect a River System: Blackfoot River, Montana

The Blackfoot River in Montana is one of the state's best trout streams, as well as a popular destination for canoeing and rafting enthusiasts. But what many who admire the river don't know is that the Blackfoot enjoys some of the most complete protection afforded by easements anywhere in the nation. This protection is the result of long-term conservation efforts by far-sighted and dedicated property owners in the valley.

Overuse of the Blackfoot River by rafters and fisherman (among others) led to a successful cooperative effort by public and private interests to manage recreational access to the river. To deal with the pressures of recreational use of the river, the landowners worked with the state to create a recreation management plan based on voluntary short-term agreements. In these agreements, landowners dedicated land along the river for public access points that were developed and maintained by the state. The state also provided a river manager to patrol the area. While the provision of public access and the river manager might have been sufficient to deal with the problems created by recreational use, the state considered that its investment for recreation required long-term assurances that the quality of the river would be maintained—the purpose of conservation easements.

A number of roadblocks to the use of easements existed, however. First, landowners had to be educated as to what conservation easements were and how they worked. Second, until a concerted effort by interested landowners resulted in passage in 1975 of state legislation permitting use of easements, their legality was open to question. Third, each landowner's decision to contribute an easement was highly individual and likely in some cases to take a long time to complete.

Source: Samuel N. Stokes, A. Elizabeth Watson, and Shelley S. Mastran. *Saving America's Countryside: A Guide to Rural Conservation.* Baltimore, MD: Johns Hopkins University Press, 1997.

Many states and private conservation organizations have bought development rights from timber companies to ensure that the forest remain intact for the species that live there and for human uses such as hunting and fishing. In return, the timber companies continue cutting trees on the land, preserving jobs and the natural resource-based economy. Under most of these easement deals, the timber companies agree to environmentally sound land practices, limiting clear-cutting and keeping logging away from streams. In 2002, an estimated 2.6 million acres of land in the

United States was protected through such conservation easements, a five-fold increase over the previous decade (see Table 6.2).

Transfer of development rights (TDR) programs are similar to PDRs. TDRs permit property owners in development-restricted areas to sell their development rights to property owners in designated receiving areas. This requires a community to have designated "sending" areas (resource or rural areas) and "receiving" areas (developed or urban areas). A conservation easement on the "sent" property is used to ensure that the resource values are protected in perpetuity. A TDR allows owners in sending areas to realize the market value of their land without developing it. Developers who purchase these rights can increase their profit margins by increasing the density of development in receiving areas.

This land-use tool has been used throughout the country. In Montgomery County, Maryland, more than 40,000 acres have been preserved by TDRs since 1980, and more than 25,000 acres have been preserved in the New Jersey Pinelands. Experts say that TDR programs are most successful in preserving smaller parcels in urban areas. Seattle's program, for example, which allows transfers from low-income housing sites to downtown office and hotel developments, has saved hundreds of low-income housing units from demolition.

Just thirty minutes southwest of Atlanta, the Chattahoochie Hill Country Alliance, which was created to protect the land from sprawling development, is

Table 6.2

Recent Purchase of Development Rights Agreements Protecting Forest Land

Seller	Acreage and location	Purchaser	Cost
Potlatch Corp., Spokane, WA	600,000 acres in Idaho astride the Clearwater and Idaho Panhandle national forests	Trust for Public Land	$40 million
Great Northern Paper, Inc., Millinocket, Maine	200,000 acres in Maine	The Nature Conservancy	$50 million, restructuring existing loans
International Paper Inc., Stamford, CT	75,000 acres in Tennessee's Cumberland Plateau	The Conservation Fund	$9.5 million
Champion International Corp.	300,000 acres in New York, Vermont, and New Hampshire	The Conservation Fund	$90 million
Plum Creek Timber Co., Seattle	142,000 acres in northwestern Montana's Thomson River Valley	Trust for Public Land	$33 million

Source: Data compiled from Jim Carlton, "Land Easements are Alliance of Big Timber, Tree Huggers," *Wall Street Journal*, November 13, 2002.

using the TDR as a tool to implement a plan that would concentrate homes and businesses in three one-square-mile, high-density conservation developments and several smaller areas, thereby preserving two-thirds of the rural land in the 100-square-mile area. Fulton County, which includes most of the hill country, has amended its zoning laws to approve the plan.

Conservation easements can be purchased or donated. In addition to ensuring the landowner that subsequent owners will maintain the land in a way that is consistent with his or her values and wishes, the main benefit of easements relate to taxes. The value of the easement can be deducted from federal income taxes as a charitable donation. In addition, the easement reduces market value, resulting in both estate and property tax benefits. By reducing the tax burden through an easement donation, landowners can help ensure that heirs do not have to sell the family farm just to pay the estate taxes.

Box 6.3

Transfer of Development Rights (TDRs) in New Jersey Pine Barrens

The New Jersey Pine Barrens is the largest contiguous tract of forest along the mid-Atlantic seaboard and is rich in biodiversity. Recognizing the ecological significance of these lands, in 1978 Congress established the Pinelands National Reserve, 1.4 million-acres of "working landscape" where farming, forestry, and other land uses are managed in a way that maintains wildlife habitat and biodiversity.

The Pinelands Comprehensive Management Plan includes an innovative transfer of development rights program designed to mitigate economic losses on property that is heavily restricted but which have important ecological values. Landowners in the plan's preservation districts are allocated Pinelands Development Credits, while developers in the growth districts get "density bonuses" if they purchase and retire credits as part of their development applications. When a landowner sells credits, his or her land is automatically deed restricted, giving that land permanent protection from development. The plan also creates a state agency, the PDC Bank, which acts as the buyer and seller of last resort to help ensure that the market in Pinelands Development Credits works well. During the program's first twenty years, sales of credits led to deed restrictions on 27,750 acres of land. The program, which supplements the economic value of land in the preservation districts, has also helped New Jersey successfully defend the plan against constitutional takings claims.

Box 6.4

Conservation Easements in Utah

Utah's preferred way to preserve open space is to establish perpetual conservation easements to maintain an area in a natural, scenic, or open condition, or for recreational, agricultural, cultural, or other use consistent with the protection of the open space. The restrictions are binding on present and future owners. In 1998, the state passed legislation to provide a dedicated funding source to support land conservation activities. The Critical Lands Conservation Revolving Loan Fund is designed to provide loans to local governments and nonprofit organizations that work to preserve open lands. It emphasizes protecting private property rights and ensuring that land-use decisions are made locally.

The fund also provides a foundation for Utah's Quality Growth Act of 1999, which the governor proposed in October 1998. The bill creates state funding incentives for local governments to conserve green spaces, make better use of infrastructure, and increase the availability of housing through more efficient land use. Leaders of the state legislature supported the measure. To help local communities conserve open lands, a 1996 executive order created the Utah Open Lands Committee to support local conservation efforts by offering technical expertise, establishing a conservation information clearinghouse, and facilitating cross-jurisdictional and multiagency partnerships.

LIMITATIONS OF EASEMENTS, PDRS, AND TDRS

Conservation easements share some of the limitations of outright purchase of the land. Like fee-simple purchase, acquiring easements can be complicated and could take years if there are many parcels in a desired hub or link. Moreover, easements are unlikely to appeal to all the people who own land in the green infrastructure network, which can leave gaps in the network. Because easements leave land in private ownership, they sometimes deny public access. Some taxpayers (and public officials) resist purchasing easements on private property without public access. Overcoming resistance may involve educating the citizenry about the benefits of protecting the land from development or undesirable use.

Many local governments lack sufficient funds to purchase development rights on all the lands they want to preserve, leaving a patchwork of open space or agricultural/forestal land. There is also no guarantee that the owners of the undeveloped

> "Improved land protection tools that reinforce
> one another are of utmost importance for success
> in the land protection game. Money is needed,
> but good practices will make it go further."
>
> S A R A H   T A Y L O R - R O G E R S
> RESEARCH ASSOCIATE, MARYLAND CENTER FOR AGRO-ECOLOGY, INC.

land will be willing to sell their development rights, which could prevent large blocks of land from being preserved. In the case of agricultural lands, most jurisdictions with successful PDR programs agree that success depends on having a strong agricultural community that wants to continue farming. However, if the agricultural sector of the economy is not strong enough to survive in the long term, a PDR program will do little on its own to maintain the economic viability of farming.

TDRs have similar limitations. A TDR program also requires the coordination of several governing bodies to set up sending and receiving zones for the development rights. A TDR program will do little to preserve agricultural lands or open space unless the broader community actively participates. The TDR has proven to be a difficult proposal to implement because people resist taking more development from the other end of the county if it means more people in their neighborhood.

Landowner education is an important element of conservation easements, as landowners may be unfamiliar with tools such as PDRs or TDRs. Education efforts need not be expensive, but they should be considered when calculating expenses.

Regulatory Approaches

Most communities already use zoning and subdivision regulations to influence the pattern of development. In many cases, however, these laws and policies are not based on a plan that clearly identifies where the community wants to grow and where it does not. In even more cases, the lands that would serve as the best locations for green space—those with high conservation values—are left out of the planning process. Many land-use decisions are based on practices and policies that have evolved over time in response to a specific need. In addition, regulations are temporary and can be affected by budgets, policy priorities, and changes in administration. Like many conservation efforts, the plans and policies that are in place result in haphazard land use. Green infrastructure plans help focus such efforts in a more strategic and comprehensive manner.

Regulations can help guide development—and the built infrastructure needed to support it—into areas best suited for it. By directing development away from environmentally sensitive areas, it is easier to protect these areas through other means and the approval process is often expedited. When developers know that they cannot build on wetlands or plan a road through an old-growth forest, for example, they tend to be more willing to protect these areas as part of the development plan. More and more developers are using easements to protect resources and create value at the same time.

The most common regulatory tools that influence development are zoning, subdivision standards, and environmental regulations. It is important to keep in mind, however, that regulating for green infrastructure involves more than simply writing new ordinances. Rather, it involves reviewing existing laws, policies, and practices to consider how they affect land-use decisions. In some cases, zoning, subdivision ordinances, or other regulations may inadvertently prohibit the use of green infrastructure tools and technologies.

ZONING

In many communities, zoning is among the most widely used tools to protect green infrastructure network components. Local zoning laws may limit nonagricultural uses or emphasize planned unit or cluster development that preserves open space, floodplains, or natural areas. Zoning may also be designed to protect a special resource like ridgetops or steep slopes. In fact, there are many different types of zoning, including sliding scale zoning, special purpose zoning, and overlay zoning.

When used properly, zoning can be a useful tool for protecting and maintaining a community's green space. Conventional zoning sets densities and determines which land uses go where. Land-use regulations can help a community create a green space network. The city of Topeka, Kansas, for example, requires developers to set aside open space at a standard of five acres per one thousand residents. The ordinance requires that the area be at least three contiguous acres unless it is an addition to an existing park. The goal of Topeka's open space ordinance is to ensure that there is enough open space to maintain quality of life and neighborhood value. It also aids in preserving open space for park systems and trail connections and for storing urban stormwater.

Reducing the number of homes that can be built per acre on a section of land, called *downzoning*, can also be used to protect green infrastructure elements, particularly agricultural lands. Landowners often object to downzoning because they worry about its effect on property values, but research has found that, when used in conjunction with a comprehensive land-use plan that identified the land with economic and natural resource value, downzoning stabilizes land values, while protecting farm and forest lands from sprawl for long periods of time. In fact, land values in Kent County, Maryland, increased after the county downzoned agriculture and forestlands.[3] Advocates of downzoning emphasize that it works best when there are very few opportunities for exceptions, such as intrafamily transfers or extra lot creation, which can undermine housing density goals.

Planned unit development zoning can be used to achieve a plan that satisfies zoning requirements while allowing density transfers or other variations. As applied to green infrastructure, program planners can encourage a landowner with significant land identified as part of a green infrastructure network to consider conservation development as a means of meeting his or her financial goals in conjunction with broader community goals. Open space zoning, sometimes called

---

Box 6.5

Downzoning in Baltimore County, Maryland

Baltimore County has an interesting history in dealing with development pressure. In 1967, the County established an Urban-Rural Demarcation Line (URDL) designating urban and rural land as distinct land uses in which rural areas would not receive county water or sewer. As the URDL proved ineffective in preserving rural land, Baltimore County enacted downzoning provisions in 1975 to help curb continued development in areas where there was a desire to keep the rural character. Downzoning was influenced by the demand for housing and "farmettes." The 1975 legislation reduced density in the Rural Conservation Zone-2 (RC-2) from one dwelling unit per one acre to roughly one dwelling unit per fifty acres. Building on this legacy, the county has downzoned an additional ten thousand acres acres from one dwelling unit per five acres to one dwelling unit per fifty acres in the past decade. A recent review of the effect of the county's efforts shows that the Rural Conservation Zone has maintained an overall density of about one dwelling unit per fifty acres. Research also indicates that the value of the agricultural land in the county has continued to increase.

Baltimore County has done an excellent job of retaining its open spaces, areas for reservoir protection, and the economic base of its horse farm sector. This is particularly impressive, as the county is located so close to the urban area of Baltimore City and has experienced unparalleled growth pressure over the last ten years.

Source: Rob Etgen, et al., *Downzoning: Does It Protect Working Landscapes and Maintain Equity for the Landowner?* Maryland Center for Agro-Ecology, Inc., 2003.

cluster zoning, requires new construction to be located on only a portion—typically half—of the parcel. The remaining open space is permanently protected, usually through a conservation easement cosigned by a local conservation commission or land trust, and recorded in the registry of deeds. To avoid disturbing the equity held by existing landowners, open space zoning allows the same overall amount of development that is already permitted.

Cluster development, also known as conservation design, conservation development, or open space development, is an increasingly lucrative option for developers because it accommodates the desire of residents to live in attractive neighborhoods with ample green space—a desire once met through "golf course developments." The cluster approach places development in less sensitive areas while preserving forested land, steep slopes, wetlands, prairies and other ecologically or visually valuable landscape features; it also helps to preserve resources such as buildings or historic sites. Typically 50 to 90 percent of a site is preserved in its existing natural or agricultural state, with individual house lots occupying the remaining acreage. It should also be noted that the cluster concept can be restricted to detached, single-family homes, each on its own downsized lot, in communities, or in specific zoning districts where this is politically desirable.[4]

The 431-acre Farmview development in Bucks County, Pennsylvania, is one of many examples of clustering. The 310 homes are built on just half of the total parcel; the developer set aside 137 acres of farm fields and 100 acres of woodland. As a result, Farmview is the fastest-selling development in its price range. Residents of Prairie Crossing, a conservation community in Grayslake, Illinois, likewise have reaped economic and health benefits from the cluster design. Prairie Crossing is linked by regional trails to the Liberty Prairie Reserve, over 3,200 acres of legally protected land. More than 60 percent of the 677-acre Prairie Crossing site is protected open land that is actively used by people and wildlife. Ten miles of trails wind through a landscape of farm fields, pastures, lakes and ponds, native prairies and wetlands and link to the trails beyond the development. A certified organic farm, in operation for over a decade, provides homeowners with views over cultivated fields of vegetables and flowers and a seasonal on-site Farm Market that sells organic produce. Residents with children can apply for admission to the on-site Prairie Crossing Charter School, a public elementary school where learning is focused on the natural environment. A cooperative of homeowners with horses manages the small stable.

Similarly, West Manchester Township, in south-central Pennsylvania, recently amended its zoning ordinance for an undeveloped portion of the township to increase the open space that would be preserved. Prior to the zoning amendment, the township made use of build-out analyses to illustrate the possible effect of the current zoning for the area—which was for single-family detached residential homes on half-acre or smaller lots. Build-out maps showing what the area could look like under the existing conventional zoning vividly illustrated the loss of existing

Figure 6.1
By clustering housing and setting aside valuable lands, conservation developments, like this one in Prairie Crossing, Illinois, offer residents permanently protected green space—an amenity that can be difficult to find in urban and suburban settings.
Credit: Sunny Sonnenschein.

farmland and open space. The township also mapped out the open space it hoped to preserve to show landowners and developers exactly what was envisioned: interconnected open space crossing parcel lines.[5]

Under West Manchester's new open space zoning provision, which applies to developments involving more than fifteen acres, a developer first prepares a sketch plan showing the number of units that could be built under a conventional development pattern. This determines the allowable density that can be used when the project is designed in a clustered manner. According to Jan Dell, the assistant township administrator, allowing the same density was important to allay the concerns of landowners who worried that a zoning change could diminish the value of their property. The zoning provision has had the opposite effect on home values, however, as preserving green space and the views they provide have made the area more attractive to home buyers.

Other zoning options that might be considered include performance zoning, which bases the uses permitted on a given parcel of land on the amount of sewage capacity available, the acceptable volume of surface water runoff, or other factors; or building permit limitations, which put quotas on the number of building permits that may be issued during a specified time period or within a specified area. Limited site development, in which landowners develop a portion of the parcel to finance the protection of the remaining land, may be another option. In addition, a buffer ordinance can prescribe the minimum width of vegetated land that must be maintained on either side of a drainage way. Larger streams require wider

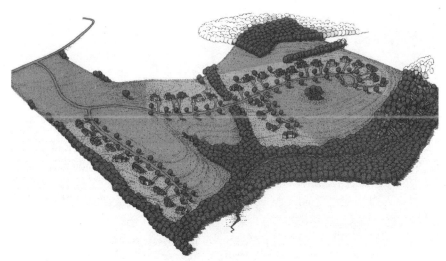

Figure 6.2
Cluster development *(above)* versus traditional development *(below)*, from Randall Arendt's landmark book *Rural by Design*. Credit: Randall Arendt.

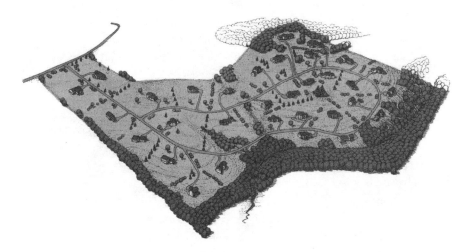

vegetated buffers to moderate peak flows and neutralize excess nutrients and contaminants. Buffer ordinances can be used to protect the linkages in a green infrastructure network.

Subdivision ordinances, which set standards for the division of larger parcels into smaller ones and specify the location of streets, utilities, other improvements, and open space, can also be used to encourage the protection of green infrastructure components. The lands set aside as a result of the subdivision process can provide valuable green infrastructure links at local scales.

Although they are not truly a regulatory tool, a local government's comprehensive plan can also be used as a green infrastructure tool. The comprehensive plan (also sometimes called a master plan, development plan, or general plan) is characterized by emphasis on physical development, a long span of time, and comprehensiveness,

Box 6.6

Cluster Development

Cluster developments differ from traditional developments in several ways. Cluster developments usually site homes on smaller lots, and there is less emphasis on minimum lot size. However, the total number of homes, or density, on a given acreage does not necessarily increase over that allowed in the traditional subdivision designs. The same number of homes is clustered on a smaller portion of the total available land. The remaining land, which would have been allocated to individual home sites, is converted into protected open space and shared by the residents of the subdivision and possibly the entire community. (It is important to note that there is flexibility on the "homes per land area" issue: some incentive-based ordinances allow for development of more homes in exchange for providing other nonrequired features that are desirable to the community.)

In most cases, local ordinances and regulations must be updated to facilitate building conservation development subdivisions. Road frontage, lot size, setbacks, and other traditional regulations must be redefined to permit the preservation of environmentally sensitive areas, rural architecture, historical sites, and other unique characteristics of the parcel of land being developed. Developers often cite local regulations as the primary reason more innovative designs are not used. Having more flexible regulations does not mean anything goes, however. Traditional codes must be replaced with new design standards that address the goals of conservation development, such as open-space preservation, and so on.

The increased common open space in cluster developments may be used for a number of purposes. The specific purposes are defined during the development's platting process. In many cases, the open space is designed to protect natural areas. One principle of conservation design is that environmentally sensitive areas must be identified first and designated as nonbuildable. Then subsequent planning can ensure that home lots do not infringe on those sites and that those sites are not calculated into the total area permitted for lots. The open space can also be used for more active recreational facilities, native habitat for plants or animals, agricultural production, or other allowable purposes. The landowner and community jointly determine how the open space will be used when the subdivision proposal is being approved.

In most of these developments, each homeowner has equal access to the open space areas. In some cases, the open space may be designed such that the whole community can share its use. Even if access is limited, the community often shares in the overall benefits of open-space preservation.

A homeowners' association is usually responsible for protecting and maintaining the open space. When necessary, the community also may have the authority to enforce the open-space provisions approved in the plat agreement. For example, if necessary maintenance of open space is being neglected, the community can create a subordinate special taxing district that taxes homeowners in the subdivision in order to fund such maintenance.

Source: University of Illinois Extension, "Local Community Resources: Cluster/Conservation Development Fact Sheet," see www.urbanext.uiuc.edu/lcr/LGIEN2000-0010.html.

covering all major aspects of the community's future. The comprehensive plan provides a guide to decision making, including zoning and/or other land-use measures that encourage (or discourage) growth. In many places, the comprehensive plan also serves as a legal document that is the basis for a variety of land-use controls.

Local restrictions regarding mountain ridges, steep slopes, streamside areas, and other natural features, whether in comprehensive plans, zoning requirements, or stormwater regulations, also can be identified and targeted as part of the green infrastructure network. In Loudoun County, Virginia, these restrictions are related to the comprehensive plan, but they can also be enacted separately from the planning and regulatory efforts of a local government. In addition, the local government can pass an environmental impact ordinance, requiring developers to assess the effects of proposed development on environmental and cultural resources that would be priorities for a green infrastructure network.

LIMITATIONS OF ZONING

Zoning is relatively easy to use and cost effective to administer. However, zoning is often under intense political pressure and represents a temporary solution. In some locations, a landowner's request for a variance to zoning laws are granted regularly; in others, zoning laws change relatively often to accommodate new growth. To be effective, the tool requires the political will to enforce zoning laws, often lacking in communities where there is pressure to grow. In addition, if jurisdictions fail to coordinate their land-use plans, zoning ordinances can create a disjointed land-use pattern across the broader region, sometimes even creating incompatible land uses at the border of two jurisdictions. As a result, the effectiveness of zoning methods varies greatly among jurisdictions.

In many communities, protecting land through zoning and other regulatory options is simply not a politically viable option, in part because landowners fear

Box 6.7

Urban Growth Boundaries

The urban growth boundary (UGB), a legal boundary separating urban land from rural land, is established in an attempt to control urbanization by designating the area inside the boundary for high-density urban development and the area outside the boundary for low density rural development. A UGB circumscribes an entire urbanized area and is used by local governments as a guide to zoning and land use decisions. In the United States, the states of Oregon, Washington, and Tennessee require cities to establish UGBs. In addition to Portland, other cities that have adopted UGBs include Minneapolis, Virginia Beach, Lexington, Kentucky, several localities in the San Francisco Bay Area, and Vancouver, British Columbia. Similar boundaries to preserve green space and constrain the area of urban development existed in London as early as the sixteenth century. In the mid-1900s, the countryside abutting the London conurbation was protected as the Metropolitan Green Belt.

The UGB is one of the tools used to protect farms and forests from urban sprawl and to promote the efficient use of land, public facilities and services inside the boundary. Other benefits of the boundary include:

- Motivation to develop and redevelop land and buildings in the urban core. This helps keep core "downtowns" in business.
- Assurance for businesses and local governments about where to place infrastructure (such as roads and sewers), needed for future development.
- Efficiency for businesses and local governments in terms of how that infrastructure is built. Instead of building roads farther and farther out as happens in urban sprawl, money can be spent to make existing roads, transit service, and other services more efficient.

they will lose equity in their property. Property owners sometimes complain that zoning restrictions don't compensate them for limitations on future use of their property. When used, zoning and other regulatory approaches should therefore be combined with compensatory approaches, such as TDRs or PDRs, installment purchase agreements, or tax credits. Similarly, in communities where cluster zoning would meet with significant opposition, a bonus or incentive can accomplish the same purpose by allowing a developer to apply for higher density or other variances in exchange for providing open space or other community amenities. Some localities offer developers the additional incentive of expedited review and approval.

CONSERVATION AND MITIGATION BANKING

A conservation or mitigation bank is privately or publicly owned land that is managed for its natural resource values. In exchange for permanently protecting the land and restoring native habitat, the bank operator is allowed to sell habitat credits to developers who need to satisfy legal compensatory requirements for the impact of development on the environment. Mitigation banking began as an effort to protect wetlands and is still used mostly to this end, but some communities have adapted wetland mitigation banking to protect other types of landscapes. Conservation and mitigation banks generally protect habitat for threatened and endangered species. Credits are established for the specific sensitive species that occur on the site.

Essentially, conservation and mitigation banks result in large, contiguous tracts of land on which creation, restoration, enhancement, and/or preservation efforts are undertaken to create a fully functioning ecosystem. Where historically there would have been a series of small, isolated mitigation sites, a mitigation bank can replace them with one large preserve. Conservation and mitigation banks are similar to the purchase of development rights, except that a community acquires fee-simple interest in the land, thereby allowing local governments to obtain, hold, and release land to control development for conservation purposes. The use of bank credits must occur in advance of development, when the compensation cannot be achieved at the development site or would not be as environmentally beneficial.

The Orchard Creek Conservation Bank, established in 1997 by Wildlands, Incorporated, a habitat development and land management company in the western United States, is one example of a successful conservation bank. The 632-acre preserve is dedicated to the conservation of vernal pools and the special-status plants and animals that depend on this habitat. Its complex ecosystem supports several unique biological elements that are protected and maintained in perpetuity through a permanent conservation easement. In creating the conservation bank, Wildlands helped the U.S. Fish and Wildlife Service to design methodology for assigning vernal pool preservation credits. It then coordinated baseline biological studies, a natural resource management plan, bank enabling instrument, conservation easements, and other documents necessary for formal approval of the conservation bank.

In addition to consolidating lands in a way that gives them greater ecological value, mitigation banking ensures a commitment to long-term management. Conservation and mitigation banks can also enhance ecological value by reducing the effects of habitat fragmentation while supporting the restoration of habitat diversity. Conservation banks help developers by reducing the time it takes to secure permits for development in environmentally sensitive areas. "[Conservation banking] encourages landowners to set aside their property for open space rather than fight for development because they can make a profit by selling the land with speed and ease," writes Michael McCollum, former Chief Deputy Director of the

California Department of Fish and Game. "Developers in need of mitigation will pay a premium for this. Conservation banks complement regional planning because land is obtained for public benefit, yet no government money is spent. For the landowner, a novel thing has happened: endangered species are now an economic asset!"[6]

LIMITATIONS OF MITIGATION BANKING

Like other conservation approaches, mitigation banks are often undertaken in a fragmented, haphazard fashion, partly because they typically result from isolated permitting issues or are focused on a specific problem or location. Having a green infrastructure network design that identifies priority natural areas and systems to be protected and/or restored can help to rectify these limitations of mitigation banks as tools for conservation.

Voluntary Implementation and Financing Tools

Federal, state, and local governments offer landowners a range of incentives to improve land conservation and stewardship. These range from a simple request to participate to financial incentives to providing technical assistance in permitting

---

Box 6.8

Mitigation Banking in Florida

The Florida Environmental Reorganization Act of 1993 directed the water management districts and the Department of Environmental Protection to adopt a mitigation-banking rule. A component of the rule encourages each water management district to establish at least two mitigation banks. These mitigation banks must:

- Improve ecological conditions
- Provide viable and sustainable ecological/hydrological functions
- Be effectively managed in the long term
- Not destroy high value ecological areas
- Achieve mitigation success
- Be compatible with adjacent land uses.

or restoration programs. Most people respond more positively to incentives than regulation. Voluntary community buy-in is preferable to issuing mandates or regulations because community support is lasting and is sensitive to the economic value of the land, private property rights, and local home rule.

NOTIFICATION AND RECOGNITION

Sometimes, simply notifying landowners of the value of green space features and explaining the purpose of a green infrastructure network are sufficient to achieve green infrastructure goals. Owners who are made aware of important resources on their properties are often willing to protect them once they learn of their existence or significance. People value what they understand and protect what they value.

Notification and recognition programs routinely and systematically provide property owners with information about conservation goals and benefits. Such a program can be spearheaded by the local government or a nonprofit organization. Essentially, the organization sends to each property owner within the area targeted for protection and/or restoration a letter describing why forest buffers, stream banks, or other important landscape features deserve protection and then follows up with a phone call or visit to answer questions. Notification can be an important first step in establishing goodwill with a property owner and may eventually result in a permanent commitment to protect a significant resource.

A recognition program takes notification one step further by announcing publicly that a property or portion of a property is significant. Presenting signs, plaques, or certificates helps an owner feel good about the role he or she is playing in the community and serves as an ongoing reminder of his or her contribution. Developing project summaries for newspaper articles or annual reports is another way to recognize the efforts of program participants while also sharing knowledge of environmental stewardship activities with peers. Awards and celebrations further reinforce the commitment to stewardship, not only among recipients but also of the broader community.

The Patuxent River Greenway, a series of connected natural areas along a twelve-mile stretch of river in Anne Arundel County, Maryland, has done a good job of offering encouragement and incentives for voluntary landowner participation. Most land in the greenway is zoned for residential and agricultural use, and property owners are told how the greenway enhances adjacent property values. The county and state use numerous voluntary land preservation and enhancement programs to encourage landowner participation, including agricultural easements, conservation easements, best management practices, and forest management measures. Agricultural economic development programs are sponsored by various levels of government to establish programs, make loans, or provide grants to agricultural producers to enhance their economic viability.

TAX INCENTIVES AND TAX CREDITS

Tax incentives can be offered by any level of government to encourage desired land uses, such as forestry or agriculture, and/or the application of best management practices, such as implementing streamside vegetated buffers or roadside grass swales instead of traditional curb and gutters.

Some states also offer reduced property tax assessments on agricultural land or forestland. The purpose of assessing such lands at reduced levels is to ensure that farming and forestry continue to be economically viable. Some states also assess at reduced value open space lands that meet specific criteria. In Texas, for example, land that meets agricultural criteria but is used for wildlife management can still be appraised as agricultural land if participating landowners implement a wildlife management plan that meets state guidelines. Conservation programs often allow lands with agricultural or forestry reduced assessments to roll over their reduced taxes, allowing landowners to participate in conservation practices without losing the tax benefits.

Some states allow income tax credits and deductions to reduce landowners' state income tax burden with a credit for part or all of the costs of a conservation practice. State tax programs are most appropriate for green infrastructure initiatives undertaken at the state scale. Landowners who permanently donate land or conservation easements may be able to deduct the value of the donation from their income for state and/or federal purposes.

TECHNICAL ASSISTANCE

The complexity of conservation programs sometimes serves as a disincentive for otherwise interested landowners. Landowners may need assistance in identifying programs and funding opportunities, understanding regulations, developing conservation plans, applying for permits, and undertaking best management practices or restoration activities. Simply providing technical assistance to landowners can facilitate the implementation of green infrastructure. Landowners may be motivated to conserve land and protect the ecosystem but they might need information about how to do so. Education and demonstration programs can help provide landowners with the knowledge and skills they need to manage their property in accordance with green infrastructure network goals.

For example, the Natural Resources Conservation Service's (NRCS) Area Wide Conservation Planning program can be used to help communities with green infrastructure planning. This community-based program involves local communities developing plans to address natural resource concerns while taking into account their economic and social considerations and needs. NRCS planning assistance to communities recognizes the interconnectedness and cumulative effects of actions taken on the land, recognizes the need for planning beyond administrative and jurisdictional boundaries, considers the community's economic needs and goals, takes into account the short- and long-term effects of actions, and acknowledges that human welfare depends on the sustainability of natural resources.

A designation program also can be used as an incentive. In Florida, for instance, a process was developed for designating lands as part of the Florida Greenways and Trails System. As a result of designation, the Department of Environmental Protection can work out a management, patrol, and protection agreement with a landowner, who thereby is protected from liability for third-party use of the land. (Public access to the designated sites is not required.) The Department of Environmental Protection may also identify opportunities for management and restoration funding for designated lands. Designation has the added benefit of bringing public recognition to a green infrastructure effort.

LIMITATIONS OF VOLUNTARY INCENTIVES

Like many other conservation tools, incentives are often applied to a specific project on a site-by-site basis in response to an application from a property owner. Although the natural resources of the individual parcel may benefit, the community or region as a whole may receive little conservation value for its investment because the conserved land is isolated from other parcels. A community, region, or state with a green infrastructure plan, however, can use this information to better target the landowners of the most important land and give preference to parcels that can be linked as part of a cohesive and strategic approach. To reach the goal of replanting forest buffers along streams, for example, outreach and funding could be targeted to contiguous parcels that would serve as a link between two conservation areas.

Many voluntary conservation programs require a significant investment of time. Landowners may need to fill out applications, develop plans, file for permits, keep records, coordinate with agencies, track expenses, and so forth. Providing technical assistance and support can help overcome these obstacles. The lack of adequate assistance can be a disincentive for landowners to participate in programs.

A "one-stop shop" where landowners can get information about incentives and conservation programs can be a powerful tool in encouraging people to sell a conservation easement, engage in restoration activities, or simply become better stewards of the land. One-stop shop services could be provided by a government agency, a nonprofit organization, or a coalition of partners—any group with the knowledge about the options and a commitment to strategic conservation.

Some state conservation programs are well below capacity in terms of landowner participation. Landowners may be unaware of these programs, may believe that the programs lack flexibility to meet their needs, or may feel that the incentives offered are insufficient. Other landowners may be wary of relinquishing control over how their land is used—now or in the future. Because the green infrastructure approach engages landowners at the outset, green infrastructure can help overcome some of these obstacles. Where the green infrastructure initiative covers a large area, trusted local groups should be tapped to lead outreach efforts. Program information should include an explanation of the benefits of green infrastructure and testimonials from landowners who have participated in voluntary land conservation and restoration programs. Promoting examples of projects through landowner recognition programs and demonstration projects can encourage peer learning and contribute to greater participation levels.

MANAGEMENT AGREEMENTS AND LEASES

Private landowners sometimes voluntarily enter into management agreements with a nonprofit organization or government agencies to achieve habitat improvements on their land. Under a management agreement, a property owner accepts the responsibility to care for a significant resource on his or her property in a specified manner for a set period of time. Some management agreements allow another organization to carry out management responsibilities. Such agreements are usually based on a cost-sharing arrangement. The landowner may receive technical assistance and/or compensation for the use of his or her land. In a restrictive agreement, the owner enters into a long-term contract with a county in exchange for preferential assessment on the land. There is a property tax penalty for developing the land covered by a restrictive agreement.

Short- or long-term leasing of land is another option. With a lease, the government or other organization pays a lower cost for land but has limited and temporary control. With a purchase/leaseback arrangement, the new owner agrees to lease back the land to the seller, but the use of the land is restricted. In a lease-purchase agreement, rents paid are applied toward an agreed upon purchase price.

There are other arrangements that can also facilitate environmental stewardship of private land. For example, agreements could be tied to a loan process so that low-interest loans are available to homebuyers or developers for homes that are built in desired areas and that have environmentally sensitive features (a smaller footprint, more open space or undisturbed land, retention of forest buffers, etc.). This is made possible through an agreement between the state and/or local government in which the government places funds, in the form of certificates of deposit, in local banks in exchange for certain criteria in loan agreements. Governments would accept a lower yield on the certificates with the understanding that the bank would pass the rate savings on to the homebuyer or developer.

LIMITATIONS OF MANAGEMENT AGREEMENTS

Management agreements involve a long-term commitment to conservation by the landowner. Restoration projects also may have highly variable results, depending on the methods used and the landowner's commitment to maintenance. These disadvantages can be overcome with close monitoring, but too often monitoring is limited to counting trees planted or miles cleaned up with little attention to the broader ecosystem goals or restoration needs. This type of information is difficult to generate or maintain in private land management programs.

Funding and Financial Considerations

Which funding programs will best meet the needs of a green infrastructure network will depend on what is available and what is needed—grants, loans, expertise, volunteers, and so forth. It is important to keep in mind that federal and state funding will most likely be insufficient for the completion of a green infrastructure network. Equally important is the understanding that local funding will help keep the project aligned—and in tune—with the priorities of local citizens. Often, federal—and state—funding programs are structured to provide matching funds for conservation activities; an opportunity for local financial and in-kind contributions and volunteerism.[7]

Some conservation initiatives have benefited from a dedicated state funding source for the protection and acquisition of priority land in the green infrastructure network. Two examples are Maryland's Program Open Space and Florida's Preservation 2000 and Florida Forever funding programs. Having a stable source of state funding can help a program achieve its long-term goals. Lotteries, general obligation bonds, sales taxes, transfer taxes or deed recording fees, as well as general fund appropriations, are common state funding sources. In addition, state incentives, such as matching grants or low-interest loans can encourage local governments and nonprofit partners to procure local funding and in-kind services, effectively strengthening the initiative.

In addition to funding, many federal and state agencies offer assistance in finding resources for environmental and other types of programs. Environmental finance centers, for example, which are funded by the U.S. Environmental Protection Agency (EPA), work with communities to develop innovative funding and financing strategies for environmental and community development projects.

Federal funding is often an important piece of the implementation quilt. For example, the Land and Water Conservation Fund, created by Congress in 1964, provides funds for the purchase of natural resource lands for conservation purposes with federal revenues obtained primarily from offshore oil and gas drilling. In addition, the Forest Legacy program provides funding for states to secure conservation easements on working forests, and the Cooperative Endangered Species Conservation Fund provides grants to states to conserve species habitat.

Among the many sources for funding green infrastructure capital projects is the State Revolving Fund (SRF), which was established through the Water Quality Act of 1987 to replace the EPA Construction Grants Program for wastewater treatment facilities. To help improve water quality, Congress appropriates funds to states, which then make loans to communities. Most states provide matching funds to increase the amount of money available. The loans to communities are for up to twenty years at or below market rates. Repaid principal and interest are then used to make new loans. The SRF could be extended to the private sector so that private and public/private partnerships would be able to use and leverage program funds to engage in environmental activities. Projects such as stormwater management, erosion and sediment control, stream restoration, structural shoreline erosion control, and agricultural runoff control may be eligible. SRF loans can provide for up to 100 percent of project costs, including planning, design, and construction. The most important criteria for selection are water quality benefits and the capacity to repay.

Federal transportation programs are yet another resource for the planning and implementation of a green infrastructure network. For example, Florida Greenways used funding from the Intermodal Surface Transportation Efficiency Act to support statewide network design and related work. Staff from Florida's Department of Transportation supported this strategic conservation effort because it also helped them better meet their environmental and planning requirements associated with transportation project planning. The U.S. Department of Transportation's Federal Highway Administration's Community Impact Analysis is a process to evaluate the effects of transportation actions on a community and its quality of life. This assessment is an integral part of the transportation project planning and development. In addition, federal transportation enhancement funds may be used to protect a viewshed or floodplain on a green infrastructure network.

Beginning in 2000, the city of Waynesboro, Virginia, successfully used federal TEA-21 funds to address one of the priorities identified in its comprehensive plan, namely, to develop a greenway along the South River, a tributary of the Shenandoah River. The South River runs for approximately ten miles through the city. The proposed greenway was designed to connect five city parks along the river, the Downtown Farmers Market, the only urban trout fishery in Virginia, and residential areas. The Virginia Commonwealth Transportation Board approved Waynesboro's TEA-21 grant request of $280,000 to begin physical improvements in the downtown area and to initiate the development of the greenway along the South River.

Federal funds may also be available for the maintenance and management of the green infrastructure network, for litter removal and cleanup, mowing grass buffers, or education and outreach activities for volunteers. Federal funds and technical

Box 6.9

Environmental Finance Centers

Environmental initiatives and programs cannot be implemented without effective financing, yet knowledge about how to fund programs is often limited, especially at the local level. The EPA's Environmental Finance Network, consisting of nine Environmental Finance Centers in EPA's eight regions, was created in response to this local level need for financing expertise. Among the issues on which technical assistance is available are rate setting, land-use planning, and sustainable development. The Environmental Finance Centers educate state and local officials and small businesses on lowering costs of compliance and pollution prevention, increasing investments in environmental protection, improving financial capacity to own/operate environmental systems, encouraging the full cost pricing of environmental services, and identifying and evaluating financing tools and options. The centers are housed at the following universities (in order of when they went into operation):

- The University of New Mexico (EPA Region 6)
- The University of Maryland (EPA Region 3)
- Syracuse University (EPA Region 2)
- California State University at Hayward (EPA Region 9)
- The Great Lakes Environmental Finance Center at Cleveland State University (EPA Region 5)
- Boise State University (EPA Region 10)
- University of North Carolina at Chapel Hill (EPA Region 4)
- University of Louisville (EPA Region 4)
- The University of Southern Maine (EPA Region 1)

Individual centers work collaboratively on national issues that are implemented at the local level and tailor their approaches to local needs to help communities develop innovative funding and financing strategies for environmental and community development projects.

EPA's Environmental Financing Program also provides the Environmental Financing Information Network, an outreach service offering electronic access to many types of environmental financing information on financing alternatives for state and local environmental programs and projects. Services include a Web site, on-line data base, referrals to an expert contact network, infoline, and distribution of Environmental Finance Program publications and some EPA publications.

- *For more information, visit www.epa.gov/efinpage.*

assistance are also available for tree planting and other forms of site restoration activities beyond the basic maintenance needs. For instance, transportation mitigation funds have been used in the Cacapon River watershed of West Virginia for streambank restoration activities in conjunction with conservation easements.

Finally, it is important to know whether any elements of a green infrastructure network qualify as national historic landmarks. The Secretary of the Interior designates as landmarks nationally significant historic places that possess exceptional value or quality in illustrating or interpreting the heritage of the United States. In addition, the National Register of Historic Places is part of a national program to coordinate and support public and private efforts to identify, evaluate, and protect our historic and archeological resources. While listing on the historic register is voluntary and imposes no direct restrictions on development, it offers tax credit eligibility and added protection from federally funded projects, such as the construction of a new highway. Such designations also protect the landscapes where the sites are located.

LIMITATIONS OF STATE AND FEDERAL FUNDING MECHANISMS

Most state incentives and federal habitat preservation programs are underfunded. The lack of funding can be an impediment to land conservation, particularly if it is influenced by political pressure rather than ecological integrity. Many legislative efforts—especially at the federal level—have focused on making relatively minor changes to existing programs rather than developing and funding new programs. Changing federal laws is a slow and laborious process; even when an overhaul of an existing federal law seems appropriate, it can be almost impossible to achieve.

TAXES AND FEES

Some green infrastructure efforts have benefited from general fund monies. Property assessments, sales tax set-asides, and real estate transfer taxes have all been used by local governments to help fund land acquisition, management, and restoration efforts. Specific taxes are often earmarked for conservation purposes. For example, some localities have implemented a tourist or hotel tax to help pay for the infrastructure needed to support visitors, including maintaining green infrastructure components that serve as attractions.

The use of taxes for conservation has a number of benefits. It can be an attractive funding source in communities that do not want to take on additional debt. Taxes typically have a broader revenue base than fees, and therefore can generate high revenues at relatively low rates. States can generate millions of dollars annually from a supplemental sales tax, and dedicating to environmental programs a surcharge on an existing tax involves minimal administrative costs. In most states, income, property, and sales data are already reported, reducing administrative costs of new surcharges. A local government might be able to pass a piggy-back tax on existing state taxes, although in some states this requires legislative authorization and voter approval.

Property taxes are the most common taxes used to fund parks and land conservation. Although the popularity of property taxes has declined over the past several decades, voters in many communities have been willing to accept property tax increases when revenues are specifically earmarked for conservation purposes. In 1997, for example, Ocean County, New Jersey, residents approved the creation of a countywide Open Space Trust Fund, funded by a property tax increase earmarked for acquisition and maintenance of open space, natural lands, and farmlands. And twice in the 1990s, Los Angeles County, California, voters approved assessments that generated over $850 million for park, open space, and recreational improvements.

Sales taxes have also been used to fund green infrastructure. Adams County, Colorado, passed a 0.2 percent sales tax that has provided the county with $6 million a year since 1999. In 1990, a twenty-year sales tax of 0.25 percent was implemented in Sonoma County, California. This tax yields $16 to $17 million per year. And in September 2000, voters in Jacksonville, Florida, approved a half-cent, local option sales tax for the Better Jacksonville Plan, a comprehensive approach to growth management, transportation, environmental protection, and economic development. Of the $2.2 billion that is projected to be raised through the sales tax, $50 million is directed toward an ambitious land conservation program targeted at guiding growth and preserving access to nature through the acquisition of 10 percent of Jacksonville's remaining developable land and improving access to the St. Johns River and other natural areas.

Another tool for funding green infrastructure is the real estate transfer tax. This tax is levied on the sale of property. Maryland's real estate transfer tax, for example, is used to fund its Program Open Space and Rural Legacy program. Due largely to the success of such efforts, Maryland is a national leader in the protection of open space and agricultural lands. Transfer taxes are also used at the community level. In Massachusetts, for example, each community has the right (with public approval) to create a transfer tax to fund land protection, and in West Virginia, under the statewide Farmland Protection Program, local governments can set aside a portion of their transfer taxes for farm and open space protection (mainly easements) once they have created a local Farmland Protection Board and once that board has established criteria and procedures approved by the county commission.

Enterprise funds are another option for funding management and restoration of green infrastructure. Topeka, Kansas, recently created a stormwater utility fund as a stand-alone enterprise fund similar to a water or wastewater utility in which residents are charged for the amount of impervious surface contributing to runoff. The stormwater utility fee is based on the square-foot area of impervious surface—roofs, sidewalks, driveways, and parking lots—that is on a property owner's land.

Box 6.10

Federal Environmental Legislation and Programs

The following federal laws address land conservation and environmental protections. Federal legislation and grant programs often can be used to support green infrastructure initiatives in a variety of ways.

- **Conservation Reserve Program.** Part of the Farm Bill, the Conservation Reserve Program allows farmers to retire highly erodible cropland or other environmentally sensitive areas to vegetative cover. The program's goals include improving water quality, restoring floodplains, reducing soil erosion and sedimentation, and establishing or enhancing wildlife habitat. The program provides technical assistance, cost-sharing, and annual rental payments.

- **Conservation Reserve Enhancement Program (CREP).** The CREP is a federal/state partnership that allows states to target local conservation priorities. Program goals are to reduce water temperature to natural levels, reduce sediment and nutrient pollution, stabilize streambanks, and restore natural hydraulic conditions. Many states target their programs toward geographic areas, such as the Chesapeake Bay watershed, while others target practices, such as farming in reservoir drainages. In exchange for retiring land from agricultural production, the program provides landowners with rental payments, cost-share assistance, and technical assistance.

- **Conservation Security Program.** Also part of the Farm Bill, this program was initiated in 2004 and rewards farmers for ongoing and planned conservation activities on working lands. The program rewards good stewardship and encourages landowners to improve their management practices.

- **Environmental Quality Incentives Program (EQIP).** EQIP provides direct funding and technical assistance to promote agricultural production and environmental quality as compatible goals. The program has four national priorities: reducing nonpoint source water pollution, reducing air emissions, reducing soil erosion, and promoting habitat for at-risk species. Each state is responsible for developing more specific statewide and local priorities. The program provides cost-share and incentive payments to assist landowners in implementing structural and management changes.

- **Forest Legacy Program.** The Forest Legacy Program protects private forest-lands from conversion to nonforest uses through purchase of a conservation easement or purchase in fee simple. Each state develops a forest conservation plan and identifies high-priority private forestlands that should be protected.

- **Landowner Incentive Program.** Usually administered by state fish and wildlife agencies, this program is intended to support on-the-ground projects that enhance, protect, or restore habitats that benefit at-risk species on private lands. The program has technical assistance and funding components.
- **Partners for Fish and Wildlife.** This U.S. Fish and Wildlife Service program provides direct funding and/or technical assistance for voluntary restoration of wetlands and other fish and wildlife habitats on private land. Projects are designed to restore native habitat to function as naturally as possible and focus on habitats that benefit migratory birds, migratory fish, or federally threatened and endangered species, or on habitats that are designated as globally or nationally imperiled.
- **North American Wetlands Conservation Act.** Administered by the U.S. Fish and Wildlife Service, this legislation was passed to encourage voluntary, public-private partnerships to conserve wetland ecosystems. Funds are available to acquire, enhance, and restore wetland ecosystems for waterfowl and other migratory birds. The Migratory Bird Conservation Fund provides additional funds to acquire migratory bird habitat and waterfowl production areas within national wildlife refuges.
- **Farmland Protection and Policy Act (FPPA).** The purpose of the FPPA is to minimize the extent to which federal programs contribute to the unnecessary and irreversible conversion of farmland to nonagricultural uses. FPPA ensures to the maximum extent practicable, that Federal programs are administered in a manner that is compatible with state and local governments, and private programs to protect farmland.
- **National Environmental Protection Act (NEPA).** The stated purposes of this legislation are (1) to declare a national policy which will encourage productive and enjoyable harmony between man and his environment, (2) to promote efforts which will prevent or eliminate damage to the environment and biosphere and stimulate the health and welfare of man, (3) to enrich the understanding of the ecological systems and natural resources important to the nation, and (4) to establish a Council on Environmental Quality. Green infrastructure initiatives may assist in mitigating the adverse effects of federal activities. NEPA often identifies mitigation activities and therefore supports green infrastructure efforts.
- **Clean Air Act.** The Clean Air Act is the comprehensive federal law that regulates air emissions from area, stationary, and mobile sources. This law authorizes the EPA to establish National Ambient Air Quality Standards to protect public health and the environment. Funding may be available for greenways or other green infrastructure elements that encourage alternative means of

transportation. The Hank Aaron State Park Trail in Milwaukee, for example, was funded in part with Congestion Mitigation and Air Quality funds.

- **Clean Water Act.** The Clean Water Act of 1977 is an amendment to the Federal Water Pollution Control Act of 1972, which set the basic structure for regulating discharges of pollutants to waters of the United States. The law gives the EPA the authority to set effluent standards on an industry basis (technology-based) and continued the requirements to set water quality standards for all contaminants in surface waters. The Clean Water Act makes it unlawful for any person to discharge any pollutant from a point source into navigable waters unless a permit is obtained. The Clean Water Act provides substantial funding through states for reducing nonpoint source water pollutions and funding stormwater mitigation and best management practices, for example.

- **Endangered Species Act (ESA).** The ESA provides a program for the conservation of threatened and endangered plants and animals and the habitats in which they are found. The U.S. Fish and Wildlife Service (USFWS) maintains the list of endangered species (there are currently 632) and threatened species (there are currently 190). Species include birds, insects, fish, reptiles, mammals, crustaceans, flowers, grasses, and trees. Anyone can petition USFWS to include a species on this list. The law prohibits any action, administrative or real, that results in a taking of a listed species or that adversely effects habitat. Likewise, import, export, and interstate and foreign commerce of listed species are all prohibited.

- **Safe Drinking Water Act.** The Safe Drinking Water Act was established to protect the quality of drinking water in the United States. This law focuses on all waters actually or potentially designed for drinking use, whether from aboveground or underground sources. The legislation authorizes EPA to establish safe standards of purity and requires all owners or operators of public water systems to comply with primary (health-related) standards. State governments, which assume this power from EPA, also encourage attainment of secondary standards (nuisance-related).

A typical homeowner fee is about three dollars per month; commercial sites with large parking lots pay more. The stormwater utility fee generates $4 million annually for Topeka. These funds are targeted to the protection and/or restoration of green infrastructure elements.

Special assessment districts can also be used to fund green infrastructure. Special assessment districts are separate units of government that manage specific resources within defined boundaries. For example, a stormwater management utility can be established as a special assessment district. Establishing the utility as a special district gives it the power to levy taxes, fees, or special assessments to pay for services and ongoing upkeep. Because special districts can issue debt independently of the state or local government, they do not add to its general debt capacity. As self-financing legal entities, they can raise a predictable stream of money directly from the people who benefit from the services they provide.

Fees charged for a service or activity are another tool for financing land conservation and restoration activities. Fees can be based on the service provided or on the benefit received and can help to offset potential negative environmental impacts. Fees establish direct links between service demands and the cost of providing services. For example, local utilities require customers to pay for the cost of providing water and wastewater services. Localities impose traffic impact fees, park fees, water and sewer fees, building permit fees, and development fees to raise funds to offset the costs of growth. Some state and local governments use fees as a source of funding for pollution control, land conservation and restoration, or other environmental issues. Given the public resistance to tax increases, this trend is likely to continue.

Fees can provide a means for paying for the restoration and/or management of green infrastructure. Of particular interest is the *development impact fee*, a one-time charge that developers are assessed on building projects. Impact fees are usually charged to offset the costs the government must incur as a result of the development, such as the costs of installing water and sewer lines, building roads and schools, or providing parks and recreational facilities. In Austin, Texas, for example, a parkland dedication ordinance requires home builders to pay a fee for parks or to make a contribution of land.

In Minnesota, a coalition of environmental, business, and farm groups called for new sewer fees to pay to clean up the state's many lakes and waterways. The 2004 "Clean Water Legacy" proposal would charge homeowners $3 per month and businesses $120 to $600 per year for each sewer hookup. The money would pay for improvements to local sewage treatment plants and other measures to reduce runoff. Some of the money would be earmarked to protect pristine bodies of water. In Martin County, Florida, each new development is assessed a one-time fee that is used to purchase beachfront property. For each project, the county estimates the number of new residents, the average amount of beach needed per person, and the market price for a linear foot of beach. In Martin County, the beaches are the natural asset targeted for protection, but development fees could be targeted to any other element of a green infrastructure network.

LIMITATIONS OF TAXES AND FEES

It is important to consider the limitations of taxes for green infrastructure projects. Public opposition to new or higher taxes often hinders legislative passage. Unlike fees, many taxes are used for general budgetary support and are only rarely dedicated to particular programs. Some states have no process for dedicating taxes to particular programs; in fact, there may even be constitutional or statutory limitations on dedication of such taxes.

Depending on the market in question, some taxes may be inappropriate for land conservation or restoration activities that require a predictable amount of revenue every year because the tax base may shrink. Moreover, unless a tax is targeted to a particular type of property, income, or sales, there is an indirect relationship between the tax base and use of funds—what is termed a weak cost/benefit relationship.

User fees have a narrower revenue base than most taxes. In an effort to raise more revenue and cover more budgetary costs, the use of fees by state and local governments has proliferated in recent years. As a result, many communities are experiencing growing public resistance to even modest fee increases.

BONDS AND BORROWING

Taxes and fees are rarely sufficient for large-scale land acquisition or preservation activities. As a result, many communities choose to borrow funds for land conservation measures. Many successful green infrastructure projects have been funded through bond measures. For example, in 1995, Portland, Oregon, passed a $135 million bond for parks and open space. Likewise, Broward County, Florida, passed a $200 million Safe Parks and Land Preservation Bond in 2000.

Where the community is reluctant to incur additional debt, a revenue bond might be received better than a general obligation bond. Revenue bonds can be repaid by development impact or user fees assessed on use of a public park, trail, or bridge. (In some cases, user fees are charged for using public parking areas adjacent to the recreation lands or natural attractions.)

Many communities fund land conservation efforts through a series of related measures, tied together by a common vision and plan. In Austin, Texas, for example, voters approved a $75.9 million bond for parks and greenways in 1998, which included $15 million for greenways and metropolitan parks connected to the greenways. Also in 1998, voters authorized a $65 million revenue bond to purchase land and easements within a fifteen-thousand-acre buffer zone over the Edwards Aquifer. The measure is funded by an increase in residential water rates. Then, in November 2000, voters approved $13.4 million in bonding authority for land conservation to prevent pollution to the city's water source. Voter-approved bonds constitute the primary source of funding for the city's acquisition of parks, greenways, nature preserves, and water quality preservation lands.

Environmental mini-bonds are another option for funding land acquisition. These bonds are issued in small denominations (e.g., five hundred dollars) available for purchase by the general public. Proceeds of mini-bonds could be designated for specific programs or activities, such as stream or forest buffer restoration, and for land acquisition programs. The state of Maryland has twice issued mini-bonds, raising $24.2 million in 1990 and $11.8 million in 1991.

Box 6.11

Criteria for Land Acquisition Priorities in Austin, Texas

Funding for land acquisition in Austin is directed toward priority lands using clearly defined criteria. The city's Smart Growth Plan designates parks and green spaces in the "desired development zone" of the city. Within these identified target areas, land is evaluated and given a numerical ranking using the following criteria.

- Park development potential (25 points): Is developable for recreational facilities; has significant natural resources; is contiguous to other parkland; has road access.
- Potential as a greenway (25 points): Has multiple-use greenway characteristics, such as recreational opportunity, potential for trails, undisturbed floodplain, wildlife corridor, natural habitat, and so on; provides connections to neighborhoods, parks, and businesses.
- Potential for aiding in neighborhood development (20 points): Adjacent land is developable for homes and businesses; is accessible to parks and greenways; infrastructure (roads, utilities, and the like) is accessible.
- Potential for watershed protection (20 points): Identified as a priority for water quality improvements; identified as a priority for flood control; pollution avoided by prevention of development; watershed benefited by land protection; protects base flow of water.
- Potential for open space conservation (10 points): Has scenic qualities; is a large, contiguous tract of undeveloped land (200 acres minimum); has historic and cultural value; has areas suitable for native wildlife.

The lands with the highest rankings are considered highest priority lands. Final selection of lands depends on land availability and affordability.

Source: *Financing Land Conservation*, ICMA IQ Report, May 2001, 9–10.

LIMITATIONS OF BORROWING AND BONDS

Borrowing can provide a community with the revenue and flexibility it needs to fund large-scale land acquisition projects as well as ongoing funding for restoration and management activities. Borrowing can take time. Months or even years can go by before a local government can get the measure on the ballot and advocates can generate sufficient support for its passage. In the case of mini-bonds, the cost of issuing the bonds (six to eight dollars per thousand dollars of bond) can be significant. It is important to remember that land conservation is a long-term investment, however. Funding for bond measures often comes from very small increases in property or sales taxes that add up to millions of dollars over one or two decades.[8]

The main disadvantage of borrowing is that bonds typically require voter approval. Local and state ballot measures have a very high rate of success, however—a clear sign of public support for protecting the green infrastructure (see chapter 8, Table 8.1). By providing concrete information about where and how funds will be used, green infrastructure advocates can help improve the success rates of bond measures even more. In Pima County, Arizona, for example, voters approved a $36.3 million open space protection bond in 1997 that specifically identified properties and showed voters exactly where their money would be spent.

PRIVATE FUNDING SOURCES

Private funding should not be overlooked. Charitable foundations, national conservation organizations, statewide and regional conservation groups, local land trusts, and historic preservation groups all devote resources to the protection of land with conservation values. Nonprofit land trusts sometimes raise funds for conservation initiatives either through fundraising campaigns or applying for grants from foundations or corporations. The Lyndhurst Foundation, for example, has contributed substantial funding to dramatically improve the environmental quality of Chattanooga, Tennessee, through a variety of initiatives including a world-class greenway system that functions as the region's green infrastructure system.

In some cases, foundations are created for the purpose of assisting a local government's conservation programs. In Jefferson County, Colorado, for example, the Jeffco Open Space Foundation is a 501(c)(3) tax-exempt organization that works with the county. It supports county programs by accepting donations of land, equipment, or other assets; it raises money by applying for grants from other foundations and private individuals.

Several national nongovernmental organizations provide significant financial and technical assistance. The Nature Conservancy, for example, a national organization founded in 1951, has played a key role in land conservation worldwide. The organization has protected over 15 million acres throughout the United States and over 100 million acres in Canada, Latin America, the Caribbean, and the Asia-Pacific region.

The Conservation Fund, a national land and water conservation organization headquartered in Arlington, Virginia, is another valuable ally in protecting elements of a green infrastructure network. The Fund works with government agencies, corporations, foundations, and willing landowners to protect America's outdoor heritage—wildlife habitat, forestlands, recreation areas, open spaces, working landscapes and historic places. Since 1985, the Fund and its partners have protected more than 5 million acres of land, including national parks and monuments, wildlife refuges, state natural areas, greenways and trails, and privately owned lands.

Founded in 1972, the Trust for Public Land (TPL) also actively acquires land and easements. Dedicated to conserving land for human enjoyment and well-being, TPL has created new parks and refuges, preserved working lands and historic resources, and provided recreational opportunities, ensuring livable communities for generations to come. Since its founding, TPL has protected over 1.9 million acres of land nationwide. In addition, TPL's Conservation Finance program assists communities and states in creating and expanding sources of public funding for land conservation. Since 1996, TPL has helped communities pass 211 local and state ballot measures that have generated more than $35 billion in new conservation-related funding.

LIMITATIONS OF PRIVATE FUNDING

Even with the commitment of many national and local land trusts and other non-profits, there will not be sufficient funding to purchase all the elements of a green infrastructure network. Moreover, it can take considerable resources—time and expertise—to identify potential funding sources, write grant proposals, and negotiate and manage any grants that result. Few local organizations have the needed expertise. By targeting priority lands, green infrastructure can help these local entities best target their limited resources to where they are needed most.

GREEN INFRASTRUCTURE IN ACTION: MOUNTAINS TO SOUND GREENWAY

Like many cities with beautiful surroundings and a high quality of life, Seattle is growing rapidly. The city has sprawled into the surrounding valleys, where farms and forests have been cleared for more houses, businesses, and roads. The sprawl threatens the environmental and cultural assets that distinguish the Pacific Northwest, including several species of salmon, the environmental hallmark of the region.

Alarmed by the threat to the area's natural resources, the Mountains to Sound Greenway Trust began work in 1990 to create a conservation corridor along Interstate 90. In just a few short years, this coalition has planned a scenic, ecological, historic, and recreation corridor that extends over 100 miles from Puget Sound to the town of Thorp in Central Washington. Along the way, the Mountains to Sound Greenway crosses a rich mosaic of public and privately owned landscapes that includes vast forests, trails of all kinds, historic landmarks, wildlife habitat, parks and camping areas, working farms and forests, and conservation lands. Together, these lands constitute a conservation network that preserves green spaces around Seattle and outlying communities and connects these green spaces to more remote, rural open spaces through an extensive trail network.

The Concept Takes Root

The Mountains to Sound Greenway is a momentous achievement born of modest origins. In 1990, a group of citizens organized a five-day march from Snoqualmie Pass to the Seattle waterfront to raise awareness of the need to protect the wild areas outside the city for scenic, recreational, and ecological benefits. The march was organized by the Issaquah Alps Trails Club and supported by corporate, state, and county sponsors. To continue the work, the Mountains to Sound Greenway Trust, a 501(c)(3) nonprofit organization, was formed a year later.

The Mountains to Sound Greenway Trust (the Trust) has a diverse and active membership that includes hikers, public and private land managers, business people, and outdoor lovers. The board of directors has grown to sixty-four people, mostly major landowners and managers, representatives of businesses and recreational interests, and elected officials. By asking who else needed to be at the table, the Trust brought together unlikely allies and fostered an inclusive partnership process.

A seventy-member Technical Advisory Committee of citizens and experts worked with a landscape architecture firm and the National Park Service to develop the Greenway Concept Plan. The goal was to connect an "already existing string of pearls into a continuous green necklace . . . interspersed with the blue waters of lakes and rivers."[9] The building blocks were lands already set aside for national and state forests, water supply and shoreline protection, and state and local parks.

The resulting concept plan outlined seventy projects that would protect land from the mountains to the sound; proposed a role for the various community organizations, governments and agencies, businesses, and private landowners in the Greenway; offered strategies to build coalitions and citizen support for the Greenway; and identified opportunities for action. The plan was carefully crafted to respect community goals and the uniqueness of each community in the region and recognized the need to balance economic and environmental values.

Implementation Strategies

The Mountains to Sound Greenway Trust has engaged a wide range of public and private organizations and used a variety of implementation strategies to accomplish its vision. Elected officials at the state and local levels have provided the needed political support, and public agencies have undertaken the planning needed to implement the vision. Boeing, Microsoft, REI, Puget Sound Energy, Osberg Family Trust, and the Weyerhaeuser Company Foundation are among the many private organizations that provided financial support and became active proponents in implementing the Greenway Plan. Boeing, for example, loaned one of its top executives to the Trust for ten years to work on furthering the mission of the Greenway, continuing to pay his salary and to provide him with office space.

The Trust's Greenway Concept Plan accommodated economic as well as ecological and recreational goals, and implementation strategies build on economic factors. Timber, for example, is a major industry in the Northwest, but timber companies have been under pressure to sell their land. The Trust's acquisition activities have focused on these forestlands, creating large tracts of working forests from properties once owned by Weyerhaeuser, Plum Creek Timber, and other timber companies. Some of these forests are now managed by the Washington Department of Natural Resources or the USDA Forest Service; others are maintained as city, county, and state parks. All the public land managers in the corridor are working toward a common Greenway vision.

Knitting together ecologically important but isolated pieces of land has required leveraging various funding sources and strategies. Land exchanges, land donations, acquisitions of public parks, and conservation easements have all been used to conserve priority land. The Mountains to Sound Greenway was one of the first recipients of Forest Legacy funding, a program sponsored by the U.S. Forest Service that supports state efforts to protect environmentally sensitive forestlands that are threatened by conversion to nonforest uses. The Trust has partnered with many other groups, including the Trust for Public Land, Cascade Land Conservancy, the Cascades Conservation Partnership, and the Washington Wildlife and Recreation Coalition, to accomplish land acquisitions.

The Greenway has succeeded in providing transportation and recreational activities without compromising its mission of protecting the environment. While encouraging recreation where appropriate, partners are actively working to protect the environmental quality of network lands. Greenway Board members and partners in Kittitas County, for example, have developed a recreation plan that will identify areas of overuse, potential recreational enhancements, and access needs. Thanks to efforts by the Greenway coalition, a planning process for the Middle Fork Snoqualmie River Valley—which was plagued by illegal hunting, dumping, and off-road vehicles—resulted in consolidated land ownership, better access for public recreation, the closing of illegal spur roads, and improvements to river access that protect environmentally sensitive riparian areas.

Management strategies also have focused on broader goals. In 1995, the Mountains to Sound Greenway Trust worked with King County to establish an innovative program to recycle treated sewage waste by land application to forests following strict EPA guidelines. The Biosolids Forestry Program fertilizes forest

Box 6.12

MISSION AND GOALS OF THE MOUNTAINS TO SOUND GREENWAY TRUST

Mission Statement:

To protect and enhance a 100-mile corridor of permanent open space lands along Interstate 90 from Seattle to Central Washington. The Greenway embraces city parks and trails, wildlife habitat, working and protected forests, recreational opportunities in nature, local history, scenic beauty, tourism, and educational activities that promote a sustainable balance between population growth and a healthy environment.

Goals:

- Enhance scenic beauty along Interstate 90 and byways
- Create an interconnected trail network from cities to the mountains
- Educate citizens about regional human and natural history
- Improve access to nature for all citizens
- Protect and enhance wildlife habitat and corridors
- Preserve working farms and forests
- Encourage communities to retain their identity and plan for sustainable settlement, employment, and natural resource protection.

soils that have been depleted by over one hundred years of forestry. The program safely recycles wastes, saves money for utility rate payers, and generates funds for land protection.

A number of organizations involved in the Greenway project sponsor environmental education programs. An education program in King County, for example, teaches students from fifth to tenth grades about the challenge of sustaining a healthy, natural environment in balance with the needs of a growing population. The Trust provides education programs designed to teach students about the Greenway, water quality, and the natural resources and processes that make the region so special. The Trust also has helped agencies and communities to develop interpretive kiosks at several sites in the Greenway.

Citizens have been involved every step of the way. Volunteers have planted thousands of trees, removed invasive plants, restored eroded stream banks, cleared abandoned logging roads, and built and maintained recreational trails. Volunteers also run a native tree nursery to provide trees for preserved lands. Some of the tree planting benefits salmon and their habitat by providing shade that helps streams stay cool in the summer. Young people have been involved in restoration activities through EarthCorps. Creating a strong network of volunteers has helped the Trust get this work done cost effectively; it also has fostered a strong sense of stewardship among the citizenry.

As another tool for fostering public awareness of and appreciation for the Mountains to Sound Greenway, the Trust kicked off the first Greenway Discovery Days in 2004. Towns and parks throughout the region hosted special events to spotlight the unique Northwest landscape and its natural and cultural assets. Events included an adventure relay race sponsored by REI, a scavenger hunt, a jazz and bluegrass concert, and the dedication of a newly renovated historic railroad station.

Results

The Trust's first public land acquisition came in 1993—1,800 acres atop Rattlesnake Mountain. Over the next fourteen years, more than 125,000 acres were acquired in the Greenway, and an additional 90,000 were protected from development by conservation easements. Today, much of the undeveloped land between Seattle and Snoqualmie Pass in the Cascades is under some form of permanent protection.

The Mountains to Sound Greenway coalition has protected many highly visible spots along the interstate highway, as well as sites prized for their ecological values. Long-closed trails have been opened to hikers, and new trails have been built to connect hubs to the more urban parts of the greenway. Existing hiking, biking, and equestrian trails have been enhanced and connected for a more exciting recreational opportunity.

In 1998, as a result of the Mountains to Sound Greenway, Interstate 90 became the first interstate highway in the country to be designated a National Scenic Byway. The Washington Department of Transportation has incorporated many

Figure 6.3
The Mountains to Sound Greenway Trust has relied on countless volunteers to restore natural landscapes. The Mount Si Trail shown here, before and after volunteers from the trust and the Student Conservation Association built steps to prevent runoff and erosion and to improve trail safety. Credit: Mountains to Sound Greenway Trust.

Figure 6.4
The view from Granite Mountain, part of the Mountains to Sound Greenway.
Credit: Mountains to Sound Greenway Trust.

Greenway projects into its long-range plan for the Interstate 90 corridor and is an active partner in the Greenway coalition, which has among its goals to monitor and guide highway expansion projects along the highway. The Greenway vision also has inspired local municipalities and public agencies to engage in more strategic approaches to land-use planning, extending the beneficial impact of the project well beyond the Greenway itself.

Success is due in part to the broad appeal of the Greenway vision. The Greenway is envisioned as a multipurpose network of conservation and open space lands—one that combines the desire to protect and enhance scenic beauty, recreational opportunities, and wildlife habitat with an interest in preserving community values and strong local economies. It also includes working landscapes where forestry and other complementary uses are encouraged.

The Mountains to Sound Greenway allows Washingtonians, including those who live in urban areas easy access to nature and all the benefits it offers. In protecting ecologically important lands and wildlife habitat from development while supporting the local economy, the Greenway will preserve the pearls of the Northwest for future generations.

• *For more information about the Mountains to Sound Greenway, visit www.mts greenway.org/index.htm.*

Notes

1. The concept of an implementation quilt evolved from the financial quilt approach introduced by the Environmental Finance Center at the University of Maryland.

2. When considering an easement, it is important to verify that the landowner does indeed own all rights; if a state or federal government, a private individual, or another third party holds mineral rights, for example, the easement cannot prohibit oil and gas exploration.

3. Rob Etgen, et al., *Downzoning: Does It Protect Working Landscapes and Maintain Equity for The Landowner?* (Queenstown, MD: Maryland Center for Agro-Ecology, Inc., 2003). See also information on downzoning on their Web site, http://agroecology.widget works.com, or www.aroecol.umd.edu.

4. For more information about open space zoning and conservation design, see Randall Arendt, *Rural by Design*, (Chicago: Planners Press, American Planning Association: 1994).

5. For more information, see Randall Arendt, "Open Space Zoning: What It Is and Why It Works." *Planners Web* (July/Aug. 1992). See www.plannersweb.com/articles/are015.html.

6. Michael McCollum, *Linkages* (Fall 1997), reprinted at www.fscr.org/html/1998-02.html.

7. For additional information about funding strategies, see Mike McQueen and Ed McMahon, *Land Conservation Financing* (Washington, D.C.: Island Press, 2003).

8. For additional information about public land conservation funding options, see *Financing Land Conservation* ICMA IQ Report, Vol. 33, No. 5 (May, 2001).

9. Mountains to Sound Greenway Trust, *Mountains to Sound Greenway: A Vision in Progress* (Seattle: Mountains to Sound Greenway Trust, 1996).

chapter seven

Management and Stewardship

G reen infrastructure is a long-term strategy, not a matter of buying land and forgetting about it. Green infrastructure lands need upkeep and management just as highways and other forms of infrastructure do. There are many factors that affect the health of land in a green infrastructure network: invasive species, overuse by visitors, water pollution, and so on. What's more, the character and health of land can change over time.

The green infrastructure approach requires assessing the status of each component of the green infrastructure network; restoring it if necessary (by planting trees, removing exotic plants, etc.), monitoring its status and the results of management actions, and modifying the original management strategy to maintain desired characteristics.

In most—if not all—cases, actions will have to be taken to complete the green infrastructure network. Habitat restoration or the creation of new habitat is often needed to connect severed network components, widen linkages where they are too narrow, fill in gaps, smooth out edges, and meet specific network goals.

For these reasons, it is critical to plan for the management and stewardship of green infrastructure lands at the outset *before* the final work on the network has been completed. Considering management issues in conjunction with other network design issues enables green space advocates to identify during the network design process which landscapes require restoration and/or have the potential for

Figure 7.1
Many factors affect the health of the land. Long-term stewardship is needed to address the land's changing needs and to enable the plants and animals that live there to thrive. Credit: Ryan Haggerty, U.S. Fish and Wildlife Service.

restoration. The design team can then include restoration costs among the factors that influence which lands should be included as part of the network.

People have been modifying or manipulating land and natural resources almost as long as they have been on earth. A land management program seeks to balance natural resource protection with appropriate public uses. There is growing consensus among professional resource managers, landowners, and the general public that a focus on a particular species of wildlife (such as deer) or a specific habitat (such as wetlands) is insufficient and often problematic. Management actions undertaken for a narrow purpose can have far-reaching, synergistic effects that are hard to predict or detect. For example, exotic plant or wildlife species introduced into an area to help with one problem sometimes create even greater problems. When kudzu, a vine native to Asia, was introduced in the Southeastern United States at the turn of the twentieth century as a forage crop, it took a lot of hard work to help it to grow. During the Great Depression, kudzu was promoted for erosion control, and the Civilian Conservation Corps hired hundreds of men to plant it. Kudzu, however, has created problems in many of the places where it has been planted. When left uncontrolled, the vine grows over almost anything in its path—derelict cars, abandoned buildings, and other vegetation. Within several years, it kills trees by blocking the sunlight, and covers paved parking lots or street signs. In the Deep South, kudzu covers over 7 million acres, and just as hundreds of people worked to plant it decades ago, hundreds of people today are working to eradicate it from the landscape.

It is not only invasive species that can disrupt the natural habitat. At Charles M. Russell National Wildlife Refuge in Montana, the six to eight thousand head of cattle that graze on refuge lands are destroying wildlife habitat and threatening the reintroduction of the endangered black-footed ferret.

Examples abound of management actions that have turned out to be expensive mistakes. In Louisiana, levees built by the U.S. Army Corp of Engineers guide the Mississippi River and its silt through a narrow shipping channel to the Gulf of Mexico. As a result, when coastal wetlands are eroded by storms, there is no sediment to rebuild them. Researchers warn that the resulting loss of natural protection increases the risk of devastating flood conditions. In Florida, many of the flood control projects begun over a hundred years ago are today considered environmental catastrophes. The interconnected waterways of the Kissimmee River, Lake Okeechobee, and the Everglades have been drained, diked, and rechanneled. By 1980, 1,400 miles of canals and levees had been carved into South Florida. The Kissimmee River is a particular problem. In 1961, prompted by seasonal flooding, the Army Corps of Engineers began converting 103 miles of oxbows and marshes into a 56-mile canal that fed into Lake Okeechobee. It was soon evident that this was an expensive mistake. Scenic bends became stagnant and separated from the free-flowing river; marshes were destroyed. In 1973, Arthur R. Marshall, a former U.S. Fish and Wildlife Service biologist, reported that the river system could not function after being carved into parts by the canals and called for the restoration of the Kissimmee River and the Everglades. In 1976, the Kissimmee Restoration Act was passed to return the river to its natural role in the South Florida system. Experts predict that undoing the $30 million channeling job and reclaiming 50,000 acres of floodplain will cost over $300 million.

So, how can we avoid such mistakes? The solution is to take a comprehensive, holistic approach to managing land and water resources, rather than managing individual species or systems. We need to determine not only what we are protecting these resources *from*, but also what we are protecting them *for*. We need a proactive approach that focuses on a clear vision of the future. We need green infrastructure.

STEWARDS OF THE LAND

Land stewardship is often seen as the responsibility of government or a land trust or some other conservation nonprofit. In reality, we are all stewards of the land on which we live, work, and recreate. Even where government has taken the lead in protecting land, private organizations and individual citizens can play an important role in its management and stewardship.

Put simply, a steward is a person who is left in charge of property by an absentee owner. Stewardship implies assumption of responsibility. Stewardship of land thus implies assumption of responsibility for the welfare of the land. Environmental stewardship implies assumption of responsibility for the welfare of

natural resources and other aspects of our environment. Environmental stewardship embodies three concepts: responsibility, care of the land, and management of
the land for the benefit of future generations. In 1996, the President's Council on
Sustainable Development concluded that "Stewardship . . . calls upon everyone in
society to assume responsibility for protecting the integrity of natural resources and
their underlying ecosystems and, in so doing, safeguarding the interests of future
generations."[1]

The notion of land stewardship goes back thousands of years. In feudal times,
wealthy noblemen owned large tracts of land that they could not possibly manage
on their own; landowners routinely put their trust in servants to run their estates.
The term also implied the responsibility of the landed gentry to ensure continued
prosperity by protecting the family's property from one generation to the next. The
Bible tells us that God put us on the Earth to be stewards of His property. As Bert
Horwood writes, "Stewardship was one of the favorite themes of gospel parables,
usually illustrating the rewards of faithful obedience to the steward's task and the
punishment for the abuse of trust. The greatest abuse was for the steward to assume
ownership and to refuse to account properly for the property entrusted to him."[2]

A recent study defines stewardship as a continuum of a wide range of activities:
"[Stewardship] is employed to describe monitoring and enforcing conservation
easements, managing land to encourage and sustain ecological health, managing
lands to maintain the diversity of earth's plants and animals, and engaging a community in more actively protecting the natural resources on which its livelihood
depends."[3]

Stewardship of the land involves everyone, both individually and collectively.
The way we care for our own house and yard can affect the natural environment
of surrounding areas. Stewardship can include management practices that recognize the benefits of the land (including ecosystems that support biodiversity, flood
control, scenic views, etc.) and maintain the land in a way that protects these benefits for future generations.

Stewardship and Sustainability

Key to the notion of stewardship is *sustainability*—the idea that we should leave
the things we care for at least as well as, if not better than, we found them. In ancient
Athens, city leaders took an oath "to leave the city, not less but greater, more beautiful and prosperous" than it was left to them. In recent years, sustainability has
become an explicit goal of government agencies charged with the management of
natural resources. In practice, however, management strategies and tactics have often
focused on maximizing short-term yield and economic gain, rather than long-term
sustainability.

There are many definitions of sustainability. Probably the most universal definition is associated with *sustainable development* and is attributed to the World Commission on Environment and Development (the Brundtland Commission): "To meet the needs of the present without compromising the ability of future generations to meet their own needs."[4] This definition has been applied to natural resource management strategies dealing with forests, wildlife, fisheries, water, minerals, and energy.

Like green infrastructure, sustainability indicates a future orientation: doing things now in a way that future generations will not be deprived of resources or opportunities. Green infrastructure management includes conservation, protection, restoration, and/or enhancement of landscape resources and processes through conscious action (or inaction) so that the landscape will function in the future as well as or better than it does now. A key part of green infrastructure management is determining how far into the future the strategy is meant to be effective and putting in place a plan for assessing the management approaches that are undertaken.

Box 7.1

Stewardship at the Core

America is blessed with an abundance of natural resources which provide both the foundation for its powerful and vibrant economy and serve as the source of aesthetic inspiration and spiritual sustenance for many. Continued prosperity depends on the country's ability to protect this natural heritage and learn to use it in ways that do not diminish it.

Stewardship is at the core of this obligation. It calls upon everyone in society to assume responsibility for protecting the integrity of natural resources and their underlying ecosystems and, in so doing, safeguarding the interests of future generations. Without personal and collective commitment, without an ethic based on the acceptance of responsibility, efforts to sustain natural resources protection and environmental quality cannot succeed. With them, the bountiful yet fragile foundation of natural resources can be protected and replenished to sustain the needs of today and tomorrow.

Source: *Sustainable America: A New Consensus for Prosperity, Opportunity, and a Healthy Environment for the Future*, President's Council on Sustainable Development, February 1996.

THE PURPOSE AND GOALS OF MANAGING GREEN INFRASTRUCTURE

Green infrastructure management is similar to other land management. Beyond public resource lands, however, many of the components of a green infrastructure network may not have a designated steward responsible for management or restoration. Lands in any green infrastructure network vary in ownership (public and private), size, landscape type, and management needs. The management of green infrastructure lands thus requires flexibility. Moreover, a green infrastructure network cuts across political, programmatic, and project boundaries. Where green infrastructure components are already managed, the current management approach may or may not be consistent with green infrastructure goals. Management approaches also need to consider the needs and desires of the wide range of stakeholders that may be affected by the implementation of the green infrastructure network. Because of these varied interests, balance will need to be struck between the overall management objectives for the network and for its individual components.

Ensuring the ecological stability of green infrastructure hubs, links, and sites requires that resources—both funding and talent—be devoted to day-to-day management and monitoring. What's more, management goals should be considered during the green infrastructure design and planning phase. It is critical that green infrastructure advocates have the support they need to implement the management strategy and a means for determining the effectiveness of the strategy over time.

Natural resource managers must balance varying perspectives, not only on what actions to take, but also on what the desired outcomes are. In the broadest sense, natural resource management starts with answering "why" questions: Why are we managing a certain area? To what end? This leads into a discussion about the purpose the land is to serve: Will it protect biodiversity or habitat for animals or plants? Will it protect groundwater or surface waters? Will it support active nature-based recreation? Will it help to sustain a resource-based industry such as silviculture or agriculture? Depending on the size of the managed area, one or all of the above could be the goal of green infrastructure management.

To some extent, the purpose behind the green infrastructure network helps to answer why the land will be managed. In general, the main reason for managing land in a green infrastructure network is to maintain, enhance, or restore landscape function and native biodiversity; this should be the primary concern when developing the management strategy. Allowing compatible human activity, such as outdoor recreation, farming, or forestry, might be part of a management approach for some components of the green infrastructure network, but it should not define the management strategy for the network as a whole.

In setting management goals, it is important not to lose sight of the goals of the green infrastructure network. From a green infrastructure management perspective, *linked*, *large*, and *unfragmented* are the key concepts because we know that large landscape components linked together are better able to sustain their natural processes when confronted with natural and human-induced perturbations. These kinds of areas tend to be ecologically healthier, more diverse, and more stable. They provide benefits not only to the plants and animals within these ecosystems, but also to the people and communities nearby.

As a result, green infrastructure management approaches should enhance landscape connectivity (by reducing fragmentation) and contiguity (by reducing the edge-to-interior ratio). In addition, management should foster and reinforce a sense of place that is consistent with cultural values and beliefs and should work toward achieving the desired future as identified in community visioning and network goal-setting processes.

GREEN INFRASTRUCTURE MANAGEMENT APPROACHES

Potential green infrastructure management approaches include *ecosystem management*, *watershed management*, and *adaptive management*. These management approaches can be applied to an individual component (a "piece" of green infrastructure) as well as integrated holistically for the entire green infrastructure network.

Ecosystem Management

The term *ecosystem* was introduced in 1935 by the British botanist Alfred G. Tansley in an article in the journal *Ecology* to describe "the whole *system* (in the sense of physics), including not only the organism-complex, but also the whole complex of physical factors forming what we call the environment of the biome—the habitat factors in the widest sense. It is [these ecosystems] so formed which, from the point of view of the ecologist, are the basic units of nature on the face of the earth."[5]

Ecosystem management recognizes and supports the connectedness of life through all the parts (biotic and abiotic), patterns, and processes. The premise of ecosystem management is that no matter how big or small an area under consideration, it can be managed as a *system*, with the understanding that the parts of the system are all connected.

An instructive example of an ecosystem management framework is the Interior Columbia Basin Ecosystem Management Project, a joint project of the USDA Forest Service and the Bureau of Land Management. In this project, which covers over 145 million acres within the Columbia River Basin, four broad principles guided the development of the management framework: (1) ecosystems are dynamic, evolutionary, and resilient; (2) ecosystems can be viewed spatially and temporally within organizational levels; (3) ecosystems have biophysical, economic, and social limits; and (4) ecosystem patterns and processes are not completely predictable.

In the Columbia Basin framework, ecosystem management is based on scientific knowledge and an understanding of the public acceptability of management actions. Scientific approaches are used to characterize biophysical and social processes and to measure outcomes. Public participation processes help determine the acceptance of possible management actions. Monitoring is used to determine baseline conditions, whether implementation achieves its objectives, and whether assumed relationships are true. The framework seeks to place planning procedures within a broad, proactive process that considers the social, economic, and biophysical components of ecosystems at the earliest stages of policy design.

The Columbia Basin framework is based on an ecosystem management approach that strives to maintain the integrity of ecosystems including long-term ecosystem health and the resiliency and vitality of social and economic systems. In addition, it takes into consideration a range of factors, including the expectations of landowners and citizens, management and ecological capabilities, scientific methods, and current scientific literature. In the end, the approach identifies ecosystem principles that can be used to develop agency procedures for interagency coordination, planning, stakeholder involvement, and management.

If your goal is to manage green infrastructure for *sustained* levels of ecosystem function and services across spatial scales (parcel, local, regional, global), it must be related to a clear understanding of how the ecosystem functions, how it responds to disturbance, and the factors that affect its function and stability. There is mounting evidence that biodiversity is a key indicator of ecosystem health. In general, loss of species diversity has been shown to negatively influence important ecosystem functions such as primary productivity, viability of keystone species, nutrient cycling, and stability. These functions are also important functions of green infrastructure; biological diversity may therefore be an important indicator of green infrastructure health, as well as of the success of green infrastructure management strategies.

Although many people believe that ecosystem management is solely focused on ecological health, it can also include the social and economic aspects of a system. Since no part of a green infrastructure network will exist in a vacuum, it is important for the green infrastructure management strategy to account for humans and their activities. Management strategies can provide economic services for individuals and communities, producing food, wood, water, or other commodities; they also need to take into account some of the less tangible services or benefits provided by the different components of the landscape.

Ecosystem management emphasizes processes and relationships, and recognizes that these change over time. It also considers both natural processes and human processes and interactions with nature. Management actions, therefore, are intended to protect, maintain, restore, or enhance the functions and values of

Box 7.2

The Ten Dominant Themes of Ecosystem Management

- All levels of natural systems are **connected**; a focus on any one level is inadequate.
- **Ecological management** must occur across administrative and political boundaries, over large landscapes for long periods of time, and across land, water, and air.
- **Ecological integrity** can only be accomplished through protecting and restoring the processes that perpetuate diversity, pattern, and function of ecosystems.
- Comprehensive and long-term **collection**, **management**, and **use** of biophysical data are required.
- Postmanagement activity **evaluation** that tracks results and assesses success or failure is critical.
- **Adaptive management** is a cornerstone concept where management is a learning process that allows for the modification of management strategies based on the success or failure of past strategies.
- **Interagency cooperation** at all levels of government and the private sector is required because ecosystems cross political and administrative boundaries.
- **Organizational changes** within resource management agencies are required due to the historic bureaucratic compartmentalization of authority and programs.
- **Humans are critical** to consider as the most influential inhabitants of ecosystems.
- **Human values** play a dominant role in developing goals and implementing ecosystem management.

Source: Florida Department of Environmental Protection, 1995.

green infrastructure as perceived by people. The connection that people feel to the land is an important consideration in determining the appropriate management approach. Emotional and spiritual ties to the area in general and to specific lands need to be considered at the outset. Failing to do so may alienate important stakeholders and sabotage the effort.

Ecosystem management applies almost seamlessly to green infrastructure. This is because both approaches encompass a large-scale focus on a future horizon, and acknowledge that people are an integral part of the system. At its core, ecosystem management assumes that intergenerational sustainability must be a precondition rather than an afterthought, not only for the continued production of "goods" or commodities, but also for the maintenance of critical "services." We rely on highly managed ecosystems such as croplands, estuarine aquacultural systems, and forest plantations to produce goods; the sustainability of such intensively managed ecosystems depends also on the matrix of less managed ecosystems in which they are embedded.

Watershed Management

John Wesley Powell, a scientist and geographer who led the first expedition through the Grand Canyon in 1869, defined a watershed as "that area of land, a bounded hydrologic system, within which all living things are inextricably linked by their common water course and where, as humans settled, simple logic demanded that they become part of the community." [6] Because watersheds are often self-contained landscapes that follow natural boundaries, they can serve as a valuable organizing system for green infrastructure design and management.

Watershed management probably has as many definitions as it does applications, but its basic premise is the management (conservation, protection, restoration, and enhancement) of water quality and quantity. Early advocates defined watershed management as "the analysis, protection, repair, utilization and maintenance of drainage basins for optimum control and conservation of water with due regard to other resources." [7] This definition is significant in that it recognizes that water is only one of the resources that need to be managed within the watershed, that other resources are affected by how water is managed, and that the management of other resources affects water resources.

Since political boundaries rarely follow watershed boundaries, different levels of government and even different agencies at the same level of government might have jurisdiction over the land and water within a given watershed, making the role of policy makers inherently difficult. Furthermore, different programs may work at cross purposes; some promoting development (or developing in a certain way) and others inhibiting it.

But watershed management has proven to be a successful unifying concept that involves many different sectors of any community. Water quality and quantity affects people in a profound and direct way. While people may not readily appreciate protecting land for its inherent value, they usually recognize the importance of keeping an adequate supply of clean drinking water. Thus, protecting water resources is often a rallying point for a community or region. The Chesapeake Bay Agreement, for example, brought together political leaders from Maryland, Pennsylvania, Virginia, and the District of Columbia to work collectively to protect their shared water resources.

Box 7.3

The T.R.E.E.S. Project: A Watershed Approach to Urban Problems

While often considered a land conservation effort in rural areas, the green infrastructure approach can also be used in more urban settings to solve a wide range of problems. The T.R.E.E.S. (Transagency Resources for Economic and Environmental Sustainability) Project, for example, brought together a coalition of government agencies and environmental organizations to address problems with drought, flooding, air and water pollution, energy costs, and urban blight in Los Angeles. Program planners believed that capitalizing on the natural processes would be a far better and more economical solution to Los Angeles' environmental problems than its current man-made solutions. T.R.E.E.S. leaders believed the solution was in treating L.A.'s droughts, mudslides, and floods as one single problem, not three different ones.

In 1997, T.R.E.E.S. held a four-day charrette that brought together city planners, landscape architects, engineers, urban foresters, and public agency staff members to design the retrofit of Los Angeles as a living watershed. The participants knew that Los Angeles had no remaining parcels of open land for conventional large-scale plants or dams and concluded that L.A.'s best chance for sustaining a water supply was convincing landowners and businesses to save rainfall. Together, they developed a series of best management practices for industrial sites, commercial buildings, schools, apartments, and single-family homes. The group designed everything from cisterns to a permeable driveway that could make a home function as its own mini-watershed.

The Sun Valley Watershed Stakeholders Group is implementing the group's plans, developing ways to save the area's seasonal rainwater. In addition to working with residents on water-saving options, the group installed a million-gallon cistern and a subterranean stormwater treatment device at a city park and is negotiating with the owners of two gravel mines to use pits as water-retention basins. The entire system as proposed simulates a natural watershed.

An interactive computer cost/benefit model was developed to help policy makers understand the economic, social, health, and safety benefits that could be derived from implementing the best management practices. Implemented citywide, advocates believed that the best management practices could:

- Decrease the dependence on imported water by 50 percent and still keep the city green
- Reduce the threat of flooding and the quantity of toxic runoff to beaches and the ocean

- Cut the flow of solid waste to landfills by 30 percent
- Improve air and water quality
- Decrease our energy dependence
- Beautify neighborhoods in ways that would create up to 50,000 new jobs.

The approach requires a paradigm shift in how urban areas think about their water supply and environmental problems—standing back and focusing on the watershed system as a whole. Initial results prove that there are enormous economic, environmental, and social benefits to be gained through a cooperative approach to designing urban landscapes as functioning mini-watersheds.

Green infrastructure can play a critical role in watershed management, and vice versa. Management of the hubs of a green infrastructure network, comprised of forest, wetlands, and native grasslands, can contribute significantly to a watershed's water and habitat quality. Upland areas promote and protect groundwater recharge while helping to slow or eliminate overland flow. And in many parts of the country, riparian corridors will comprise many if not all of the corridors connecting hubs within the green infrastructure network. Vegetated riparian corridors provide many benefits to aquatic systems, including shading for temperature control, channel stabilization, sediment reduction, spreading of surface runoff, nutrient uptake, and providing roots and woody debris for habitat.

Adaptive Management

Adaptive management is an approach that acknowledges that scientists and land managers do not know everything about how ecosystems function and therefore cannot be sure how best to manage them. *Adaptive* refers to learning about ecological and social systems as they are managed. Adaptive management uses the responses of a system to management actions to determine future actions. The goal of adaptive management is to learn from what is being done to reduce the uncertainty about the impact of future actions. In adaptive management, learning is not simply a by-product of the management process, it is an integral objective.

Implicit in adaptive management is the idea that management actions are experiments, the results of which are fed back into the iterative process. The process views each new management decision as an experiment within a series of experiments, each of which is based on one or more hypotheses about the behavior of critical ecological systems.

Adaptive management has long been an approach to dealing with salmon issues in the Pacific Northwest, bringing together scientific and democratic processes that reflect the viewpoints of natural resource managers, the public, resource users, and scientists. Adaptive management has also long been used as part of an attempt to control white-tailed deer in suburban communities in Rochester, New York, where science-based information about the characteristics of the deer population and a population change model were used to develop population management options and to project their outcomes, as well as to estimate the management effort and costs of each option.

In addition to recognizing limitations in our knowledge, adaptive management acknowledges differences in perspective among resource managers, citizens and other resource users, and scientists. Advocates of adaptive management argue that bringing diverse perspectives to bear on the management strategy improves the outcome because alternative perspectives inform and challenge one another, enhancing the management process with creativity and robustness. This is one of the many ties that adaptive management has to green infrastructure, an approach that builds on the work of many different disciplines and relies on input from a cross section of stakeholders.

Monitoring is a critical component of adaptive management, but the approach does not require rigorous scientific monitoring or data analysis. Monitoring could be as simple as asking the local bird-watching club to conduct yearly surveys focused on specific bird species that would indicate the effects of the management strategy. It is also important to recognize that the adaptive management approach is continuous. While this may sound daunting, it allows for incremental changes to be undertaken gradually, reducing the need for costly changes in management practices every twenty, thirty, or fifty years. Like green infrastructure, adaptive management is proactive, rather than reactive. Imagine how much public money would have been saved if adaptive management had been employed fifty years ago in the Everglades.

Quilting Together Management Strategies

As with funding and other implementation approaches to green infrastructure, no one management approach will suffice. Green infrastructure management can take a variety of forms. Ecosystem management, watershed management, and adaptive management may each play a critical role. The best green infrastructure management strategies identify the parcels most in need of restoration or other management activities and match them to the available management approaches, while also capitalizing on existing management already underway.

Green infrastructure allows for holistic management of various landscapes and parcels. The ecosystem and watershed approaches enable landowners, land managers, and other stewards of the land to connect watersheds and eco-regions in a way that benefits the lands most in need of restoration and management. Management of the green infrastructure network is critical to maintaining a watershed's integrity and its ecosystem services. Meanwhile, adaptive management is critical to ensuring that the management approaches employed are meeting their objectives and the broader green infrastructure goals.

RESTORATION AND ENHANCEMENT

As we have seen, some components of green infrastructure networks might be heavily degraded. Restoration needs should be analyzed during the network design phase and prioritized according to the anticipated ecological benefits, reclamation ease, and institutional opportunities. Restoration opportunity evaluation—or restoration *targeting*—should consider a variety of factors, ranging from the cost and likelihood of success to ecological factors relating to the characteristics of the ecosystem to be restored. To the extent possible, these factors should be quantified to help prioritize the restoration activities at different sites.

In a nutshell, *gaps* are areas within the network that lack natural vegetation. Man-made gaps are often a logical starting point when identifying opportunities for landscape restoration. For example, land that has been cleared for agriculture or mining could be targeted for conversion to wetlands or forests. Field investigation and a method of ranking parameters that reflect function can help to identify what restoration action should be taken. For example, any gaps considered for wetland restoration should contain hydric soils; an agricultural field surrounded by forest that ranks high for potential gain in interior forest and contains hydric soils could be reclaimed as a forested wetland. Other restoration projects that can use landscape and watershed targeting include in-stream habitat restoration, nutrient and sediment load reduction, and other stream remediation projects. Still other restoration projects might focus on the removal of blockages to allow fish passage; constructing road or railroad underpasses to permit wildlife passage, hydrologic continuity, and other ecosystem processes; closing roads or utility corridors; ditch removal; or the removal of invasive exotic species.

Man-made gaps should not be confused with gaps created in tree canopies or other vegetation by natural disturbances like storms, fire, or tree falls. Natural gaps are a vital part of healthy ecosystems and are rarely targeted for restoration.

The cost and ease of restoring each gap should be estimated. It is not necessary to calculate a dollar figure for each project, but a crude estimate of restoration ease by land cover, the area involved, ownership, and access can be helpful in making restoration decisions. Consider also indirect costs, such as the increased flooding that may result from removing a ditch or the loss of economic return from converting a cornfield to a forest or wetland. Such costs should be compared to restoration benefits.

The Maryland Department of Natural Resources used the results of its statewide green infrastructure assessment to work with partners on targeted restoration projects. Among its efforts was a fifty-two-acre wetland restoration and tree planting project at Chino Farms, the largest farm on Maryland's Upper Eastern Shore. Like

Figure 7.2
In-stream habitat restoration, nutrient and sediment load reduction, and other stream remediation projects can be used to restore watersheds within a green infrastructure network. Removing debris from waterways can prove helpful in maintaining riparian ecosystems. Credit: Conservation Resource Alliance.

the green infrastructure assessment, these restoration and planting activities were based on scientific landscape ecology principles and were designed to increase the connectivity between land parcels, reduce forest edge, and increase interior forest area. The restoration project was a partnership between Queen Anne's County, the Upper Eastern Shore Tributary Team (a governor-appointed nutrient management group), and a consulting firm. The Maryland Department of Natural Resources and Washington College (located in Chestertown) monitored the site to learn about changes in the use of the area by birds. This project demonstrates how government agencies at all levels can work together with private landowners and private business to make habitat improvements without infringing on private property rights.

DEVELOPING A GREEN INFRASTRUCTURE MANAGEMENT STRATEGY

The process used to develop a management strategy for a green infrastructure network or one or more components of the network will vary from place to place; no one process will work everywhere. The general steps include forming a group of stakeholders, inventorying resources, developing goals, evaluating options for achieving stated goals, selecting the best option, monitoring outcomes, and using the information to refine the management strategy.

It is important to emphasize that management needs should be considered in the planning and design phases of a green infrastructure project. Projects that do not consider management issues up front usually cost more in the long term and may not achieve the desired goals or objectives.

Step 1: Form a Group of Stakeholders

For any green infrastructure initiative, countless people and groups can be tapped to plan management and restoration activities. In some cases, a subcommittee or working committee of the larger leadership group can take the lead in addressing management issues and making recommendations on how to proceed. As management activities are pursued over a longer term, this group will likely expand and become independent of the initial leadership group. In addition, it is important to recognize that different stakeholders might be involved in monitoring or managing different components of the network and incorporating the various management approaches into an overall implementation plan.

Step 2: Conduct an Inventory of Natural Resources

Before you can develop a management strategy with goals and objectives you need to know the natural resources that are found on the green infrastructure network and assess their condition. Taking an inventory of these natural resources coincides with the steps of designing a green infrastructure network. (See chapter 5 for further discussion.)

Step 3: Identify Measurable, Outcome-Based Goals and a Strategy for Achieving Them

Green infrastructure management activities need to be directed toward one or more outcomes, such as protecting the water supply, increasing the number of migratory birds, restoring a specified area of wetland habitat, and so forth. Consider making your goals relevant to the community as a whole, so that citizens will readily grasp their importance and become excited about participating. Goals should deal not only with ecological restoration, for example, but also with the ways in which the green infrastructure enhances quality of life and supports the local economy. The primary ecological goal might be protecting streamside or woodland habitat; an associated sustainable economy goal might to work with landowners to sustainably manage their woodlands by planning timber harvests to protect forest connectivity and species diversity, reintroducing native plant species, and minimizing impacts to water flow. Quality-of-life goals might combine protecting wildlife habitat with construction of nature trails.

Stating goals in measurable, outcome-based terms enables you to determine whether your strategy is working. A goal to protect and increase forest interior-dwelling birds, for example, might include specifics about the number of birds and a year for measurement to take place (e.g., the community could seek to double the neotropical migrant bird population by the year 2010). Assessing progress would require monitoring the number of neotropical migrant birds using certain patches of forest. If the goal is to enhance the economic health of the community through ecotourism, the goal statement might be to expand ecotourism by 50 percent in ten years, as measured in revenues from outdoor recreation businesses, motel and hotel receipts, and user fees at local attractions.

Step 4: Evaluate Options for Meeting Goals

Once consensus is reached on the desired management outcomes, the next task is figuring out how to reach them. Activities should be based on sound technical principles and address the specific needs of green infrastructure network components. Although some management approaches might encourage risks to be taken, this must be weighed against the potential effects; the presence of a healthy population of a globally rare plant or animal, for example, would eliminate management experimentation—and possibly even active management altogether.

As discussed in chapter 6, many tools can assist in the long-term management of a community's green infrastructure. In addition to acquisition, regulatory approaches, and major programs, consider low-cost voluntary options that can produce immediately visible results and engender community support, such as tree or grassland planting, river or stream cleanup, or trail clearing.

Step 5: Select and Implement the Appropriate Management Option

The various alternatives should be prioritized based on stated goals and outcomes, and the best approach selected for implementation. As discussed earlier, the appropriate management action will depend on the goals for the green infrastructure network as a whole and for each parcel under consideration, the costs of alternative approaches, the available time and money, the management approaches already being used, the expected timeliness of results, and a host of other factors. It is important to consider the pros and cons of each management option, based on the management goals and outcomes. Ultimately, such evaluation requires a mix of professional judgment, insight, and technical information.

Step 6: Monitor the Outcomes of Management Options

Monitoring results involves determining the ecological and community response to implementation of the management option that has been chosen; that is, determining whether the actions taken to protect, restore, or enhance any component of a green infrastructure network have been successful in achieving desired goals. How the monitoring and evaluation are done will depend on the resources available, but they do not need to be expensive or cumbersome.

Evaluating ecosystem health can be accomplished by measuring the diversity and abundance of plant and animal populations in an area. Most techniques rely on specific indicator species selected due to their sensitivity to pollutants or other habitat changes. In aquatic systems, for example, fish and insects are good indicators of water quality. Measuring the effects of green infrastructure should take into account biodiversity and *carrying capacity*, usually defined as the maximum population of a given species that can be supported indefinitely in a habitat without permanently impairing habitat productivity.

It is critical to choose indicators that reflect green infrastructure goals and desired outcomes and that accurately indicate the effects of management action. Indicators act as early warning systems for management activities that are not producing the desired effects. With an early warning system, management activities can be changed before causing damage that is expensive—or even impossible—to rectify. Indicators should be based on adequate sample sizes to ensure accurate statistical analyses, but keep in mind that some indicators, such as the population of rare, threatened, or endangered species, may be too small to allow for statistical analysis.

Finally, traditional cost-benefit analysis can be expanded to take into account the benefits produced by green infrastructure, including social and environmental factors. Although the quantification of many green infrastructure benefits is extremely difficult, there are tools that can be used to analyze numerically or graphically the benefits associated with natural and working lands. For example, the Land Evaluation and Site Assessment (LESA), developed by the USDA Natural Resources Conservation Service, is designed to determine the quality of land for agricultural uses and to assess sites for their agricultural economic viability. LESA sites are initially evaluated for their soil suitability for cropland and forest, and then for their compatibility with relevant plans and zoning, access to public infrastructure, and other factors. The LESA system can be used to facilitate decision making by state and local policymakers, planners, landowners, and developers.

Step 7: Feed Information Back into the Management Strategy

An effective monitoring program tests major assumptions and enables changes in management approaches when warranted. Central to monitoring is using the information that results to refine management actions. Information about whether the actions that were planned have been taken, whether the assumptions made are correct, and whether management objectives have been met can then be used to reassess actions, alter decisions, change implementation, or maintain current management direction.

THE ROLE OF CITIZENS

Land stewardship activities are a popular and effective way to get people involved in land conservation. By planting trees, removing exotics, cleaning up litter, and so on, stewardship fosters a link between humans and the natural environment in which they live.

Community education is an important aspect of any stewardship approach. Sometimes simply informing citizens of the benefits of land or water resources can drastically reduce the impact of human uses on natural resources. Educational seminars, workshops, nature walks, brochures, and pamphlets can all be used as part of this citizen education strategy. Residents can be informed about how to live with nature. For example, many people do not understand the repercussions of cutting down an old shade tree or using nitrogen fertilizers to encourage their greenery to grow. Residents may also be unaware of what happens when exotic plants or animals are introduced into an ecosystem. Educating residents about how they can be better environmental stewards by composting or natural mulching, for example, can help them recognize that the land they own is part of a larger ecosystem.

In many communities, environmental education is a proactive activity undertaken by a specific group. For example, the Rocky Mountain National Park has developed a brochure for homeowners in neighboring communities to help them avoid activities that degrade park resources. Entitled, "Hey, There's a National Park in My Backyard," the brochure offers a range of suggestions for landowners, from keeping pets on a leash, to using native plants for landscaping, to designing homes in harmony with nature. In Ashland, Wisconsin, a gateway to the Apostle Islands National Seashore, realtors provide new owners of waterfront property with information packets that describe how to minimize their impact on the nearby loon habitat. In addition, hundreds of local volunteers work to protect loon habitat, track loon populations, and educate adults and children about loons. Similarly, in the Thousand Islands region of the St. Lawrence River, volunteers with the nonprofit group Save The River help monitor common terns, a threatened species, and "adopt" tern-nesting colonies. Volunteers also help with habitat restoration activities, maintaining and improving the few suitable nesting locations available to the common tern population.

Environmental education helps people to be better citizens. It is also the first step in encouraging their involvement in the stewardship of conservation lands. Nonprofit land trusts, community groups, and volunteers often can manage or restore parks and trails at a lower cost than can government. In Boulder, Colorado, for example, an active group of trained volunteers helps with everything from wildlife monitoring to mapping nonnative and exotic plants, and serve as educators at local schools and guides for nature walks.

In Australia, New Zealand, and other areas around the world, Landcare has taken hold as an organizing concept for environmental action. Landcare Australia is a network of people who are committed to the more sustainable management and use of natural resources. Landcare encompasses many networks with improved natural resource management ideals, including Waterwatch, Coastcare, and Bushcare.

The movement is led by community-based Landcare groups, independent and autonomous groups that work with government, community organizations, or businesses to achieve results. Landcare groups are formed by volunteers with a common concern about the quality of the land and water in their local area and undertake a wide range of activities, including on-the-ground projects, research, education, and community education. Problems being addressed by Landcare groups include salinity, soil degradation, plant and animal pests, vegetation loss, stream bank erosion, poor water quality, coastal degradation, and urban land degradation. Coastcare groups tackle problems like dune erosion, loss of native

Figure 7.3
Environmental education and hands-on habitat management programs can help young people appreciate their responsibilities as stewards of conservation lands. Credit: Conservation Resource Alliance.

plants and animals, stormwater pollution, exotic plants and control of human access to sensitive areas. Coastcare groups are revegetating, building boardwalks and access paths, and removing exotic plant species, as well as educating visitors and locals alike. By promoting conservation at the community level, Landcare can play a role in designing, planning, and managing green infrastructure networks and individual green infrastructure components.

GREEN INFRASTRUCTURE IN ACTION: WILDLINK AND RIVER CARE PROGRAMS, NORTHWEST LOWER MICHIGAN

Nestled on the shores of Lake Michigan, the Traverse City region has been undergoing rapid population growth. The population of this thirteen-county region grew by 12.8 percent from 1990 to 1997; forecasters predict the population to increase another 58,100 between 2000 and 2020, a 21 percent increase in just twenty years.[8] In addition, more than 500,000 tourists flock to the area each year, drawn by outdoor recreational activities that include hunting, fishing, and wildlife viewing. The dense forests prevalent in the region provide shelter and sustenance for a rich diversity of wildlife, including deer, elk, beaver, and several species of migratory birds, while the cool waters teem with a variety of fish.

Although still predominately rural, this part of Michigan is beginning to feel the effects of this growth. New development is fragmenting forests and converting agricultural lands, interfering with the traditional patterns of the wildlife that live there. Moreover, the area continues to grapple with problems stemming from the logging practices of a century ago, when steep banks were used as log slides and logs were floated down rivers. The sandy soils, steep slopes, heavy recreational use, and resulting erosion prevent the stream banks from revegetating and stabilizing naturally. Eroded stream and riverbanks can dump hundreds of tons of sand into the water every year, smothering the spawning beds and feeding grounds of fish and making the rivers shallower and thus warmer, further affecting the delicate ecosystems on which some species depend.

Established in 1968 as part of a nationwide network of Resource Conservation and Development Councils, the Conservation Resource Alliance (CRA) is a private, nonprofit organization committed to "sensible stewardship of the land" in northwest Lower Michigan. CRA serves the thirteen-county area and cares for over 4 million acres of land. Dedicated to maintaining the natural beauty and ecosystems of the area while simultaneously nurturing the economic vitality of northern Michigan, CRA has played an especially active role in watershed restoration, working with a variety of local partners in stream bank stabilization, road/stream crossing repair, fish and wildlife habitat conservation, and erosion inventory projects.

Because of CRA's long-term commitment to regionwide ecosystem protection, it was a natural partner when The Conservation Fund and the National Park Service's Rivers, Trails, and Conservation Assistance Program (RTCA) sought to apply the concept of green infrastructure in this part of Michigan. The vision for the Northwest Michigan Greenways project was to "identify and promote a system of ecological and recreational linkages to protect and enhance the natural beauty and integrity of northwest Lower Michigan." The three partners worked with local and regional agencies and private groups to develop a plan for greenways protection in the region. RTCA provided technical assistance to coalesce various greenways efforts already under way and tie them into a plan for an interconnected system of greenways throughout northwest Lower Michigan.

As a result of this project, CRA identified and mapped important ecological corridors in the area's seven fastest growing counties and then used this information to focus its two main programs, WildLink and River Care, on the areas where there is the most urgent need for management and restoration actions.

WildLink

Begun in 1998, WildLink aims to "preserve the rural character of northwest Michigan for outdoor recreation, hunting, and simply viewing wildlife in natural surroundings." To do this, the WildLink program works to protect ecological corridors —the streams and rivers and the wetlands and forested areas along them—that provide connections between larger blocks of wildlife habitat. The goal of the program is to provide linkages between habitats where various species live. The ultimate goal is to keep animals off the endangered species list by allowing them safe access to the land they need for food, mates, and shelter.

Creeks and rivers and the adjacent buffer areas are critically important elements of the ecosystem. In fact, although they account for only 5 percent of the land in the forest ecosystem, they typically contain 75 percent of the forest's plant and animal diversity. CRA tries to maintain a 300-foot-wide riverine and other corridors to accommodate black bears, bobcats, and otters, which are *umbrella species*—so named because if the habitat needs of umbrella species are met, other species will also be protected.

WildLink works with private landowners to protect wildlife corridors between public lands. The goal is to help landowners to manage property that animals use to travel from one large parcel of land, such as a state forest, to another. In partnership with local landowners, a biologist evaluates the private property's potential to provide wildlife and timber benefits and to improve water quality. The biologist then develops a ten- to twenty-year land management plan to help the landowner achieve those goals. Other land management goals under WildLink

"We're not one of those groups that thinks
it's either people OR the environment. We believe
healthy habitat is highly compatible with human activity
and economic growth. For example, fishing adds $2 billion
annually to Michigan's economy. To us, sensible stewardship
means balancing human activity and economic growth
with a healthy environment. And a healthy environment
must start with healthy habitat."

CRA WILDLINK PROGRAM

include deer management, promoting old-growth forests, managing timber for profit, providing firewood, producing specialty agriculture or forestry products, and attracting songbirds. The land management plans often include recommendations for planting crops that can provide food for wildlife, installing nest boxes, planting native shrubs and trees, selective timbering and/or pruning, and stream or river habitat improvements. All of these tactics enhance wildlife corridors and provide associated ecosystem benefits.

Green infrastructure mapping also plays a role in setting management and restoration priorities. In deciding on protection areas, the CRA targets ecological corridors that face the greatest development threats. They also focus on areas where land protection would provide a better return on investment than restoration. For example, the Maple River corridor in rural Emmet County was chosen as a pilot for the WildLink program because there were large, ecologically rich hubs of public land nearby, there was significant investment in land acquisition and conservation easements through the local land conservancy, it was of manageable size, and it faced increasing development pressure. Although the corridor is still relatively intact, the development of private lands threatened to fragment high-value habitats into isolated pieces that would no longer be able to sustain their ecological functions. Protecting and rebuilding corridors in the watershed will link more than 120,000 acres of ecologically valuable public or protected lands.

The program is entirely voluntary, but finding willing landowners has not been a problem; rather, it is finding professionals who can assess properties and develop and carry out plans that has proved challenging. CRA biologists typically work with more than twenty property owners in a summer. To relieve some of the pressure and sustain landowner interest, CRA publishes habitat management tips in its newsletter and produced a CD-ROM with information about WildLink and tips on getting started in habitat management. These strategies allow landowners to begin implementing sensible land management practices, such as pruning to benefit fruit and nut trees, even if they are not official participants of the WildLink program.

River Care

Like wildlife, rivers and streams do not respect political boundaries. Too often, what is not the responsibility of one jurisdiction becomes the responsibility of none. To address this issue, in the 1980s, CRA began convening local residents to undertake an innovative form of river restoration. In 1998, CRA named the program River Care. The program combines a network of local watershed committees, CRA's technical expertise, and financial support from the private sector to implement long-term, consistent river management that crosses political boundaries. CRA leverages financial and in-kind support to perform habitat improvement and restoration projects on the region's waterways, including its world-class trout streams.

River Care is a proactive program that works to maintain a consistent and prioritized action plan for each river. It identifies and repairs physical problems before they become worse and maintains coordinated local watershed partnerships. Like WildLink, the work of the River Care program is focused on ecological corridors identified through a mapping process. River Care staff and partners look at the big picture by prioritizing watersheds and then break the work down into manageable projects, such as the restoration of a single stream bank. The program's main concerns are the restoration and management of stream and river crossings and banks, erosion control, fish habitat improvement, and river and stream quality monitoring. To accomplish these feats, the program engages in a wide variety of restoration actions. To reduce stream bank erosion, for example, tactics include placing large stones on the bank, terracing steep banks, and planting shrubs and trees. The River Care staff always considers the effects on the local economy as well as local ecology. To this end, River Care has built timber bridges to improve the market for forest products in the area and has improved access to rivers for anglers and paddlers.

Another important aspect of River Care is citizen education regarding watersheds and the impact of alternative land uses on water quality. River Care Kids, which is funded in part by a grant from the General Motors Foundation, involves children in hands-on habitat improvement projects. The goal of the program is to heighten children's innate curiosity and concern for the natural world, especially the health of rivers and watersheds. In one River Care Kids program, schoolchildren raised salmon in the classroom and then witnessed their release into the wild.

The Role of Citizens

Each of CRA's projects begins with a diverse group of partners who share a common interest in improving the watershed or river corridor. For each watershed or corridor, CRA facilitates a steering committee that understands the problems, solutions, and available resources. Some steering committees have worked with CRA for more than twenty years. CRA is proactive about keeping all parties engaged and attracting new interest. River float trips and driving tours are used to showcase project results and provide a unique opportunity for private landowners and volunteers to host a groups of landowner participants and describe the projects in their own words.

CRA staff and partners spend significant time and energy networking with landowners, local interest groups such as hunting and fishing clubs, and civic organizations. To spread the word about its projects and engage citizens as stewards of the land, CRA holds open houses and public meetings, publishes a newsletter, maintains a Web site, and routinely informs the press and interested parties about its activities. CRA offers annual memberships for citizens and businesses and has designated outstanding partners for their work with River Care and WildLink.

Results

In the first two decades of river restoration efforts, CRA restored more than four hundred degraded stream and riverbanks, and improved nearly one hundred road crossings and a number of degraded recreational access, agricultural, and residential sites. Its flagship project, the restoration of the Pere Marquette River, a world-class trout stream and a federally designated wild-scenic river, was a $2-million, ten-year project. Working with partners, CRA coordinated the treatment of more than two hundred damaged and eroded stream and river banks. CRA started by scientifically identifying several tiers of ecosystem impacts along the river and then worked on the most severely degraded sites, repairing over five hundred problem sites in more than fifteen watersheds. CRA has inventoried and prioritized more than three thousand sites in the thirteen-county area that need treatment to reduce severe erosion.

CRA's WildLink and River Care programs provide innovative approaches to land management and restoration activities. Priority ecological corridors are carefully defined by wildlife ecologists in conjunction with local residents. These corridors tend to emphasize riparian areas and wetlands as well as upland ridges and coastal shorelines, critical habitats for songbirds, migratory waterfowl, and shorebirds. WildLink has succeeded in protecting wildlife corridors for umbrella species, thereby helping to ensure that animals have access to an adequate food supply and mating partners.

Figure 7.4
The River Care Program uses a mapping process to set priorities for watershed restoration and management activities and break the work down into manageable projects, such as stream bank restoration. These before and after photos clearly show how these efforts can transform an area and greatly reduce the potential for erosion. Credit: Conservation Resource Alliance.

CRA uses science-based ranking to proactively address problems and identify priorities for restoration. Local volunteers are given stewardship responsibilities and are empowered to complete on-the-ground conservation work. That the approach engages the voluntary support of private landowners is testimony to the love of residents for the land and their respect for the environment. Together with the greenways activities in northwest Lower Michigan, these programs have helped to identify, protect, and restore important ecological and recreational connections in northwest Lower Michigan, which conserve the environment and benefit its people and wildlife.

• *For more information about CRA's Wildlink and River Care Programs, visit www.rivercare.org/index.php.*

Notes

1. President's Council on Sustainable Development, *Sustainable America: A New Consensus for Prosperity, Opportunity, and a Healthy Environment for the Future,* February 1996. See http://clinton4.nara.gov/PCSD/Publications/TF_Reports/amer-top.html.

2. Bert Horwood, "Stewardship as an Environmental Ethic," *Pathways: The Ontario Journal of Outdoor Education* 3(4), 5–10:6.

3. See Marty Zeller, *Stewardship of Land: An Investigation into the State of the Art* (Menlo Park, CA: The INNW Fund, 1999). See ftp://cnlm.org/pub/stewardship.pdf.

4. The concept of a sustainable future was defined in 1987 by the World Commission on Environment and Development in its report entitled, *Our Common Future* (New York: Oxford University Press).

5. Alfred G. Tansley, 1935, "The Use and Abuse of Vegetational Concepts and Terms," *Ecology* 16(3), 284–307.

6. New Concepts in Watershed Management. *American Society of Agronomy Special Publication* 4 (Madison, WI: Soil Science Society of America, 1969):55–65.

7. Ibid.

8. Northwest Michigan Council of Governments, *1997 Population Characteristics of Northwest Lower Michigan,* August 1998. See www.nwm.cog.mi.us/data/nwmpop97.pdf.

chapter eight

Building Support for Green Infrastructure

Look at any successful green infrastructure or strategic conservation program, and you'll find active volunteers. During the planning process, citizens and other stakeholders serve on leadership groups and advisory committees; during implementation, they are instrumental in planting trees, building trails, restoring natural areas, monitoring wildlife or water quality, and sharing information about the importance of conservation. Motivated by the changing landscape and character of their communities, community groups can help create a program, steer its direction, and oversee its implementation. By providing support as well as a variety of perspectives and talents, stakeholder participation is crucial to developing a plan that reflects the priorities of residents and stakeholders alike. Stakeholder involvement is also critical in the local decision-making process by urging favorable support for green infrastructure.

Perhaps most important, engaging citizens generates support for the project and expands the pool of potential volunteers for land protection and management activities. Local businesses and residents can play a key role in land protection and management, by donating or putting easements on their land or by funding land conservation or restoration activities. A local business may be willing to pay for the protection, restoration, or maintenance of a specific park, trail, or other piece of priority network land, particularly if the business can post a plaque to advertise its good deed. Local businesses have also spearheaded campaigns to raise awareness of a green infrastructure effort and offered the time or expertise of staff to support an effort.

Citizens have already demonstrated their support for the conservation of land and water resources. From 1996 through 2004, voters in states and localities across the United States approved 1,065 referenda, raising over $27 billion for parks and open space (see Table 8.1). A strategic approach to conservation—one that employs green infrastructure principles and practices—can help ensure that these conservation funds are spent in a way that will effectively protect natural systems and address community priorities.

PUBLIC INFORMATION TOOLS AND TECHNIQUES

Throughout the network planning and implementation phases, it is important to keep the public apprised of your plans and progress. Which methods to use and when to use them depend on the nature of the community; citizens' attitudes toward growth and development, land conservation, and green infrastructure; and the mission and goals of the green infrastructure leadership group.

A press release is perhaps the easiest and most inexpensive public information tool. Effective press releases provide information in a brief, easy-to-read format. All

Table 8.1

Local and State Ballot Measures for Land Conservation

	Measures passed	Measures on ballot	Passage rate	Amount for conservation
1996	60	74	81%	$1.1 billion
1997	54	64	84%	$0.6 billion
1998	144	190	76%	$6.6 billion
1999	93	102	91%	$2.2 billion
2000	174	208	84%	$4.4 billion
2001	137	196	70%	$1.6 billion
2002	140	190	74%	$5.4 billion
2003	101	135	75%	$1.3 billion
2004	162	217	75%	$4.1 billion
Total	1,065	1,376	77%	$27.3 billion

Trust for Public Land data, published in Reid Ewing and John Kostyack, *Endangered by Sprawl: How Runaway Development Threatens America's Wildlife*, National Wildlife Federation, Smart Growth America, and NatureServe, 2005, 17.

press releases—and all other public information pieces—should include the date and contact information for those interested in following up.

Since you have no way to control media coverage, fact sheets and brochures should be designed and provided to key constituencies. A fact sheet is a simple one-page document that provides information about the green infrastructure group's composition, vision, mission, and activities, and gives answers to frequently asked questions. Fact sheets can be updated as goals are accomplished and milestones met. A brochure often contains the same basic information as a fact sheet, but presents this information in a more colorful and polished format. Today's computerized self-publishing programs make it fairly easy and inexpensive to produce high-quality brochures, but care should be taken to make sure they look professional.

Radio and television stations may also be interested in a green infrastructure initiative. They may cover special events or project milestones on the local news or run public service announcements about community visioning workshops, green infrastructure planning meetings, and the like. If possible, book a green infrastructure advocate to appear on a radio or television talk show to discuss the project and/or to answer call-in questions from citizens.

Written information is important, but it cannot replace face-to-face meetings with those who have a stake in the green infrastructure initiative. Green infrastructure advocates should attend meetings of constituent groups to discuss the vision and mission, answer questions, solicit feedback, and encourage citizen involvement. An open public forum at the outset of the project—perhaps held in different neighborhoods or regions—can help to get the project off on the right foot.

In addition, it helps to hold small, informal meetings with key people in places that are comfortable, safe, and convenient for attendees. A neutral location, such as the community center, fire hall, or local school, should be used if project leaders do not know attendees well or if attendees represent diverse interests. Finding a local host and including refreshments can further encourage attendance.

Regardless of the specific methods used to get the word out about the green infrastructure initiative, there should be a well-conceived communication plan centered around a simple, convincing message. Involving people with marketing expertise, skilled writers, graphic artists, and other communication professionals can help ensure that the message reaches the intended audience. Green infrastructure advocates should also prepare speaking points, a slide show, or a PowerPoint presentation that clearly illustrates the goals of the initiative and how a green infrastructure network would benefit the community. Special events, such as a hike along a major corridor of the green infrastructure network or a rally that takes place on a priority piece of land, can help to highlight components of the green infrastructure network and generate enthusiasm for the initiative.

Between 1991 and 1995, members and staff of the Florida Greenways Program and the Florida Greenways Commission worked hard to educate the public. They designed and distributed a quarterly newsletter and a series of fact sheets about greenways issues and projects, sponsored workshops and roundtables, and routinely issued press releases on project milestones. The Florida Greenways Program also partnered with Walt Disney World, Inc., to produce a video and slideshow about the proposed statewide greenways system, and with the National Park Service's Rivers, Trails, and Conservation Assistance Program (RTCA) to design and distribute a Florida Greenways poster. This poster had an artistic mosaic depicting the different benefits and uses of greenways on one side, and on the other, the commission's vision and concept of a statewide network and its benefits.

RTCA also worked with the commission and the Florida Greenways Program in the fall of 1994 to design and facilitate five public forums around the state to inform the public about the concept of a statewide greenways system, to supply information on existing and proposed greenways in surrounding areas, to provide an overview of the Commission's mission and work, and to seek input on its draft findings and recommendations. A critical public awareness campaign involved a celebration of "150 Greenways across Florida" to coincide with Florida's sesquicentennial in 1995. The celebration included events held at existing greenways around the state.

BUILDING CITIZEN ENGAGEMENT

There is no one right way for engaging citizens; it is important to note, however, that public engagement is much greater in projects where citizens play an active role in decision making. The greater the role of citizens, the more they will support the project. Equally important, maintaining an engaged citizenry provides the public conscience necessary to sustain a long-term initiative like green infrastructure.

Public participation is mandated for most public planning processes. But even in situations in which citizens take the lead, it is critical for leaders to ensure that a broad range of citizen input is sought so that the process is not skewed unduly by a specific interest group. Too many programs convene a citizen advisory committee at the beginning and ask for input on the preliminary design, but do little to sustain citizen involvement throughout. True success depends on the active involvement of citizens throughout the planning and implementation of the green infrastructure project and the resulting network design.

Citizen involvement is easy in theory but often difficult in practice. Many places have a diminished sense of community, resulting from a more mobile and increasingly isolated population. Residential lots are bigger and farther apart, many families have two working parents, and neighbors may go for days without ever seeing one another. Television lures people away from social engagements. With the rise of cable and satellite stations, television is even making the local movie house obsolete. Advances in technology—most notably the personal computer and the Internet—have resulted in less face-to-face interaction in both work and leisure activities.

Figure 8.1
The Florida Greenways poster uses an artistic mosaic to educate residents about the diverse benefits of the greenway system for people and for nature. Credit: Florida Greenways Commission.

In any community, different people have different perspectives of the present and visions for the future. Differing perspectives too often pit different factions of the community against each other—old-timers versus newcomers, retirees versus families, developers versus conservationists. If not addressed, these antagonisms can grow over time and become a divisive wedge in the community. Yet, people from all walks of life tend to have a number of important goals in common: clean air and water, economic vitality, quality of life, and so on. These shared goals give green infrastructure advocates a place from which to build solid partnerships and to forge lasting change.

Social Capital

Political scientists, practitioners, and activists have worked for decades to rebuild the fabric of communities—to build what Harvard University professor Robert Putnam coined *social capital*. Social capital can be defined as the norms and networks of social relationships that build mutual trust and a spirit of reciprocity among community residents, organizations, and institutions. Social capital is the glue that holds a community together.[1]

The power of social capital is unmistakable. Unlike financial capital, social capital increases with use. The more social capital exists in a community, the more it will build. Or, as sociologist Judy Gruber puts it, with social capital, the rich get richer. Yet, for many communities, building social capital remains elusive.

In any community, people interact and organizations facilitate community interaction in a variety of ways: church groups, block watches, citizen advisory councils, neighborhood associations, the PTA—these are all parts of a community's civic infrastructure. However, these interactions do not always lead to the creation of social capital. Social capital also requires social relationships that are mutually reciprocal and inclusive. For social capital to exist, people must not only participate in community activities, but they must also be meaningfully involved in decision making. Social capital requires mutual trust and reciprocal relationships.

Communities are a complex web of formal and informal groups. The same people and groups tend to be involved in a wide range of community affairs and leadership activities, while others are seldom heard from. Building social capital requires balancing the interests at both ends of the activist spectrum.

It is not easy to balance the needs of various federal, state, and local agencies, businesses, environmental organizations, landowners, and other groups and individuals with a stake in green infrastructure. Many communities find themselves grappling with the need to involve citizens against a backdrop of mistrust. In some cases, such mistrust is built on a long history of antagonism between different groups or neighborhoods, between citizens and government, between conservationists and developers, or between any number of other factions.

To mitigate this mistrust, it is important to be as inclusive as possible. A citizen advisory committee or other community group should have a diverse membership that includes underrepresented sectors of the community. Citizen committees can lend credibility to a government program—or what otherwise may be seen as a government program. They also serve as a system of checks and balances on a government-led program.

Strong identification with a geographic location or community can provide the foundation for trust and open communication. Once participants sit down and talk about a specific piece of land, they can move beyond theory and beyond their predefined notions to begin to see how specific actions (or inaction) will affect the landscape. Field trips, clean-up activities, and similar events can help promote a sense of community and demonstrate the potential of a place.

Science can provide a common language and procedures that are comfortable for everyone. Joint research and fact-finding can facilitate this process; engaging technical advisory committees as an adjunct to stakeholder groups can provide a source of credible, nonpartisan scientific review. Performance measures can be used to help assess whether the actions taken are achieving what was expected.

Act Locally

Regardless of the scope of a green infrastructure initiative, success is achieved locally; successful leaders build broad stakeholder support through a consensual, open, fair, and transparent process. Residents and other stakeholders should have opportunities for input throughout the planning process, to offer feedback on the green infrastructure network design, and to participate in the implementation of the green infrastructure network. Public involvement is not the goal; it is a tool for achieving tangible, on-the-ground results. This means giving people a voice and listening to what they have to say, even if it's not what you want to hear. Involving citizens after key decisions have been made undermines trust and can give rise to opposition.

Green infrastructure can be a tool for building social capital. Because green infrastructure initiatives bring together people with different perspectives, it helps to forge bonds where they did not previously exist. Building trust takes time. By taking baby steps and widely publicizing each success, green infrastructure advocates can gradually build the trust needed to take larger steps. By highlighting the involvement and contributions of once opposing players, a project can find common ground and build the foundation for future dialogue.

Finding Volunteers

In the search for people and organizations that can contribute money and/or expertise, other valuable resources—including social capital—are too often overlooked. As important as money and expertise are, it may be more important to make sure that people involved in the green infrastructure project have real and

Box 8.1

Secrets of Success

To effect community change and enlist support for green infrastructure:
- Develop a widely shared vision.
- Engage all interests and sectors.
- Create an inventory of local assets and resources.
- Provide opportunities for leaders to step forward.
- Target the message for different constituencies.
- Be clear about program needs, and create opportunities for involvement.
- Recognize nongovernmental organizations and reward volunteers.
- Meet the needs of landowners and the broader community.

lasting commitment to the goals. In many projects, volunteers freely give their time—an important consideration when calculating a project's costs. In green infrastructure projects, it is often a few committed people that make the difference between success and failure.

Community outreach requires creativity. Volunteers can be found in unexpected places and come in all shapes and sizes. Senior citizens may have more time to volunteer than busy professionals and can play a powerful role in any effort designed to ensure that the community they love will be preserved for generations to come. Corporations also often engage their employees in improving the communities in which they live, particularly if they can reap the benefits of good publicity. A high school or college also may be a good source for volunteers, particularly if the green infrastructure initiative can be tied to the school's curriculum.

People are often willing to take on responsibility for planning or managing green space when given the opportunity and the knowledge to do so. Teaching residents about the implications of their own land-use decisions, such as the advantages of using native plants, may be a good place to start. Educational markers at parks or other green infrastructure sites can be used to teach visitors about wildlife populations and how to enjoy the natural environment without leaving a human footprint.

Volunteerism is also enhanced by making involvement rewarding. Some volunteers are motivated by an altruistic spirit. River restoration, tree planting, trail construction or clean-up—all of these have tangible results that enable people to see a difference. Making the work fun is also important. People are far more likely to participate as part of a team than on their own. Recognizing their efforts is another important motivator. The Wisconsin Community Open Space Partnership, for example, holds Green Ribbon Awards to honor "the people, places, and policies that make Wisconsin's communities more livable through creating and promoting vibrant green infrastructure." The awards are celebrated at receptions for program staff, volunteers, and other invitees held in different parts of the state; the program helps to recognize the work of these people as well as publicize the mission and goals of the green infrastructure program. From a simple letter of thanks to a potluck dinner celebrating project milestones to a hike through a newly restored trail, there are many ways to ensure that volunteers know that they are appreciated.

There are often unintended benefits of community outreach. In 1991, when a cooperative education student at the Corpus Christi field office of the U. S. Fish and Wildlife Service visited a sixth-grade class to talk about the importance of wetlands, a student asked what the class could do to save wetlands. The result was a new Adopt-A-Wetland program in which students learn about wetlands through monitoring a wetland, conducting classroom activities, and surveying sites or restoration projects.

Getting Citizens Involved

The first step in citizen engagement is to generate enthusiasm and identify common interests. Interactive displays in public places can be used to show what the community could look like if action is not taken to protect green space. Special kick-off meetings or events can be used to generate publicity. These can be followed up with information sessions where people can ask questions and sign up as volunteers.

Informational meetings and planning sessions need to be well organized. It is important to consider the optimum size of the meeting and tailor this to what you hope to accomplish. While informational sessions should be targeted to as large a group as possible, true dialogue and consensus building is difficult to accomplish with groups of more than twenty-five or so.

Of course, people won't attend if they don't know about the meeting. A variety of methods can be used to publicize the meeting and encourage attendance. Send flyers to residents, place posters in local businesses, post information on related Web sites, and ask the local newspaper to run articles or ads. Make sure that people understand the purpose of each meeting and how it fits into the green infrastructure effort.

Facilitate attendance by making sure community meetings accommodate different lifestyles. If a series of meetings is to be held, schedule meetings on different days and different times (on a weekend morning and a weekday evening, for example). Consider providing on-site childcare; sometimes this is the only way parents of young children are able to attend. Make an extra effort to reach out to underrepresented sectors of the community and to those who may be skeptical about what you are trying to accomplish.

Box 8.2

Ten Ideas for Recruiting New Leaders and Volunteers

1. **Ask the question, "Who's not here?"** Find those groups and constituencies that have eluded your attempts to be broadly representative of the community. Invite them to join local committees and organizations.

2. **Look for skills not names**. Find individuals who have important skills and talents, as well as those with key positions.

3. **Try involvement by degrees**. Start volunteers on simple, finite tasks that require less time. This allows volunteers to become comfortable with the committee or organization and its members, and to take on additional responsibilities.

4. **Appeal to self-interests**. Find out whether the potential volunteer is motivated by social activities, a position of leadership, altruism, or enlightened self-interest. Assign them a role that suits their motivation.

5. **Use a "wide-angle lens."** Welcome all volunteers and volunteer efforts no matter how humble or large. A volunteer's contribution should never be belittled nor taken for granted.

6. **Define the task.** Be certain to accurately describe the time commitment and task requested of volunteers. Describe the task in the context of how it will contribute to the overall effort.

7. **Use current leaders to recruit new leaders**. Use the snowball effect of visible and motivated leaders recruiting new leaders through friendship, recognition, and encouragement.

8. **Be known for efficient use of people's time**. Do not waste people's time with disorganized meetings or work sessions. Define tasks in detail and hold meetings with clear agendas and time limits.

9. **Offer membership premiums.** Give symbolic recognition and real rewards to leaders who dedicate themselves to committees and organizations. Reward leaders with newspaper profiles, certificates, letters to employers, exclusive social affairs, or travel to a workshop or convention.

10. **Market your wares**. Make the community aware of progress being made. Publish newsletters and press releases and work hard to get media coverage of your successes. This will provide another reward for volunteers.

Source: *Building Gateway Partnerships*, Rivers, Trails, and Conservation Assistance, National Park Service, Seattle, Washington.

In addition to sharing information about your plans and activities, public information strategies should be used to actively involve citizens during various phases of the green infrastructure planning process. For example, after a preliminary green infrastructure network design has been developed, citizen groups should be asked to review it to make sure that it meets desired goals. This critical aspect of public involvement in green infrastructure network design is discussed in chapter 5.

COMMUNITY VISIONING AND GREEN INFRASTRUCTURE

Green infrastructure initiatives have a greater chance of success when a common vision is developed and all interests are actively engaged. Building community consensus on what should be done requires identifying core values—those essential and enduring tenets that can help guide plans and activities. Groups with staying power believe that they have a fundamental reason for being, a perpetual guiding star on the horizon, and faith that what they are doing will make a difference.

Communities that are successful in preserving what they love actively involve a broad cross-section of residents in planning for the future. An essential part of this process is bringing citizens together to assess the current situation, consider trends that may affect the community, and develop a common vision for what they want the community to look like in the future. Community visioning usually involves one or more workshops or charrettes in which citizens try to reach consensus on goals for the community and how to achieve these goals. Visioning can also include written surveys or other methods used to get feedback from a broader constituency.

> "A sustainable world can never come into being
> if it cannot be envisioned. The vision must be built up
> from the contributions of many people before
> it is complete and compelling."
>
> DONELLA MEADOWS

Visioning not only helps a community identify what it wants to look like in the future, it also helps the community identify the steps needed to make its dreams a reality. A community vision may result in recognition of the need for tools to protect cherished landscapes and to plan for development in a more comprehensive and proactive way. In 1999, more than 180 residents in Fluvanna County, Virginia, for example, developed a common vision: "It is the hope that Fluvanna's heritage and character will shape the course of change and development instead of

Box 8.3

What Is a Vision?

A vision is a community-based strategic planning effort in which citizens and leaders work together to identify a series of shared goals encompassing a broad range of common interest, such as a community green infrastructure initiative. In addition to community goals, the visioning process defines specific strategies for each goal and a short-term action plan to "jump-start" the implementation phase of the vision. There are five principles that lead to implementing a successful vision:

- **A vision must be inclusive**. It must seek out and involve the broad range of interests. Inclusiveness creates ownership of the vision and its goals. This sense of ownership leads to (1) support for the implementation, (2) continuity over time and consistency in the decision-making process, and (3) a strong sense of community identity.
- **A vision must deal with all aspects of concern**. A vision will provide a complete picture of all the needs and aspirations of a community, and it will link issues across traditional, professional, and institutional boundaries.
- **A vision must be community-driven**. It must be implemented by a steering committee that reflects the economic, sociocultural, and environmental make-up of the community. The leadership of the vision must include citizens, stakeholders, and community leaders.
- **A vision must be carefully orchestrated.** There are four specific areas to be addressed: (1) outreach to ensure broad involvement, (2) marketing to create a general awareness of the initiative's goals, (3) logistics to oversee the specific elements of visioning workshops, and (4) meeting design to ensure that meetings are "safe," structured, accessible, consistent, and fun.
- **A vision must lead seamlessly into actual implementation**. The participation of the initiative's leadership must be engaged to move beyond defining a strategic plan.

Source: "The Vision Thing: Tools to Get It in Focus," the American Communities Partnership.

new development shaping the character of our community." A subsequent forum, held three years later, was conceived and designed by local organizations to obtain citizen perspectives and recommendations for the county's future open space needs and specific tools that could be considered for protecting open space. The forum was marketed as an opportunity for citizens "to discuss protection of open space in Fluvanna as a way of preserving our rural character in the context of change." The resulting Open Space Plan was formally adopted by the Fluvanna County Board of Supervisors as a component of the county's comprehensive land-use plan. The county also undertook the revision of its zoning ordinances and subdivision codes, in part to implement actions recommended in the Open Space Plan.[2]

Green infrastructure visioning is not that different from other community visioning efforts. In fact, protecting green space and preserving community character are often priorities that come out of community visioning workshops, fueling the drive for green infrastructure. For example, in 1995, the town of Pittsford, New York, a suburb of Rochester, embarked on a visioning process aimed at building consensus on the issues of concern to the community, including the town's character. The process confirmed a shared understanding among Pittsford residents that "the working agricultural and natural landscape is a living testament to the history, scenic beauty, and natural resource wealth of the community." Citizens agreed that these resources were part of the essential character of Pittsford. They also agreed

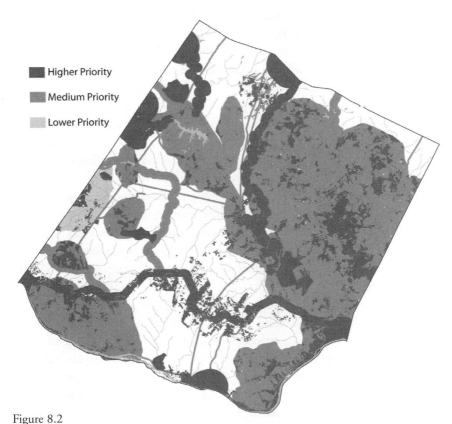

Figure 8.2
Open space priorities identified during the third Fluvanna Heritage Forum (Virginia).
Credit: The Fluvanna Heritage Forum 2002.

that development pressures would soon consume this landscape if the town did not intervene to protect these resources. Consensus building continued through the comprehensive planning process. As it worked to implement the recommendations from the Pittsford 2000 visioning sessions, the town benefited significantly from the ongoing participation of several special interest groups and landowners and from the active involvement of the general public.

Green infrastructure visioning workshops also provide an opportunity for residents to come together and talk about things they don't usually discuss and to focus on the long-term future of the community rather than on its immediate problems. In some cases, new relationships may be forged: between government and business, developers and environmentalists, old-time residents and newcomers. In others, the relationship building may take place between one community and another, between different public agencies, or between different levels of government.

The Mapping Charrette

Just as some communities use community visioning as a means for focusing on the future and creating a shared vision, so too communities are using green infrastructure *mapping charrettes* to envision a desired future in terms of green space. Mapping charrettes can result in new personal and professional relationships that can lead to better coordination of ongoing conservation and/or recreation efforts.

A mapping charrette is a short, intense, concentrated design session. It can be targeted toward specific sectors of the community that have a vested interest in green space planning, such as natural resource, parks, and recreation staff, land trusts, hiking or hunting clubs, and other outdoor recreation business owners, or it can be open to any members of the community interested in planning for the future. Like community visioning workshops, green infrastructure mapping charrettes can succeed in bringing together diverse segments of the community to share their different perspectives and come to consensus on shared values and vision.

The concept is simple: invite individuals with relevant expertise and/or experience to work together to record their knowledge on a common base map and accompanying data sheets. The result, after one or two days of intensive work, is a map depicting lands to be protected and a blueprint for potential future action.

A mapping charrette hosted in 1991 by the Florida Chapter of The Nature Conservancy, the Florida Audubon Society, and the Florida Department of Natural Resources played a key role in setting the stage for Florida's statewide greenways initiative. At this charrette, a group of forty experts in ecology, botany, zoology, geology, hydrology, and land planning and management were invited to Tallahassee to identify priority ecological resource conservation areas for Florida. The two-day workshop resulted in the preparation of the Preservation 2000 Charrette Map.

In addition to depicting existing federal, state, regional, local, and private conservation lands, the map identified priority lands recommended for acquisition by the state of Florida, as well as broad areas of conservation interest, not proposed for acquisition but considered important for the movement of wildlife and the maintenance of biological diversity and ecological processes. Taken together, the results of the charrette defined important ecological parameters for a statewide conservation system consisting of large ecological hubs and broad landscape linkages. The 1991 charrette was followed by a number of regional land acquisition planning workshops. These regional workshops provided useful information for updating the statewide concept and coordinating ongoing conservation land acquisition activities. A recreational greenways mapping charrette sponsored by the Florida Greenways Program in June 1992 complemented and expanded upon the results of the Preservation 2000 Map Charrette by identifying existing, proposed, and potential hiking, biking, and canoeing corridors statewide.

As part of its Massachusetts Community Preservation Initiative, the Massachusetts Executive Office of Environmental Affairs held twenty-four summits across the state to get citizens thinking about what they wanted to preserve in their communities and what they wanted to change. Citizens were shown a series of maps representing the land-use changes over time, concluding with a build-out analysis that showed maximum development permissible under current zoning laws. Summit leaders also presented analyses of jobs, housing, and drinking water supplies at build-out, demonstrating, for example, that full build-out would result in a statewide deficit in public water supplies of 241 million gallons per day.

Participants also looked at maps of the resources that were present and at maps projecting how those resources would change in the future. The participants then took part in a vision mapping exercise focused on creating a map of both green and gray infrastructure. In the final step of the workshop exercise, participants discussed the various options and funding programs that might help to achieve the future vision. Project leaders encouraged the use of these maps to create community development plans. Staff also organized five regional "super summits" to encourage analysis of growth issues at a regional level. The momentum generated through the summits was used to encourage passage of local community preservation funding initiatives.

THE MAPS

Central to mapping charrettes are the maps. Mapmaking requires researching and compiling information on the landscapes and the associated native and nonnative features. If GIS is used, digital databases on ecological and human-dominated landscape features are compiled, converted to the same format, trimmed to fit the area of focus, and categorized using selected criteria. The data layers are stored electronically and can be viewed by the charrette participants on a computer terminal or as hard-copy printouts. Data layers and analysis outputs used in the initial network design process can also be used in community visioning charrettes or workshops.

Base maps and overlays can also be created by hand. The base map should depict the entire geographic area to be considered during the mapping charrette, and usually will include political and administrative boundaries as well as major geographic features. Map scale is an important consideration, the advantages afforded by having more detail with a large-scale map will need to be balanced with convenience and manageability of a map at a smaller scale.

The next step is to develop overlays, typically using clear drafting film (like Mylar). A separate overlay should be developed for each of the landscape features and criteria to be considered during the mapping charrette. Overlays may present ecological features, physical attributes, and ownership patterns, including data that demonstrate the geographical features that affect growth: steep slopes, wetlands, the built landscape, and conservation restricted lands. The maps should also distinguish the areas that are most (and least) at risk of development. This mapping process enables the community to get a realistic image of the amount, nature, and possible location of future change.

The overlays need to be at the same scale and for the same geographic area as the base map, allowing workshop participants to build the overlays to see a graphic representation of various features and elements. This process can be used to identify relative priorities for land conservation and/or restoration activities and to create a map of green infrastructure hubs and links.

Mapping charrettes can come at almost any stage of the community visioning process. Wyoming Township, a small Minnesota community, used a community values mapping process to help address concerns expressed in visioning sessions conducted from 1998 to 2002: namely, how to manage growth while preserving the township's rural character. As part of its 2003 community visioning process, the township developed a set of maps showing GIS data at township and subwatershed scales to look at current physiographic features, land use, and ecological patterns. Workshop participants broke into four groups to review the maps and to look at the community through four different lenses: natural habitat value, water quality value, social resources value, and development suitability value. When overlaid, these green infrastructure-related layers showed a composite picture that leaders hope to use to help organize and direct the township's growth so that both the best locations for development and for protection are identified.

By its interactive nature, the design process itself can be a useful forum for community discussion about development and change. The findings of Wyoming Township's community visioning process will be used in a second phase in which local citizens will visualize alternative development scenarios to determine a preferred scenario. They will also identify design principles to guide future land-use

Box 8.4

Healing Waters Retreat, Cacapon and Lost Rivers Land Trust

Quite often, land trusts respond to requests for conservation easements from individual landowners rather than actively seeking out lands with the highest resource values. This approach typically results in individual, scattered easements rather than the conservation of large, contiguous areas that tend to provide superior ecological benefits. The Cacapon and Lost Rivers Land Trust, which is dedicated to preserving land in the largely rural eastern panhandle of West Virginia, sought to address this problem.

To initiate a shift toward strategic conservation, the Land Trust, with the help of staff from the Canaan Valley Institute (CVI) and the National Park Service's Rivers, Trails, and Conservation Assistance Program, assembled resource experts and conservation professionals, along with local residents and stakeholders, for a workshop called the Healing Waters Retreat. The Land Trust organized participants into groups to focus on the four resource categories specifically referenced in its mission statement: forest ecology, water quality, farmland, and rural heritage. Each group was asked to delineate priority lands in its category by defining protection goals, developing criteria to identify important areas, and weighting the relative importance of each criterion.

The process was greatly enhanced with results from a pre-meeting survey of participants regarding the criteria they believed to be important in targeting lands for conservation. These criteria were then used by CVI staff to prepare thematic reference maps (e.g., land cover, topography, row crops on prime agricultural soils, forested floodplains, large tracts of forested lands, and lands with high conservation value) to familiarize participants with the region.

This workgroup exercise resulted in a series of maps depicting high-priority lands for each of the four resource categories, along with a fifth map illustrating the aggregate of all high-priority resource lands. Participants also mapped special places and other known watershed features, identified locally viable conservation practices and implementation techniques, and various initiatives to advance land conservation throughout the watershed.

Following the Retreat, an Implementation Workgroup was organized to establish a decision-making process to aid the Land Trust in targeting conservation throughout the watershed, to develop one or more focused conservation initiatives, and to identify tools and potential funding sources for implementing each initiative. On behalf of the Land Trust, CVI funded West Virginia University staff to develop a GIS-based decision support system to identify those parcels that encompass priority lands delineated in the mapping workshop. Land Trust staff used this decision system, which resides on a laptop computer, daily to make decisions about conservation easements and restoration activities.

Since the Retreat, the Land Trust staff has been using the decision support system to evaluate the relative resource values of parcels whose owners wish to donate conservation easements as well as to target priority landowners through workshops and educational forums. By providing local leaders with a factual and objective assessment of the region's resources, the Retreat helped the trust move toward a more strategic approach to conservation in which the top resource priority lands are given priority for protection. This approach also assures that more informed and balanced land conservation decisions will be made in the future. In the three years since the Retreat, the Land Trust has successfully established a forestlands protection program and a farmland preservation initiative and has negotiated conservation easements on more than 7,500 acres of land.

policies. The final phase will translate the preferred development scenario, design principles, and community values into new language for the Township's Comprehensive Plan and Zoning Ordinance.

Planning and Conducting Visioning

The success of any community visioning process—whether a broad effort that includes many communitywide workshops or a more targeted mapping charrette for the leaders of or participants in a green infrastructure effort—requires understanding the overriding purpose and tailoring the event to accomplish this purpose. At what point(s) in the visioning process workshops will be held, what types of information will be requested of citizens during these workshops, and how the results will be used are important considerations. These choices are followed by logistical decisions about when and where workshops will take place and who will be invited. Visioning workshops and mapping charrettes both offer an opportunity to seek out a diversity of opinions and expertise.

Depending on the nature of the issues or concerns prompting the visioning process and the purpose visioning is designed to accomplish, different groups may take the lead. Sometimes, a local government spearheads a visioning effort as part of its planning process. In other cases, citizens take the lead through an established community group or coalition of groups. For example, Jackson Hole, Wyoming's visioning workshop was sponsored by forty-seven different organizations, from

Box 8.5

Tips for a Successful Visioning Workshop

As you plan for your visioning workshop, consider the following suggestions:

- **Use a facilitator.** An experienced facilitator is critical to keeping a group on track as it moves through the process. Effective facilitation is needed to ensure that all participants have an opportunity to express their views, to resolve conflicts and differences in perspective in a mutually satisfactory manner, and to ensure that the final product is a true representation of the consensus of the group, rather than its most vocal constituents.

- **Invite a wide range of stakeholders.** Broad-based participation is critical. The visioning workshop should welcome any and all interested persons and seek out underrepresented segments of the community.

- **Have clear expectations.** Clarify your expectations prior to the workshop and make sure to repeat them at the beginning of the first day.

- **Keep the group manageable.** The group must be large enough to represent the community but small enough so that everyone can be heard. Breaking into small groups also enables people to have a voice. If there is considerable interest in the community, you may need to have more than one workshop.

- **Plan the workshop(s) at a convenient time.** If you are tapping volunteers, evenings or weekends are usually a better option than during the week; if you are engaging experts for a mapping charrette, it may be preferable to do this during regular work hours. If you are holding more than one workshop, plan them at different times to encourage the attendance of a broad range of people.

- **Plan ahead.** Make sure the people you have invited have time to prepare. Send information ahead that describes what you hope to accomplish and the process you will use to reach a shared vision.

- **Prepare small groups for their roles.** Make sure you have recorders and resource people for each small group. Some visioning charrettes provide a brief orientation or training session for small-group facilitators.

environmental organizations to the chamber of commerce. Participants credit the success of Jackson Hole's endeavor to the fact that the impetus came from the community.

Following a visioning workshop or mapping charrette, a report of findings should be widely disseminated. The final report should include a summary of the environmental, economic, and social resources and will serve as a public statement on the community values for conservation and development and how the citizenry wishes to guide the rate, type, intensity, and location of development. The local newspaper, a flyer or poster, and/or other communication venues can be used to publicize results, discuss next steps, and solicit volunteer involvement. A final report not only captures the findings for future reference, it also helps to reinforce a sense of partnership and common ground.

GREEN INFRASTRUCTURE IN ACTION: SAGINAW BAY GREENWAYS COLLABORATIVE, MICHIGAN

The mid-Michigan region—encompassing Saginaw, Bay, and Midland counties—is known for its tremendous natural beauty. The area boasts scenic lakeshores and sparkling rivers, lush forests and rich farmland. Despite decades of population growth and development pressures, approximately 50 percent of the land in the three counties is agricultural working lands. In addition, the area is blessed with a national wildlife refuge, a state forest, and one of the largest intact coastal wetlands in the Great Lakes region. The Saginaw Bay Watershed is home to more than 138 endangered or threatened species.

The residents of the tri-county region had great respect for the land and an interest in preserving it. But growth was coming to Michigan. At the turn of the twenty-first century, land in the state was being developed at a rate that was eight times faster than the rate of population growth, and the rate in Bay County exceeded the state average by 27 percent. Saginaw County was the most heavily influenced by human-centered development, which had left little outside of currently owned state and federal land in a naturally functioning state. In 2001, the Michigan Land Resource Project predicted that if current land-use patterns continued, the state's built or developed areas would increase by 178 percent by the year 2040.

In 1998, representatives of more than two dozen agencies and organizations met to explore the potential of a nonmotorized trail network in Bay, Midland, and Saginaw counties. The result was the Tri-County Trail Guide, which identified thirty-three existing parks, nature preserves, state and national wildlife refuges, and trails in the region. Over time, the focus of the initiative transitioned from an emphasis on recreational trails to greenways to green infrastructure, forming the framework for a more proactive and holistic approach to conserving the area's ecological resources, as well as its recreational resources.

From Trails to Greenways

The Saginaw Bay Greenways Collaborative (the Collaborative) formed in 1999 to develop a plan "to connect communities to the area's natural and cultural amenities for the benefits of recreation, transportation, education, health, and well-being of its citizens." The Collaborative is a voluntary association with representatives from national, state, and local governments, nonprofit organizations, and concerned citizens.

The Dow Chemical Company started the Saginaw Bay Watershed Initiative Network (WIN) to fund sustainable development projects. The Conservation Fund administers the program. Members of the initial planning group brought in staff of the National Park Service's Rivers, Trails, and Conservation Assistance Program (RTCA), which was already working on similar regional greenways initiatives in Michigan, to serve as the project facilitator. RTCA staff worked with the Collaborative to develop a public planning process, a public education plan, and a work plan for the project and helped facilitate public meetings and the greenways charrette.

Fed by previous Saginaw Bay Watershed and sustainable development initiatives and by the people's genuine love for the community and its heritage, the greenways project soon evolved from a regional greenways planning effort to planning a regional green infrastructure network that could be used to strategically direct and influence development and conservation initiatives.

The Collaborative used a scientific and community-based approach to identify land best suited for conservation and recreation throughout Bay, Midland, and Saginaw counties. Extensive tracts of the Au Sable State Forest in Midland County form the largest land-based hub in the three counties. Saginaw Bay and remnants of coastal wetlands on its edge form another important hub. The Shiawassee National Wildlife Refuge and the adjoining Shiawassee River State Game Area form the third major hub for the region. Most of the green infrastructure links identified by the Saginaw Bay Greenways Plan follow the network of rivers that flow into the bay.

A Science- and Community-Based Approach

The Collaborative based its greenways and green infrastructure planning process on three key elements: (1) a thorough resource inventory and analysis of the project area, based on the most accurate and current information available; (2) public input from diverse stakeholders in the identification and development of a green infrastructure vision; and (3) public outreach to inform citizens about the project and the benefits of greenways and green infrastructure and to build support for implementation.

The planning process was facilitated by RTCA and was guided by a steering committee, with representatives from WIN, the Saginaw County Metropolitan Planning Commission, Ducks Unlimited, Bay County Department of Environmental Affairs, East Central Michigan Planning and Development Region, Little Forks Conservancy, Saginaw Basin Land Conservancy, Bay Area Community Foundation, The Conservation Fund, and others. The Collaborative also set up a thirty-member technical advisory committee responsible for ensuring

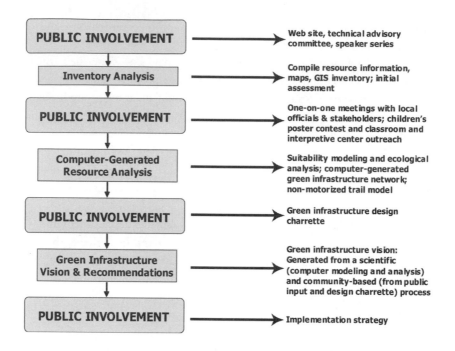

Figure 8.3
Engaging the public was a priority of the Saginaw Bay Greenways Collaborative in the state of Michigan. Shown here is the organization's plan for public involvement steps and outcomes. Credit: Saginaw Bay Greenways Collaborative.

that the resource inventory criteria, methods, and data used in the GIS analysis were scientifically correct. Several members of this committee contributed valuable GIS data to the effort, which helped to reduce duplication.

From the beginning, public outreach and involvement were priorities. The first undertaking of the Collaborative was a speaker series designed to generate media coverage and excitement about the idea of a greenways plan. The Collaborative also developed a Web site (www.saginawbaygreenways.org) and a brochure, made presentations, conducted television and radio spots, and staffed an educational display at various community events.

The Collaborative met one-on-one with more than fifty local officials and land managers in the three-county region to provide an overview of the project; identify important social, cultural, historic, and environmental resources; and verify inventory and mapping data. At these meetings, leaders of the Collaborative emphasized that growth was not bad—it was in fact inevitable and advocated planning for growth and conservation. The Collaborative later indicated that these meetings were crucial in getting local stakeholders to buy into the concept of a regional green infrastructure system.

Collaborative members also introduced teachers and students to the greenways concept through programs at the Saginaw Bay Visitor Center and through classroom visits. More than 150 elementary and middle school students submitted artwork for a poster contest based on the theme, "Greenways in our Community." The winning drawings were featured in a poster called "It's Great to Be Green."

The biggest public involvement event was the Saginaw Bay Greenways Charrette, a day-long event that attracted over a hundred community participants. The morning was spent learning about the values and principles of green infrastructure and the basic components of a green infrastructure network. During the second half of the day, participants worked in teams using acetate overlays of the resource assessment data layers, base maps, and aerial photos to develop and present their own versions of a green infrastructure network for the region. The designs from each of the nine charrette work groups, along with the computer-generated models, were evaluated and consolidated into a green infrastructure design for each county. The county designs were then assembled and assessed to create a "Vision of Green."

In comparing the computer-generated analysis and design with the analysis and design from the work groups, the results were strikingly similar. The benefits of the charrette extended beyond reinforcing the information in the computerized inventory and database, however. As citizens contributed their intimate knowledge of the community and its landscapes, they also added a human perspective and set priorities. The involvement of stakeholders encouraged a participatory environment that blurred the boundaries between public and private, between community planners and the community, fostering community support and buy-in.

Figure 8.4
One of the posters submitted by elementary and middle school students for the Greenways in our Community contest sponsored by the Saginaw Bay Greenways Collaborative. Credit: Saginaw Bay Greenways Collaborative.

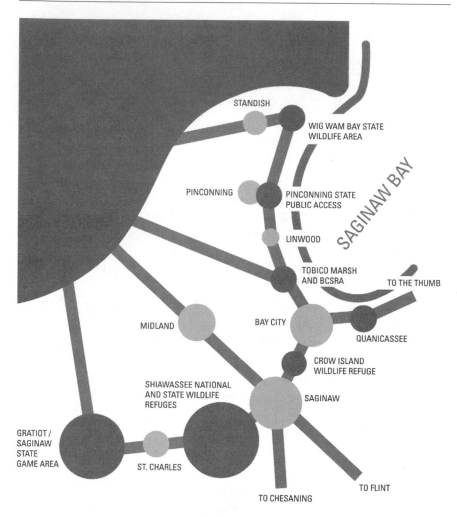

Figure 8.5
Schematic of a green infrastructure network for the Saginaw Bay region
(green infrastructure hubs and links in black, the region's cities in gray).
Credit: Saginaw Bay Greenways Collaborative.

Results

The Collaborative developed a visionary green infrastructure network design and
resource assessment that incorporated sound scientific findings with public input.
As stakeholders were involved, they not only informed the decision-making
process but changed the very nature of the project—from one based on recreational
trails to one that encompassed a larger green infrastructure vision. Program
advocates are optimistic that the plan will stimulate projects to protect, restore,
and manage the area's green infrastructure resources.

The work of the collaborative got people thinking and talking on a regional basis. As Michigan's first green infrastructure project, the Saginaw Bay initiative is helping to market green infrastructure benefits throughout the region and the state. The project leaders are also hopeful that the project will serve as a model for green infrastructure design and planning in other Michigan communities.

Box 8.6

Educating the Public about Green Infrastructure Benefits

The Saginaw Bay Greenways Collaborative's educational materials note that green infrastructure provides the following benefits to the Saginaw Bay region:

Ecological
- Provides connections to maintain biodiversity
- Filters pollutants from air, water, and soil
- Aids in cooling streams and soils through shading
- Protects and enhances the water quality of rivers and lakes
- Recharges groundwater aquifers
- Buffers developed areas from floodwaters, saving lives and property
- Protects water resources such as riparian corridors and aquifer recharge areas

Economic
- Increases property taxes and residential values because properties near and adjacent to green infrastructure often increase in value and generate greater overall revenue
- Encourages corporate relocation to an area by increasing quality of life
- Increases tourism and new business generation, such as bed and breakfasts, rental facilities, restaurants, and art galleries
- Attracts environmentally sensitive development

Social
- Provides an alternative to crime and drugs
- Increases socialization and celebrates diversity
- Improves human health and eases mental fatigue
- Ensures access for urban residents to large green spaces
- Enhances local residents' sense of connection with nature and to each other
- Expands opportunities for recreation

Already, a group of Michigan counties has obtained funding to initiate a green infrastructure network design for the Titibawasee River corridor. Organizers of the Collaborative hope that these and other efforts in Michigan can eventually be linked.

The Collaborative has done a remarkable job of blending the interests of local, state, and federal agencies, nonprofit organizations, and concerned citizens united around the goal of developing a green infrastructure system in Saginaw, Bay, and Midland counties. The Collaborative created a vision for a green infrastructure network by using a scientific and community participation approach to identify land best suited for conservation and recreation throughout the Saginaw Bay region. The Collaborative then identified and mapped important green infrastructure elements (hubs, corridors, links) across the tri-county region and is making this information available to municipal leaders and decision makers to include in pertinent land-use plans at all scales and jurisdictions. The project began with a focus on transportation, recreation, and human interaction with natural areas, but gradually evolved to include a focus on protecting ecosystems and water resources and decreasing habitat fragmentation. By enabling the initiative to grow as people became more comfortable with resource conservation and protection concepts, the Collaborative proved that the flexibility a green infrastructure approach provides can be a powerful tool.

• *For more information about the Saginaw Bay Greenways Collaborative, visit www.saginawbaygreenways.org.*

Notes

1. Robert Putnam discussed his research findings on social capital in "Bowling Alone: America's Declining Social Capital," *Journal of Democracy* (6:1), 65–78. For more information, see also Robert D. Putnam, *Bowling Alone: The Collapse and Revival of American Community* (New York: Simon and Schuster, 2000).

2. More information about Fluvanna's visioning process and plans can be found at the Fluvanna Heritage Web site, www.fluvannaheritage.org.

chapter nine

Making It Happen

G reen infrastructure requires foresight, political will, and sustained effort on the part of a state, region, or community to change the way conservation and land-use planning are undertaken. But savvy states and localities are starting to recognize the benefits of focusing strategically on land use. Communities are coming together to create a vision for the future—a vision that is based on preserving what is most important to the residents who live there—and identify strategies for making this vision a reality. Green infrastructure should be at the heart of these efforts.

To make sure your work does not simply become a map in the file drawer and a plan on the bookshelf, you cannot stop after you have a green infrastructure design and an implementation plan. You must work in an ongoing fashion to ensure that the design and plan are adopted, incorporated, and used in a diversity of programs and delivery platforms. This requires incorporating your plans into community plans and seeking out programs that are in place that will support your initiative.

INTEGRATING GREEN INFRASTRUCTURE INTO THE PLANNING PROCESS

Governments of all sizes—states, counties, cities, townships, and regional entities—engage in planning. Most public planning focuses on gray infrastructure and takes place at all scales: neighborhood, city, county, regional, state, and even the federal level, as in our system of interstate highways. Just as there are opportunities to plan for gray infrastructure at every scale, there is an opportunity to plan for green infrastructure at every scale.

State and federal agencies, for example, have planning processes that could be aligned with green infrastructure goals. Public land management agencies each have their own planning processes that could facilitate green infrastructure goals. States are sometimes required to complete various types of plans as a requirement for federal funding. The State and Tribal Wildlife Grants Program established in 2001, for example, required states to develop a comprehensive wildlife plan by October 2005 in order to be eligible for funding. The plans were to address the "species of greatest conservation needs" and the "full array of wildlife and wildlife issues." This is just one of many opportunities to integrate green infrastructure into a broader statewide planning effort.

At the local level, green infrastructure planning can fit in many places—a revision to a local comprehensive plan, passage of the annual budget, a new transportation plan, a community visioning process, a new zoning ordinance, or subdivision regulations. These planning efforts can serve as a forum for green infrastructure advocates to introduce the network design, the implementation plan, the management plan, or other key outputs of the green infrastructure planning and implementation process. Where the government has not been an active supporter of green infrastructure, the leadership group must make a concerted effort to educate elected officials and citizen planning board members about the benefits of green infrastructure and how a green space network can help the community. On the other hand, green infrastructure initiatives sometimes come out of these planning processes. A comprehensive plan update, for example, may lead to the creation of a citizen advisory committee to explore the possibility of developing a green infrastructure network.

Most local governments have comprehensive plans—sometimes called a general or master plan—that describe a community's goals and priorities. The comprehensive plan is used to develop zoning and land-use regulations. In addition, local governments engage in short-range planning in conjunction with the annual budget cycle. Green infrastructure should be integrated into all these phases of the planning process. Since comprehensive plans are updated rather infrequently, green infrastructure should also be considered in short-term and project planning efforts, including zoning changes and amendments; review and approval of subdivisions with respect to stormwater retention areas, walking paths, density transfer, and open space dedication; GIS databases and maps; parks and recreation planning; upgrades to or extension of roads and other gray infrastructure; capital improvement planning, including the development of schools, public buildings, corridor and drainage projects, recreational facilities, and other public infrastructure; heritage, farmland, and open space protection efforts; watershed planning; and smart growth, urban revitalization, and other initiatives seeking to guide the pattern of growth or development.

Green infrastructure can become part of a community's day-to-day planning process in many ways. For example, some communities build bike trails on top of new water lines. Others use highway mitigation funds to buy green space. Still others manage natural gas pipeline rights-of-way as wildlife movement corridors. Planning green infrastructure in conjunction with transportation corridors also provides an opportunity to maximize the use of scarce resources—both money and land. Integrated planning and design connects green and gray infrastructure in a more cost-effective and workable network.

In addition to traditional community planning efforts, there are many programs that can support a green infrastructure effort. Flood protection projects, floodways, floodplains, and adjacent wetlands are ideal starting places to begin assembling a green infrastructure network. In most urban areas, flood protection and stormwater management are accomplished by building a vast network of underground storm sewers and detention ponds or levees—solutions that are not only costly to construct but have substantial ongoing maintenance needs. Flood protection thus presents a major opportunity for the development of green infrastructure. Keeping residential and commercial development out of flood zones can not only save the public money by reducing storm damage, but it can also filter runoff and trap pollutants, provide critical habitat for wildlife, and provide land for green infrastructure corridors.

Milwaukee, Wisconsin, for example, is using stormwater management as a tool for creating green infrastructure. Responding to studies that indicated that demographic trends will intensify local flooding, the Milwaukee Metropolitan Sewerage District (MMSD) is implementing a Conservation Plan to complement traditional stormwater management techniques. The Conservation Plan identifies undeveloped private properties that are potentially at risk for development and that could provide future flood prevention benefits. The MMSD, which provides wastewater treatment and flood management services to 1.2 million people in twenty-eight southeastern Wisconsin communities, is working with The Conservation Fund to contact landowners in the forty-two highest priority sites to determine whether they are willing to sell a conservation easement on their land or sell their property outright. MMSD will partner with local governments and/or land trusts to provide management on the properties that are acquired under this program.

Greenway planning is also a viable starting point for a green infrastructure initiative, and the linkages of a green infrastructure network often include greenway

Box 9.1

Integrating Green Infrastructure into Community Planning

Just as gray infrastructure planning is linked together at different levels of government, so should green infrastructure be. Just as city streets connect to county and state roads, and then to our system of interstate highways, so could local parks connect to a county or regional park system tied together by trails and greenways. Like gray infrastructure, green infrastructure should be an integral part of the community's land-use planning process. Green infrastructure can become part of a community's day-to-day planning process in myriad ways. Here are just a few suggestions:

- Provide land for passive recreation opportunities as part of the parks and recreation department's goals.
- Change subdivision development policies to protect and connect green space and provide for sound water management practices that depend primarily on natural functions of the land.
- Encourage and facilitate conservation or cluster development.
- Link green infrastructure and watershed planning. Just as watershed planning looks at ecosystem boundaries rather than political boundaries, so too green infrastructure focuses beyond jurisdictional boundaries.
- Incorporate green infrastructure principles into heritage development and historic preservation efforts.
- Encourage the dedication of existing easements for open space as green infrastructure.
- Incorporate green infrastructure principles into community revitalization, brownfields redevelopment, and other development initiatives.
- "Borrow" green infrastructure from highway or stormwater rights-of-way. The restructuring of utilities may result in changes in land ownership that provide a unique opportunity for obtaining lands that could be used as green infrastructure corridors.

components such as bike paths, trails, or parkways. In fact, many green infrastructure efforts have begun as efforts to create walking paths or recreational trails. These efforts often expand to include conservation corridors and then to focus on the protection and restoration of water flows or other ecological functions. This is a logical progression that many communities go through before reaching green infrastructure as the ultimate goal. The Saginaw Bay, Michigan, initiative, for example, began as an effort to design a recreational trail system. The project soon evolved into a greenways approach. Currently, Saginaw Bay is focused on adding ecological values to its network, making it consistent with the principles of green infrastructure. In communities that already have greenways plans in place, five- or ten-year plan reviews or updates could offer a tremendous opportunity to incorporate into the plan green infrastructure principles and ecological elements.

In the past decade, conservation development that sets aside natural lands has become a common approach to planning walkable communities with ample green space. Homebuyers have proven that they are willing to pay for green space, and developers are responding by incorporating green space into their subdivision plans. Recent studies have also shown that conservation development, in contrast to dispersed development, can reduce the impact of development on wildlife habitat.

Box 9.2

ArborLinks Golf Course

Golf courses are not always antithetical to green infrastructure. Many golf course designers are working with environmentalists and landscapers to make their courses part of a healthy, functioning landscape, which may be an optimal solution in communities that want golf courses rather than nature areas.

The Arnold-Palmer designed ArborLinks Golf Course in Nebraska City is an example of how conservation, natural beauty, and the challenge of an eighteen-hole championship golf course can be combined. Built and managed by Landscapes Unlimited, of Lincoln, Nebraska, in cooperation with The National Arbor Day Foundation, ArborLinks is setting the standard in environmental sensitivity, both in its construction and ongoing operation. The 320-acre course was built on wooded hills and old cornfields northwest of Arbor Day Farm. Each of ArborLink's eighteen holes tells a conservation story, ranging from "Black Cherry Row" for the first hole, demonstrating field windbreaks and their value, to hole eighteen, "Cottonwood Creek," which illustrates the use of bioengineering in restoring and protecting the banks of South Table Creek.

The course was designed with environmental principles in mind. Narrow fairways and wild rough of native grasses will require less fertilizer and pesticide use. During construction, existing trees were spared wherever possible, and many new trees have been planted. Wildlife protection and compatibility have also been important concerns; areas not in play are preserved as wildlife sanctuaries.

Source: ArborLinks Golf Course Web site, www.arbordayfarm.org/arborlinks.html.

Clustering decreases fragmentation and perforation of habitat due to roads and houses, leaving the remainder of the landscape in a condition more suitable for wildlife that is sensitive to human contact.[1] Conservation development not only protects green space and natural systems, but also encourages residents to consider how to plan for a community that includes ample space and how open space preservation relates to development. In doing so, conservation development helps further the goals of green infrastructure.

In effective conservation development, developers divide the land according to how appropriate it is for development, planning the open space before the developed land uses. Conservation subdivision planning identifies and protects the most desirable green or open space in order to connect that space within and beyond the subdivision, and to protect, restore, and use natural processes such as water flow. Integrating green space with development clusters and setting aside the most appropriate land as open space not only reduces the amount of impervious surfaces but also enhances the ability of nature to perform its functions.

Communities can support green infrastructure principles by eliminating common obstacles to conservation development, such as lot size minimums, by sharing knowledge about successful and profitable examples of conservation developments elsewhere, and by offering incentives, advice, and support to developers interested in applying conservation planning principles to new developments.

Figure 9.1
With five miles of trails and wide expanses set aside for open space, the conservation development of Cooke's Hope in Easton, Maryland, offers a pastoral setting and recreational opportunities for residents, habitat for plants and animals, and attractive views and natural amenities to adjacent neighborhoods. Credit: Ed McMahon.

FROM GRAY TO GREEN

If incorporating green infrastructure in new development is a challenge, retrofitting green infrastructure in areas that are already built may seem next to impossible. Some communities, however, have been successful in reclaiming vacant lots as open space and abandoned rights-of-way as corridors. Even if these lands are not physically connected with the green infrastructure network, they can play an important role in the environmental, social, and economic health of a community and may make it easier to identify other land that should be set aside for its conservation value. A revitalization project's chances for success are greatly increased by the inclusion of green and open space.

There are several ways to increase the amount of green space in a community renewal or development project. Communities can encourage in-fill development; in addition to protecting isolated green patches within an urban environment, conservationists can work with community leaders to protect lands beyond the urban setting that may serve as hubs or links in a conservation network. Providing incentives for developers to select land in already developed areas can help protect lands in more rural settings.

The Parramore Greenprint Program in Orlando, Florida, is one example of how a community has incorporated land use, the desire for open space, and the use of natural systems (in this case for stormwater management) into redevelopment plans. The Parramore Heritage Neighborhood, an historically African-American neighborhood on the western edge of downtown Orlando, faced many problems, including incompatible land uses, the need for more recreational facilities, a dearth of parkland, and the lack of a comprehensive stormwater system. The city of Orlando included an element in its 2000 plan to address Parramore's needs in these areas by calling for the development of a master stormwater management system that would handle current and future development runoff and attenuation, incorporating stormwater retention facilities into park facilities to create new green space, and establishing incentives to encourage new development and compatible land uses adjacent to green spaces.

Brownfield redevelopment may be an overlooked opportunity for integrating green infrastructure into an urban landscape. Although highly contaminated sites may be unsuitable for redevelopment as parks or open space, many brownfields have low levels of contamination that can be easily mitigated. Portland, Oregon's Greenway in the North Macadam Urban Renewal Area, for example, included the rehabilitation of industrial land near the Willamette River to serve as parkland and open space. The project restored natural conditions along the bank and on adjacent uplands, integrated stormwater flows with the natural and built environment, protected linear wildlife corridors, and provided access to the water's edge in a way that supports the natural resource and accommodates human activity.

Another brownfield redevelopment project that is part of a broader green infrastructure effort is Emscher Park in the Ruhr Valley of Germany. Once

Germany's industrial heartland, the Ruhr Valley was badly degraded. Its rivers were polluted, and the main features of the landscape were large industrial buildings and slag heaps the size of small mountains. In 1989, the state of North Rhine-Westphalia initiated a project to revitalize the region's economy and environment. Clean-up of the Emscher River, which, with its tributaries, flows for about 218 miles, provided a common focus for seventeen local authorities in an area of approximately 200 square miles. Using ecology as the central organizing focus, the project aimed to turn industrial wastelands into a regional park system with seven green corridors connecting the parks. The result—the largest renaturalization project in Europe—was innovative in its regional, rather than site-specific, approach to brownfield restoration. The open space at the heart of the network comprises former industrial sites, their connecting transportation system, and the old slag heaps. Thematic driving and biking routes help to create and improve green infrastructure, provide recreational opportunities, appeal to tourists, and increase the understanding of and respect for the region's heritage.

Abandoned railroad lines and utility rights-of-way can sometimes be converted to trail systems linking people to larger tracts of the green infrastructure network. These multipurpose trails can also serve as alternative transportation routes, linking commercial and residential areas and thereby reducing a community's dependence on automobile travel.

Retrofitting gray infrastructure requires looking at the larger landscape. In some places, highways have cut off important wildlife migration routes—the routes animals use to move across the landscape and that are needed for wildlife populations to remain healthy. Fences, a solution to reduce the deadly collision of cars and animals, aggravate habitat fragmentation. Some transportation planners are working with wildlife biologists and conservationists to find solutions that benefits both motorists and animals. A wildlife underpass or overpass is one solution. In Canada's Banff National Park, for example, several wildlife crossing structures were installed under and over the TransCanada Highway as part of an ongoing attempt to mitigate habitat fragmentation. The most notable of these structures are two fifty-meter-wide wildlife overpasses that allow animals to safely cross the TransCanada Highway between the town of Banff and Castle Junction, but twenty-one less visible underpasses are also in place. The structures vary from small culverts, suitable for rodents and reptiles, to open-span underpasses, to creek bridges, to the two wide overpasses.[2]

In the Critter Control Project, a pilot project funded by the Orton Family Foundation, students at Hayden Valley Elementary School in northwestern Colorado produced a map of road-kill patterns along U.S. Highway 40 to pinpoint wildlife-crossing trouble spots. The results are being used to help state officials decide where to place new signs, as well as devices that emit high-pitch sounds to scare off wildlife. In the Santa Monica Mountains, less than twenty miles from downtown Los Angeles, wildlife advocates and land managers are considering building an underpass that would enable mountain lions to safely cross Interstate 101 at Liberty Canyon, one of fifteen critical biological linkage sites identified by a coalition of two hundred land managers and conservation ecologists. At about one hundred feet long, Liberty Canyon is considered the mountain lions' best chance to cross the freeway because it is the only area with undeveloped wildlands on both sides. Planners recently scrapped plans for development at the Coal Canyon exit of Highway 92 near San Diego, after scientists realized that a mountain lion was using the underpass to get to the other side of the freeway and move between suitable parts of his habitat. The underpass is now protected as a wildlife corridor and is being restored to its natural state. Advocates believe that the underpasses will provide an important way for animals to travel from one location to another, maintaining the gene pool needed to sustain healthy populations.

The Wyoming Department of Transportation has explored the possibility of using overpasses to facilitate the movement of pronghorn antelope across highways and has tested an underpass for the pronghorns. The antelope shows the complexity of planning for wildlife, however. Because the pronghorns rely on eyesight to detect predators, it is thought they will generally resist using underpasses; the fences needed for overhead passes are dangerous for antelope because they can get caught in fences during blizzards.

To maximize the use and benefits of wildlife corridors, wildlife crossings should be located within movement corridors where quality habitat exists. Wildlife crossings also must be numerous enough to serve entire populations of a species and must provide the mix of cover and openness that various species desire. Burying or elevating sections of the highway and providing at-grade crossings for wildlife can also help facilitate the movement of many species.[3] Although these wildlife crossings cannot restore the freedom that animals have before a highway is built, incorporating the need for wildlife corridors into a transportation plan can facilitate the survival of a species.

SELLING GREEN INFRASTRUCTURE

Building support for a green infrastructure effort relies on effective public education and citizen engagement. First, you need to sell the benefits of green space. Then, you need to explain why an interconnected system of green space is better than isolated parks or natural assets. A good way to start is to gather data on how many acres of land are being converted to development each year. Such data can document the loss and degradation of important resource features and values and can demonstrate the need to change the pattern of development.

One way to illustrate this is through a *change detection analysis*. Aerial photographs or satellite images of selected areas over a period of time—for example,

1975, 1985, 1995, 2005—can be used to calculate and demonstrate changes in land use. The result is a visual picture of the loss of valuable landscapes and features and the increase in developed or altered lands. It is also possible to generate a computer analysis of the change in native habitats over time, highlighting which are the most vulnerable to future development. In addition, professionals can conduct surveys on wildlife population size, changes, and viability to detect "problems." For example, The Nature Conservancy conducts natural areas inventories to identify threatened species and habitats. The need for a better approach to conservation and development might also be demonstrated through data on water quality, chemical levels in marine life, or other indicators that reflect the health of natural systems. Such data, presented in an easily understandable graphic and/or text format, can be quite useful in selling the need for green infrastructure. The BioMap Program in Massachusetts, for example, portrays complex data in a way that is easy for the average citizen to understand. Program leaders identified critical natural areas and then created maps to show projections of what areas would look like if current trends continued.

It is important for citizens to understand that open space can provide more in revenue than it costs in services. A fiscal impact analysis can demonstrate the costs to taxpayers of various types of land uses. Cost of Community Services (COCS) studies, pioneered by the American Farmland Trust, for example, can help a community assess future tax liabilities for different types of land uses. These studies demonstrate the economic advantages to a community of preserving green space and working lands. A recent COCS study in Bandera County, Texas, for example, revealed that ranch and open land generates almost four times more dollars for the county than what they require in county services (i.e., for every $1 generated by ranch and open land from property taxes, sales taxes, and other revenues, they demand only $0.26 in services). Conversely, although residential land contributes the largest amount of revenue to the county, its net fiscal impact is negative; residential development in Bandera County requires $1.10 in services for every tax dollar it generates.

In Loudoun County, Virginia, costs to service one thousand new development units exceeded their tax contribution by as much as $2.3 million. Marshall Township, Michigan, also learned that it was losing money by converting working lands into residential developments. Its COCS study found that for every $1 in revenue generated by residential development, $1.47 was required in public services. For every $1 generated by farms and open land, on the other hand, only $0.27 was required for associated services, and for every $1 of revenue from commercial/industrial uses, $0.20 was spent in services. Studies in DuPage County, Illinois, and Morris County, New Jersey, suggest that even commercial development may fail to pay its own way. In addition to making its own demands on community resources, commercial development can attract costly residential sprawl.

In Bucks County, Pennsylvania, a similar study focused on the costs of schools. The study looked at the school district costs associated with developing a hypo-

Box 9.3

The Cost of Community Services Study

Cost of Community Services (COCS) studies are becoming a common approach to evaluating fiscal impacts of local development. These studies examine a community's overall balance of revenues and expenditures at any given point in time and attempt to determine the proportion of municipal revenues and expenditures attributed to major categories of land use (residential; commercial and industrial; farmland, forest, and open land). For example, the costs of a parks and recreation program would be classified as costs of residential development; the costs of roads would be allocated across all types of development; local expenditures on the farm services agency would be assumed to be benefiting farm and forestland. The resulting totals for revenues generated and expenditures incurred can be presented as a ratio of expenditures-to-revenues for different land-use types.

Over seventy COCS studies have been undertaken nationwide. Results of COCS studies consistently show that for residential land, the cost of service ratio is greater than one—usually between 1.05 and 1.5. In other words, for every dollar generated in revenue from suburban residential development, it costs a community between $1.05 and $1.50 in services. COCS ratios for commercial and industrial properties are typically below one, ranging between $0.30 and $0.65 for every dollar generated. For agricultural land and open space, ratios are even smaller, ranging from $0.10 to $0.15 for every dollar of revenue. COCS studies have concluded that farmland and open space provide more revenue to a community than is incurred in expenditures, resulting in a net fiscal benefit to the community.

• *For more information and examples of findings from COCS, see Clyde F. Kiker and Alan W. Hodges,* Economic Benefits of Natural Land Conservation: Case Study of Northeast Florida, *Gainesville: University of Florida, Food and Resource Economics Department, December 30, 2002.*

thetical 100-acre farm as compared to purchasing the land or a conservation easement. The researchers found that developing a 100-acre farm in the county would result in a $273,834 shortfall per year, whereas the community would break even in 8.5 years if it purchased the land and in 6.2 years if it purchased a conservation easement on the farm (see Table 9.1). The results have been replicated in a number of other communities in and beyond Pennsylvania, where this data has helped to convince elected officials and citizens to initiate local green space protection programs.[4]

Table 9.1

The "100-Acre Farm"—
Public School vs. Preservation Costs

Development of the Farm—Costs to the Community		
Calculate the Public School Costs for the Development		
	100	Acres developed
x	0.66	Dwelling units per acre
	66	New homes
x	$7,526	Public school costs per home
	$496,716	Public school costs for the 66 new homes per year
Calculate the Public School Revenues from the Development		
	66	New homes
x	$3,377	Average school tax revenues per home
	$222,882	Public school revenues for the 66 new homes per year
Calculate the Annual Net Shortfall from the Development		
$222,882 (revenues) − $496,716 (costs) = − $273,834 per year (shortfall)		

Preservation of the Farm—Savings for the Community		
Calculate the Cost to Purchase the Property for Public Use		
	100	Acres purchased
x	$23,303	Average cost per acre for fee simple purchase
	$2,330,300	Purchase price of the farm
Calculate the Break-Even Period		
$2,330,300/$273,834 (shortfall) = 8.5 years break-even period		
Calculate the Cost to Purchase Conservation Easements		
	100	Acres purchased
x	$16,982	Average cost per acre for purchase of easements
	$1,698,200	Purchase price of the easements
Calculate the Break-Even Period		
$1,698,200/$273,834 (shortfall) = 6.2 years break-even period		

Source: Michael Frank, *Opportunity Knocks: Open Space Is a Community Investment*, Doylestown, PA: Heritage Conservancy, 2003, 3.

Alternative Futures

Alternative futures assessments are another common approach. These GIS-based studies use different assumptions to investigate the possible outcomes of current policy options and decisions. An alternative futures assessment provides a compelling framework for visualizing possible future landscapes, leading to more effective planning and better-informed decision making. The approach is flexible and can enable community leaders and policymakers to consider a range of possible future conditions based on the specific concerns of the community or region.

In a scenario-based study of alternative futures, each single policy option either alters a spatially varied characteristic that can attract or repel future development or alters a parameter in one of the several process models that assess the impacts of future change. Choices are made, and the resulting scenarios are used to direct the allocation of future land uses using a model of the process of development. The alternatives are then assessed for their consequences. Using a hypothetical example, three different population projections—one based on present trends, one based on lower-than-forecast growth, and one based on higher-than-forecast growth—and three different building scenarios—one concentrating development in a central area, one allowing it to spread at random, and one creating satellite communities in outlying areas—could be combined to create nine reasonable future scenarios.

The most common alternative futures approach puts forth several alternative plans for future land use and/or land cover and then assesses and compares their potential consequences. The scenarios are often based on different development patterns or political priorities. A more comprehensive approach to alternative futures aims to identify the most important issues responsive to policy and planning decisions, along with the widest range of options pertaining to each issue. The analysis does not look at these decisions independently, but rather as a simultaneous set, so that each decision is considered in the context of others. A scenario is then created to reflect choices among the possible options for each policy in the set.

This latter alternative futures approach was used to help crystallize land use and growth issues in the Upper San Pedro River Basin of southeastern Arizona and northern Sonora, Mexico. This three-year research project examined nine alternatives for land use and evaluated the impact of these scenarios on surface and subsurface water quantity—an issue of primary importance in this area—as well as both direct and indirect impacts on various wildlife species. The outputs of the scientific research were hundreds of maps representing planning scenarios and the resulting water table and species habitat changes.[5]

In addition to providing a means for envisioning how different policies and approaches to land use will affect the future of a community or region, alternative futures can bring together people with very different perspectives and can help citizens articulate and understand their different viewpoints, priorities, and goals. In the San Pedro River Basin, for example, stakeholders include the United States Army based at Fort Huachuca, the copper mining industry, the farming and ranching communities, land developers, residents, and environmental groups. These stakeholders have played a critical role in turning the data generated from alternative futures analyses into action—planning and policymaking. The concerns of these different groups vary widely; alternative futures can help people better understand the trade-offs they are making in choosing one path over another and the consequences of their decisions.

The Willamette Valley, Oregon, Alternative Futures project similarly has contributed to more informed decision making about land and water use in the region. Land allocation modeling identified a shortage of commercially zoned land basinwide, providing an example of the value of large-scale planning. The alternative futures project also stimulated two future related analyses, which relied in part on the initial scenarios and data but assessed different endpoints. The Willamette Valley Livability Forum evaluated alternative transportation futures and effects on traffic congestion, while 1000 Friends of Oregon assessed the implications of landscape futures for infrastructure costs and losses of farm and forestry lands. Alternative futures can be used to show residents what their community would look like if unchecked and unplanned growth and development were allowed and can thus be a valuable tool for building support for green infrastructure.

A number of communities across the United States have also used Community Viz, a software program developed by the Orton Family Foundation, to help evaluate how development will affect everything from infrastructure systems, to endangered species, to the economy. Community Viz, a suite of integrated software tools, uses GIS technology to provide a three-dimensional look at the future. It has been used by communities to support spatial decision making and land-use scenario analysis, as well as to engage citizens in the process of planning for the future. Lyman Orton, a Vermont businessman, described his experience as a planning-board member in the town of Weston as the inspiration for the software project. "When growth occurred, citizens were surprised at the way it happened," he said. "I began to think deeply about how we could better paint a picture of the future and the outcome would be different."[6]

CITYGreen, developed by American Forests, is another GIS-based software tool that communities have used to map urban ecosystems and measure their values. The software can be used to show planners, government officials, and others the benefits of urban forest resources and provides a tool for including trees in community plans.[7] Perhaps more important, the data relating to the loss of trees and their associated benefits can be a powerful tool for helping citizens to understand why preserving green space is important even in urban areas.

Program planners need to clearly demonstrate to the community the benefits of green infrastructure. But the benefits of green infrastructure will differ from place to place. In suburban communities, the discussion might focus on how a green infrastructure plan can help the community avoid sprawl and the associated problems of traffic congestion, declining air quality, and other concerns. Citizens in urban areas might appreciate the mental and physical health benefits of having open space available for passive recreation. Those in areas where the water supply is short might be particularly interested in how green infrastructure can help ensure clean water, while residents in areas prone to flooding might be persuaded by the flood protection afforded by natural systems.

CREATING AND SUSTAINING GREEN INFRASTRUCTURE PARTNERSHIPS

Green infrastructure is not a government program. Nor is it just a conservation NGO program or a land trust's responsibility. Successful green infrastructure programs depend on partnerships—real and lasting relationships between business, government, citizens, and nonprofit organizations.

Building green infrastructure partnerships begins with identifying the stakeholders (e.g., landowners, community organizations, businesses, and government agencies) and learning about what resources—time, expertise, and money—they might be able to contribute. You need to know who should be at the table to carry the project from planning to implementation. Who might be able to help with restoration activities? What organization should take the lead on monitoring the network? Be inclusive. Reach out to homeowner associations, businesses, landowners, and conservation organizations. The key is to establish a network of people who can accomplish your objectives.

The benefits of partnerships are clear. By pooling their efforts, organizations can reduce duplication and accomplish more with the same level of effort. By bringing together people with a variety of experiences and perspectives, partnerships can foster innovative solutions. Partnerships can provide public agencies with support for their legislative or programmatic agenda, by increasing community understanding of agency goals and methods. Organizations report improved morale from involvement with partnerships that increase productivity or otherwise help the organization to fulfill its mission. Partnerships may also improve the public's perception of participants.

People join partnerships to accomplish what they cannot do alone. A partnership that benefits just one party will quickly collapse, but it is important to recognize that different partners often derive different benefits from the same project. For instance, a new greenway can mean habitat to a natural resource agency, corporate stewardship to business, a biodiversity reserve to a conservation group, an outdoor classroom to the school district, and a tourist attraction to the local chamber of commerce. The benefits may differ for each partner, but they should be clearly understood by all.

Although effective partnerships often start informally, lasting collaborative efforts are put in writing. This helps each partner understand the desired outcomes and what resources it is expected to contribute. Each partner must feel vested in the partnership and the issues, problems, and solutions that the partnership has been organized to address. As individuals become part of a team, their self-interest tends to become fused with, or even subservient to, the interests of the project involved. It is at this point that great strides toward the goals of the partnership can be made.

Another key to successful partnerships is letting them grow over time. Successful partnerships recognize that different constituencies have different perspectives. They

Box 9.4

"Do's and Don'ts" of Partnership

Do:

- **Take the initiative**. Talk to people. Think creatively about ways to work with others to achieve common goals.
- **Put ideas in writing for people who may be interested**. Make sure to represent these as ideas rather than an agreement.
- **Set partnership parameters**. Clearly define the objectives of a potential partnership, the resources that each participant would bring to the activity, and the benefits that each stand to gain.
- **Be inclusive**. Early on, involve people whose approval or participation will ultimately be required.
- **Learn about prospective partners**. Be comfortable with their reputations and capabilities before joining the partnership.
- **Be realistic**. Lengthy time periods are often required to initiate and implement a partnership.
- **Investigate alternative strategies for achieving the objective**. Are other avenues or other partners better suited to accomplish the objectives?
- **Focus on the end result.**

Don't:

- Limit the ways you use partnerships to further agency objectives.
- Endorse an external product that will be put up for sale.
- Wait until the last minute to bring in supervisors, public affairs, or agreement specialists to review the contemplated partnership.
- Exceed your authority to solicit partnership funding from private sources.
- Get into turf battles.
- Get frustrated if there are delays. Time periods are estimates only.

Source: Management Institute for Environment and Business, *Conservation Partnerships: A Field Guide to Public-Private Partnering for Natural Resource Conservation*, Washington, D.C.: U.S. Fish and Wildlife Service, 1993.

respect and appreciate the different perspectives each brings to the table. Public/private or public/public collaborative efforts often require people to look at one another with a fresh eye. Clear ground rules for group decision making can require participants to truly listen to one another without prejudice or presumption. It is critical to encourage open and honest communication that identifies and shatters misconceptions. As people work together, they learn about each other, understand each other better, and often trust each other more. A flexible process that allows the partnership to evolve as needed over time enables the partnership to meet the goals of individual partners while working toward joint goals and objectives.

The city of Bellevue, Washington, for example, accomplished multiple objectives by coordinating its stormwater management program with its citywide system of parks. Today two city agencies, the Storm and Surface Water Utility and the Parks and Recreation Department, use the same land to accomplish multiple objectives. The utility bears responsibility for water resources and has a budget for land acquisition. The parks department manages much of the utility's land as parks, ball fields, playgrounds, interpretive areas, and trails. Many of these open space assets are also elements of the stormwater system. As a result of this partnership, both agencies have reduced their costs while achieving their seemingly dissimilar objectives.

The Yellowstone to Yukon Conservation Initiative (Y2Y), a joint Canadian-U.S. network of over 340 organizations and individuals, benefited from its gradual evolution. The initiative dates back to 1993, when a group of top scientists and conservationists met near Calgary, Alberta, to talk about the possibility of applying the principles of conservation biology to the Rockies. The discussion continued off and on until 1996, when the group hired a coordinator. By fostering an open exchange of ideas and coordinated action among its participants, Y2Y has grown to be a powerful force in energizing and inspiring others to work on behalf of land conservation and stewardship in the Rocky Mountains.

Partner organizations must provide decision-making entities with the flexibility, support, and follow-through they need to try innovative solutions. Avoid "that isn't the way we do it" or "we tried that and it didn't work" mentality. Effective partnerships recognize that change does not happen overnight. Plans must be in place to ensure that the partnership continues as long as needed to accomplish the partnership's goals beyond any individual's tenure.

In Florida, the statewide greenways program was aided by strong and active support organizations that helped lead the effort. In addition to The Conservation Fund and 1000 Friends of Florida, the leadership groups reached out to many nongovernmental organizations, including The Nature Conservancy, the Florida Trail Association, Southeastern Trail Riders, Rails to Trails Conservancy, local land trusts, and others. Public agencies involved included Florida's natural resource and planning departments, water management districts, regional planning councils, and local governments. The University of Florida's contribution was also essential. University professors and staff developed a database of Florida's conservation lands and trails and used innovative GIS mapping techniques to define and identify the ecological and recreational hubs and links that could make up the statewide system. University personnel then developed and applied an objective method for identifying the lands of highest priority for protection in the ecological network.

Several private foundations, the Florida Department of Transportation, and the Florida Department of Environmental Protection, provided important financial support, but in-kind contributions were just as valuable. Walt Disney World, the National Park Service's Rivers, Trails, and Conservation Assistance Program, and other organizations provided invaluable technical assistance.

KEEPING THE INITIATIVE ALIVE

Change is inevitable. Growth will occur in communities whether they have planned for it or not. Landscapes also undergo changes as part of their natural processes and ecological systems. A green infrastructure design that is developed today will not look the same as a design developed a decade from now. In most cases, there will be fewer options for hubs and links in the future, as land continues to be converted to housing developments, shopping centers, and roads. With each day, we lose opportunities to prioritize our natural assets and protect those that are most valuable.

It is not enough to simply design a green infrastructure network. This is just the first step in a long and continuous process. It may take years to acquire, protect, or restore priority conservation lands. Changing community attitudes and amending zoning laws to better guide growth to more suitable locations may take even longer. Planning and implementing a green infrastructure approach provides a means for changes in community attitudes to occur gradually, even as advocates work to protect the most threatened lands from the negative effects of change. Moreover, the network design model will need to be rerun periodically so that it reflects new data on resource values and areas and accommodates the changes in the landscape that occur naturally.

In communities facing the immediate pressure of population growth, the issue of where to build homes, offices, or shopping centers sometimes polarizes the community. Green infrastructure provides a means for changing the very nature of the debate. In rural communities, the debate regarding growth and planning often centers on property rights. By providing ways for protecting the landscape and its valuable ecosystems without changing the property ownership structure, green infrastructure can change the nature of the debate in these communities as well. In short, green infrastructure enables people—regardless of how they feel about growth, land conservation, and related issues—to focus on their shared values and to work together toward a desired future.

Every state and local government has a long-range transportation plan. Communities undergoing growth also have detailed plans for improving their stormwater systems, sewage treatment plants, telecommunications facilities, utility lines, and other public infrastructure. Just as communities need plans to upgrade and expand their gray infrastructure, so too do they need plans to upgrade and expand their green infrastructure. Green infrastructure plans provide a blueprint for conservation and development. They create a framework for future growth while ensuring that important natural resources and community assets will be preserved for future generations. States and localities are beginning to realize that green infrastructure is not a frill; it is smart conservation for the twenty-first century.

GREEN INFRASTRUCTURE IN ACTION: METROPOLITAN GREENSPACES PROGRAM, PORTLAND, OREGON

Over one hundred years ago, citizen park boards in Portland, Oregon, and Seattle, Washington, collaborated in bringing John Charles Olmsted to prepare park master plans for both cities. Olmsted's plan included a forty-mile-long trail system for Portland that would circle the city and link public parks.

A regional approach to planning in the Portland metropolitan area reaches back almost as far. In 1925, a citizen committee expressed concern that the automobile was allowing rapid and unplanned suburbanization and recommended the consolidation of Portland and Multnomah County. Although this recommendation did not come to fruition, for the next five decades, local government coalitions, appointed commissions, and regional planning agencies drafted regional plans and issued reports encompassing the area, often focused on transportation and other infrastructure needs.

> "The key to urban conservation is to find the balance between the seemingly conflicting goals of allowing development density and protecting natural resources."
>
> METROPOLITAN GREENSPACES PROGRAM

Concern for planning and environmental protection at the state level further encouraged a regional approach. In 1969, the Oregon Senate passed a bill requiring cities and counties to engage in comprehensive land-use planning, laying the foundation for the land-use planning system that was detailed in later legislation. Portland's urban growth boundary was established in 1979, and the Portland Metropolitan Area Local Government Boundary Commission was given the authority to approve or disapprove both major boundary changes (formation, merger, consolidation, dissolution) and minor boundary changes (annexations and withdrawals) of cities and eight types of special districts. The Boundary Commission became a major force in implementing land-use planning by testing boundary changes against plans for land development and the provision of public services.[8]

With the establishment of the Metropolitan Service District (MSD) in 1977, regional planning became institutionalized. The MSD was combined with the Columbia Region Association of Governments a council of governments representing cities and counties in the area, and began operation in 1979. Now called Metro, the agency was given responsibility for the urban growth boundary, solid waste planning, and operating the Washington Park Zoo. Metro's scope gradually increased over the next several decades, with environmental protection and regional planning among its many added responsibilities.

In the late 1980s, a group of representatives from Metro, nonprofit organizations, local governments, and citizens formed to collaborate on the protection of green space in the Portland, Oregon-Vancouver, Washington region. As a result of their efforts, Congress allocated funding for Metro and the U.S. Fish and Wildlife Service to partner to initiate the Metropolitan Greenspaces Program. The program is one of two national demonstration projects to develop new and innovative ways to preserve natural areas including wildlife and fish habitat in metropolitan regions. (The other demonstration project is in Chicago.)

In 1989, Metro inventoried and mapped the remaining natural areas in urban Multnomah, Clackamas, and Washington counties. At that time, approximately 29 percent of the metropolitan region's land was considered natural, including the Columbia Gorge between the Sandy River and the Mt. Hood National Forest. Only about 8.5 percent of these natural areas were publicly owned parks or were protected as open space.

Box 9.5

The Fast Pace of Growth in the Portland Metropolitan Area

- Metro estimates that the region will grow by an average of 70 people per day, adding up to a population increase of 465,000 people between 2000 and 2017.
- Between 1997 and 2000, vacant land was developed at an average rate of 1,100 acres per year.
- A 1997 study of natural areas showed that 16,000 acres of the natural areas identified in 1989 were lost or substantially changed.
- Over 400 miles of natural streams in the Metro area have been culverted or lost.

Figure 9.2
The Metro Greenspaces Master Plan called for cooperative efforts to acquire and
protect a system of green space for wildlife and people. Credit: Portland Metro
Greenspaces.

Gaining Commitment through the Master Plan

In 1992, voters approved a home-rule charter defining Metro's most important
service to be "planning and policy making to preserve and enhance the quality of
life and the environment." This same year, the Metro Council adopted the
Greenspaces Master Plan to serve as the policy guide for the Metro Regional Parks
and Greenspaces Department. The plan identified fifty-seven urban natural areas
and thirty-four trail and greenway corridors that define green infrastructure for the
Portland metropolitan region.

The Master Plan called for cooperative efforts to (1) acquire and protect a system of green space for wildlife and people throughout the metropolitan area
including areas of ecological and aesthetic value and a system of trails and greenway connections; (2) prepare management plans and standards for the green spaces
system to guide the facility development and management of sites to ensure that
public access and passive recreational opportunities are provided while protecting
the natural areas; and (3) operate and maintain major components of the green
space system.[9] With its emphasis on interconnected green spaces that would serve
as habitat for wildlife and people, the Master Plan essentially called for the design
and implementation of a green infrastructure network.

The Master Plan recognized the need to carry out restoration activities as part of the Metro Regional Parks and Greenspaces Department's ongoing work. "By carrying out the recommendations in this plan," reads the foreword, "this region will keep its special sense of place. Future generations will inherit a legacy of natural areas protected forever for all to enjoy."[10]

Funding for Green Space Protection

In 1995, the Metro Council adopted a long-range growth management plan to be used to guide regional land-use decisions, and citizens voted in favor of a $135.6 million bond measure to purchase natural areas, trail corridors, and greenways to be held for future use as parks, trails, and fish and wildlife habitat. Metro has used the funds from the bond to acquire property in fourteen regional natural areas and six regional trails and greenway corridors. In addition, a "local share" portion of the bond monies has funded more than 100 local park projects, located in almost every city, county, and park district in the region. As of October 20, 2004, Metro had acquired more than 8,000 acres of land for regional natural areas and regional trails and greenways in 258 separate property transactions. These properties protect nearly seventy-four miles of stream and river frontage.

A variety of integrated regulatory and nonregulatory tools are being used to protect green space, water quality, floodplains, and fish and wildlife habitat. One of the priorities of the Metro-U.S. Fish and Wildlife Service partnership was habitat restoration. Conservation and restoration grants (of up to $30,000 in 2004) were available for a wide array of projects and programs designed to address high priority fish and wildlife conservation issues. Federal funding was set aside for local governments and 501(c)3 nonprofit organizations to submit grant requests through a competitive process. Grants required a one-to-one match for the federal dollars transferred through Metro. Objectives of the grant program included carrying out needed restoration and enhancement projects that might not otherwise be completed. These projects have increased public awareness about the importance of maintaining healthy urban natural resources, wetlands, and streams. Implementation of projects that include numerous "friends" groups, jurisdictions, and agencies show that cooperative and regional approaches offer real solutions to natural resources management issues.

Partnerships in Action

Metro Greenspaces has brought together more than sixty governmental agencies, nonprofit organizations, and businesses working cooperatively to establish an interconnected system of natural areas, open spaces, trails, and greenways in the four-county Portland, Oregon-Vancouver, Washington metropolitan area. Success is due in part to the unique partnership of Metro and the U.S. Fish and Wildlife Service. The partnership allowed for the pooling of resources and expertise to implement a multifaceted program aimed at conserving sensitive species while providing recreational trails for area residents.

The purpose of the Greenspace program is "to provide long-term protection of the natural areas that lend character and diversity to the region . . . and to balance an urban landscape with wildlife habitat in the midst of a flourishing cosmopolitan region." The program focuses on environmental education, habitat restoration, public outreach, and cooperative planning throughout the region.

The Metro Greenspaces program builds on Portland's legacy of regional planning. When originally conceived over a century ago, Portland's trail system was going to be forty miles long, circling the city and linking public parks. The vision for a regional system of trails and greenways that was described in the 1992 Metropolitan Greenspaces Master Plan expanded the concept to twenty-five cities and four counties within the Portland-Vancouver metropolitan region. Today, plans call for an 950-mile network of regional trails, including water trails and greenways. As of 2003, nearly 30 percent of the land-based trails are complete.

Different trails are designed to meet different needs. Some, like the Interstate 205 Corridor Trail, are designed for bike commuters and people on the go; others

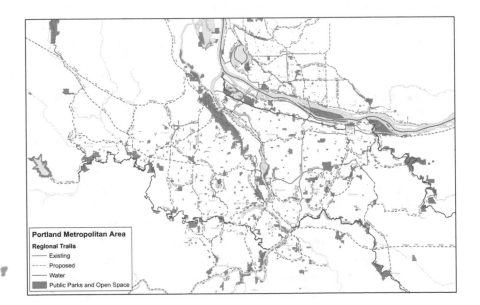

Figure 9.3
Plans in metro Portland call for a 950-mile network of regional trails, including water trails and greenways. The system of trails is being built in phases as funding becomes available and trail alignments are secured. Credit: Portland Metro Greenspaces.

take hikers into a more natural setting. In some cases, greenways allow for an environmentally compatible trail, viewpoint, or canoe launch site, but others are a swath of protected habitat along a stream with no public access. In addition to land trails, the network includes trails on rivers and other riparian linkages.

The Portland Greenspaces system is anchored by hubs that support a variety of plant and animal species. Portland's Forest Park, for example, encompasses more than 5,000 acres, making it one of the largest natural forested urban parks in the United States. The park contains old-growth trees, a wide variety of plants, and over 100 species of mammals and 100 different types of birds.

Making It Happen: The Implementation Phase

As Portland's experience illustrates, regional trail and greenway projects can take years to move from concept to reality. Metro Portland's system of trails is being built in phases as funding becomes available and trail alignments are secured. Some projects have received big boosts from a special dedicated funding source, such as Metro's 1995 open spaces, parks, and streams bond measure. Other projects have been built one section at a time.

The regional trails system has also benefited from state and federal funding programs. A number of regional trail projects have been funded through the Metropolitan Transportation Improvement Program, which disburses federal and state transportation money in the Portland metro region. In addition to paying for trail construction projects, funds from Metro's 1995 bond measure supported the acquisition of a

---

Box 9.6

Forest Park

The history of Portland's Forest Park goes back even further than that of the city itself. William Clark, of Lewis and Clark fame, took a side trip up the Willamette in 1806, making note of the many types of wildlife and huge old growth trees found in the forested western hills along the river. Despite the many changes that have occurred in and around Portland in the past two centuries, preservation efforts of Forest Park have paid off. In her 1982 survey of Forest Park wildlife, biologist Marcy Houle identified more than 112 species of birds and mammals. According to Houle, while most city parks have a steady decline in native wildlife, the assemblage of species she found in Forest Park was very similar to that noted by William Clark in 1806.

Box 9.7

Metro's Green Trails Guidebook

Metro's Green Trails guidebook, produced in 2004, provides a comprehensive source of information about planning, construction, and maintenance of environmentally friendly or "green trails"—trails that avoid or minimize impacts to water resources and fish and wildlife habitat. The guidebook is a resource for citizens, trail planners, designers, builders, and maintenance staff. It focuses on trails in environmentally sensitive areas and recommends strategies for avoiding or limiting the impacts on wildlife, water quality and water quantity. It also provides an extensive bibliography of other sources that give more specific guidelines for trail planning, design, construction, and maintenance.

number of river trail access points. Local cities and park districts also have used local funds to acquire, plan, and build new trail segments throughout the region.

For each project, different strategies are used. Pieces of trails are built, gaps are filled, key acquisitions are made, and local landowners agree to participate. Each step moves Metro and its partners along the path to their goal of a regional trail network.

Citizen Involvement and Education

Citizen outreach and education are key elements of the Metro Greenspaces project. During the program's fledgling years, numerous public forums were held in the region's four counties to involve citizens in deciding the scope and direction of the program. Today, the effort to protect and preserve an interconnected network of green space is guided by a number of citizen groups, including a fifteen-member citizen advisory committee. A number of other policy and technical committees and working groups continue to advise Metro of the Greenspaces program.

Extensive public information efforts have included many public presentations and meetings, a Greenspaces display, a slide show, an insert in *The Oregonian*, and other fact sheets and brochures. Parks forums are scheduled quarterly to encourage information sharing among parks providers, conservation groups, and the public.

As part of the Metro Greenspaces Program, environmental education grants of up to $10,000 were made available to build comprehensive environmental education programs around urban natural areas that encourage field and hands-on learning experiences for people of all ages. As with the conservation and restoration grants, grant recipients were required to provide matching funds. The program funded 183 regional environmental education projects totaling over $860,000. An additional $2.5 million has been generated through local matching contributions. Funds have been used for environmental education and habitat restoration projects designed to engage thousands of people in hands-on outdoor studies that include collecting environmental data, improving habitat for fish and wildlife, mapping, conserving water, and training teachers. Many projects offer volunteer opportunities.

> "I think we are building a more holistic kind of citizenship with these modest investments in environmental education. Nature is in every neighborhood and environmental education is the key to knowing how to find it."
>
> DAVID BRAGDON
> METRO COUNCIL PRESIDENT

These and other environmental awareness programs sponsored by Metro encourage local citizens to become active and involved stewards of natural areas. Metro also engages young people in environmental stewardship activities. In the Green City Data Project, for example, twelve teams of middle and high school students were trained to do field inventories and analysis of plants and animals in urban natural areas. A "GreenScene" series of guided hikes and other activities in the urban outdoors help connect people to nature and promote the goals of the Greenspaces program.

Restoration and management projects have brought together cities, counties, special districts, schools, colleges, state and federal agencies, and neighborhood organizations working to protect and enhance wetlands, streams, river banks, riparian zones, and upland greenspaces. Volunteers, school children, property owners, and neighbors have all participated in the actual work. Volunteer work parties at project sites have identified and removed invasive species of plants, built and removed fences, and planted trees and native plants. Trained volunteers also track data on plants and animals and lead nature hikes and other citizen outreach activities.

Complementary Activities

The Portland-Vancouver area supports habitat and migration corridors for a number of at-risk species including native salmonids, migratory birds, amphibians, mammals, and plants, and the Metro Greenspaces Program recognizes and protects this habitat while building a network of trails primarily for human use. In doing so, the program complements other objectives and planning activities of local and state governments, including urban growth management plans outlined by the state government. Confining growth to reduce urban sprawl will protect fish and wildlife habitat *outside* the urban growth boundary (UGB). Maintaining healthy streams, natural areas, and movement corridors *within* the UGB will help to ensure that urban land uses contribute toward conservation efforts within the larger landscape.

The Metro Greenspaces Program dovetails nicely with the Metro 2040 Growth Concept, which defines the region's growth management effort. Metro 2040 was initiated in 1990 as part of a visioning effort to plan fifty years into the future. The 2040 Growth Concept includes land-use and transportation policies that will allow the Portland metropolitan area cities and counties to manage growth, protect natural resources and make improvements to facilities and infrastructure while maintaining the region's quality of life. Policies in the 2040 Growth Concept encourage efficient land use, the protection of farmland and natural areas, a balanced transportation system, a healthy economy, and diverse housing options.

Recognition and protection of open spaces, including important natural features and parks inside and outside the UGB, are reflected in the 2040 Growth Concept. The program includes a map highlighting future land-use alternatives. Green areas on the Growth Concept Map may be designated as regional open space, which removes these lands from the inventory of land available for development. Rural reserves, already designated for farms, forestry, natural areas or rural-residential use, are further protected from development pressures.

An essential element of the Metro Greenspaces program is its cross jurisdictional approach. The program draws its strength from its focus on interconnectivity—between natural areas, between people, and between programs. The regional approach crosses political boundaries and embraces the principles of landscape ecology that emphasize the interdependency of ecosystems by taking context into account. The structure and use of the surrounding landscape and how each natural area fits within the region as a whole are used to help determine priorities for the Greenspaces program.

The Metropolitan Greenspaces Program plays a role in ensuring that citizens are knowledgeable about and involved in natural resource issues that affect their own communities and that decision makers are provided with the best conservation information that is available. Program staff works proactively with local communities and partners on a variety of efforts designed to protect and restore natural areas. These activities build support for land conservation and facilitate citizen stewardship of the land.

• *For more information about the Metropolitan Greenspaces Program, visit www.metro-region.org/pssp.cfm?progservID=5.*

Notes

1. See, for example, Eric A. Odell, David M. Theobald, and Richard L. Knight, "Incorporating Ecology into Land Use Planning: The Songbirds' Case for Clustered Development," *APA Journal* (Winter, 2003):72–79. This study examines the impact of two types of residential development, clustered and dispersed, on songbird habitat in Pitkin County, Colorado.

2. For more information, see CPAWS, Calgary/Banff Chapter, What's Happening in Our Mountain Parks? at www.cpawscalgary.org/mountain-parks/managing-impacts.html.

3. For more information on the design of wildlife corridors, see Paul Beier and Steve Loe, "A Checklist for Evaluating Impacts to Wildlife Movement Corridors," *Wildlife Society Bulletin* 20 (1992):434–440; Monica Bond, "Principles of Wildlife Corridor Design" (October 2003), www.biologicaldiversity.org/swcbd/programs/sprawl/wild-corridors.pdf; and the American Wildlands' Corridor for Life program, www.wildlands.org.

4. For more information, see Michael Frank, "Opportunity Knocks: Open Space Is a Community Investment," Heritage Conservancy, 2003, at www.heritageconservancy.org.

5. Carl Steinitz, et al. *Alternative Futures for Changing Landscapes: The Upper San Pedro River Basin in Arizona and Sonora* (Washington, D.C.: Island Press, 2003).

6. Quoted in Montana Associated Technology Roundtable, "Communities Can See Future in 3-D," *News* (April 18, 2003). See www.matr.net. Information on Community Viz and case studies on how it has been used in other communities can be found at www.communityviz.com.

7. Information on CITYGreen and case studies on how it has been used can be found at the American Forests Web site, www.americanforests.org.

8. The Portland Metropolitan Area Local Government Boundary Commission was abolished in 1999, and Metro assumed authority over boundary changes.

9. As defined in the report by Metro, *Metropolitan Greenspaces: Master Plan Summary*, 1992.

10. Metro, *Metropolitan Greenspaces: Master Plan Summary*, 1992, 2.

GLOSSARY

Adaptive management: A land management concept or approach that uses the responses of a system to management actions to determine future actions, allowing for ongoing modification of management strategies.

Agricultural district: Legally recognized geographic area formed by one or more landowners and approved by one or more government agencies; voluntary and created for fixed, renewable time periods, agricultural districts grant enrolled landowners specific protections from farmland conversion pressures.

Biodiversity: The variety and variability within and among living populations and the ecosystems within which they occur; a gradient including genes, species, ecosystems, and landscapes.

Bioregion: Assemblage of native landscapes and ecosystems that can be defined by topographic or climatic features or watersheds; a place defined by its life forms, its topography and its biota.

Bond: An interest-bearing certificate issued by a government or business, promising to pay the holder a specified sum on a specified date; it is a common means of raising capital funds.

Buffer: Natural area or open space used to minimize the impacts of adjacent lands and their uses on core areas or areas selected for a particular management strategy.

Charrette: A concentrated design session involving a small group of experts and other interested participants in a targeted exercise with a clearly defined objective; in green infrastructure, mapping charrettes are often used to identify elements that should be included in a green infrastructure network.

Cluster development: A development approach that preserves ecologically valuable open space and other lands by grouping buildings and other built infrastructure in less environmentally sensitive areas; a site-planning technique in which lot sizes, setbacks, and frontage distances are minimized to allow for open space; also called *conservation design, conservation development,* or *open space development.*

Coarse filter approach: Biodiversity conservation that involves identifying and conserving entire native communities and ecosystems.

Community visioning: A strategic planning effort in which citizens work together to envision a desired future and identify a series of shared goals encompassing a broad range of common interests.

Compatible human use: Any use that protects, sustains, or enhances the underlying natural, recreational, cultural, and/or historic resources of a specific area.

Comprehensive plan: Used by most local governments, a plan that includes the guidelines, principles, and standards for an area's orderly, coordinated, and balanced future economic, social, physical, environmental, and fiscal development; also called a *general plan* or *master plan.*

Connectivity: The creation of functionally contiguous blocks of land or water through linkage of similar ecosystems or native landscapes; the linking of trails, communities, and other human features.

Conservation banking: See *mitigation banking.*

Conservation biology: A discipline that explores and applies biological and ecological principles to the conservation of biological diversity and related critical habitats.

Conservation corridor: A linear feature that serves as an ecological connector that facilitates the movement of animals, plants, and their genes into other populations. They are primarily managed for the conservation of biological diversity, renewable resources, water flow, and water quality protection.

Conservation easement: See *easement.*

Core area: A large area within a reserve network that is managed solely or primarily as an ecological reserve for the conservation of biological diversity; such areas will often be the central units within the network—they may include several ecosystems.

Corridor: A narrow or linear segment of land that differs from the matrix on each side; they may serve as biological and/or hydrological connecting corridors and/or provide outdoor, resource-based recreational opportunities.

Development rights: The right of property owners to develop their land in accordance with applicable local, state, and federal laws; this right may be exchanged for a conservation easement.

Disturbance: Any relatively discrete event in time that disrupts an ecosystem, community, or population structure and changes resources, substrate availability, or the physical environment.

Easement: A legal restriction contained within a deed that prohibits certain land uses in perpetuity; landowners voluntarily place a conservation easement on their property to protect natural resources, such as water quality, wildlife habitat, or scenery, or to protect the land for a certain type of use, such as farming; the landowners retain rights to use the land for any purpose that is not prohibited by the terms of the easement.

Ecological degradation: The interruption of ecological functions and processes and/or loss of ecological structure necessary to maintain the integrity and adaptive nature of native landscapes and ecosystems.

Ecological network: A network of lands that is designed to conserve native ecosystems and landscapes, restore connectivity among native ecological systems and processes, and maintain the ability of native ecosystems and landscapes to function as dynamic systems and to allow biota to adapt to future environmental changes; also known as a *reserve network.*

Ecological process: The interactions of living organisms with one another and with their physical/chemical environment. Ecological processes, which include predation, pollution, and landscape change due to fire, flood, and other natural and man-made occurrences, can have far-reaching effects on plant and animal populations and the quality of their habitats.

Ecology: The scientific study of the relations between living organisms and their environment.

Ecosystem: The living and nonliving components of the environment that interact or function together, including native plants, animals, and peoples, as well as the physical environment and the energy systems in which they exist.

Ecosystem integrity: The ability of an ecosystem to maintain essential ecological processes, functions, and structures and to adapt to spatial and temporal changes.

Ecosystem management: An integrated approach to the conservation, restoration, and ongoing management of native landscapes and communities that recognizes the interrelationship of the biological, physical, and chemical elements of discrete environments.

Ecotourism: Tourism based principally upon natural and archaeological/historical resources; the segment of tourism that involves traveling to relatively undisturbed or uncontaminated natural areas with the specific object of admiring, studying, and enjoying the scenery and its wild plants and animals, as well as any existing cultural features, both past and present; ecotourism approaches often focus on preserving the integrity of the location and the land.

Edge: An outer band of a patch or corridor that has an environment and/or structure significantly different from the interior; an area of transition between two types of land cover.

Environment: All the conditions, circumstances, and influences surrounding and affecting the development and survival of an organism or group of organisms.

Exotic species: Those species not native to the existing ecosystems or geographical area. They are often detrimental to native ecosystems, flora, and fauna and are also known as *nonnative species* or *invasive species*.

Fee-simple acquisition: Acquisition of all the interests in a property resulting in ownership.

Fine filter approach: Biodiversity protection focusing on a single species and its habitat.

Floodplain: Area that is in the path of water as it flows naturally from higher to lower elevations during periods of heavy rain.

Focal species: Plant and animal species that are critical to maintaining ecologically healthy conditions.

Geographic Information System (GIS): A computer system for integrating, storing, and using information describing places and features on the earth's surface.

Gray infrastructure: Man-made systems that support communities, including roads and other transportation systems, stormwater management systems, and utilities. Also called *built infrastructure.*

Green infrastructure: Our world's natural life-support system—an interconnected network of waterways, wetlands, woodlands, wildlife habitats, and other natural areas; greenways, parks, and other conservation lands; working farms, ranches, and forest; and wilderness and other open spaces that support native species, maintain natural ecological processes, sustain air and water resources, and contribute to the health and quality of life for communities and people.

Green infrastructure network: A physical network that links conservation areas and other types of open spaces to maximize the natural functions of the landscape and protect the species that live there; often, green infrastructure networks also provide diverse benefits and services to people and communities.

Green infrastructure plan: A plan that identifies green infrastructure resources within a community, region, or state and describes the methods that will be used to protect, restore, and maintain those resources for the benefit of nature and people. Green infrastructure plans often identify and rank green infrastructure resources in terms of ecological value, vulnerability, and human benefits and thereby can help in determining where conservation and development should take place.

Green space: Natural areas, parks, trails, greenways, and other types of open space that are not developed; green space can preserve natural ecological values and functions and provide places for resource-based recreation and other forms of human enjoyment.

Greenbelt: A linked network of protected natural or working lands that surrounds a city and buffers areas beyond the city from urban and suburban growth.

Greenway: A linear open space established along either a natural corridor, such as a riverfront, stream valley, or ridgeline, or over land along a railroad right-of-way converted to recreational uses, canals, scenic roads, or other routes; any natural or landscaped course for walking, biking, and other recreational use that links parks, nature reserves, cultural features, and/or historic sites with each other and with populated areas; locally, a strip of land or linear park designated as a parkway or greenbelt.

Habitat: The natural environment of an organism; habitat contains the elements of a landscape that the plant or animal needs for survival.

Habitat fragmentation: Human activity such as agriculture, road building, and land development that results in the creation of small, isolated areas poorly suited to maintaining ecological functions and supporting smaller populations of remaining species; there are two components of habitat fragmentation: (1) reduction in total habitat area, which affects population sizes and increases extinction rate; and (2) redistribution of the remaining area into disjointed fragments, which affects dispersal and decreases immigration rates.

Hub: An area that anchors a green infrastructure network and provides space for native plants and animal communities, as well as an origin or destination for wildlife, people, and ecological processes moving through the system; hubs range in size from large conservation areas to smaller regional parks and preserves.

Impact fee: A charge assessed to private developers, usually used to compensate local governments for the cost of new infrastructure and capacity of new development.

Keystone species: Plant or animal species occupying important niches that have major impacts on ecological structure and function and/or specifically create necessary habitat for other species.

Land ethic: The desire humans have to conserve, protect, and respect the native landscape and other natural resources; a recognition that the well-being of all life—including human life—is dependent upon the proper functioning of the ecosystem.

Land leasing: An arrangement whereby a government or organization pays a lower cost for land in exchange for limited, temporary control; with a purchase/leaseback arrangement, the new owner leases the land to the seller, but the use of the land is restricted.

Land trust: A privately supported, nonprofit land conservation organization whose purpose is to protect human and natural resources including productive farmland and forests.

Landscape: A mosaic of ecosystems or land uses that possess common attributes that are repeated across a large area.

Landscape ecology: The study of native landscape structure, function, and change at the scale of entire landscapes, as well as the application of the results to the design and management of both natural and human-dominated areas.

Landscape linkage: Large linear protected area that connects ecosystems and landscapes and provides sufficient space for native plants and animals to survive.

Link: The connection that enables a system or network to function and multiplies the utility of existing components by connecting them together like beads on a string. Includes greenways of varying size and function to smaller conservation and trail corridors, often considered synonymous with *corridor*.

Mapping charrette: See *charrette*.

Mitigation banking: Preserving and/or restoring large natural systems or areas for the purpose of mitigating in advance the adverse effects of development or other land alteration activities; mitigation banks allow developers and landowners with eligible sites to transfer mitigation responsibility to multi-acre "bank" sites of degraded lands that bank operators enhance or restore to carry out their clients' mitigation responsibilities.

Most suitable path: The best option for a path connecting ecological hubs or trailheads, as identified by a GIS algorithm or similar tool; sometimes called a *least cost path*.

Native ecosystems: Protected, managed, and/or restored biotic communities and composite ecological processes that are relatively unaltered by human activity in comparison to human dominated environments.

Native landscape: Relatively natural juxtaposition or interaction of protected, managed, and/or restored native ecosystems, compared to landscapes that have been altered for human use; lands that function naturally.

Open space: Undeveloped lands suitable for passive recreation or conservation uses.

Patch: An area of uniform habitat that is surrounded by significantly different land, such as a woodlot among cornfields; a nonlinear surface area differing in appearance from its surroundings.

Purchase of development rights (PDR): A method by which landowners place a deed restriction on their land in exchange for payment.

Recreational corridor: A linear open space used primarily for outdoor recreational activities.

Reforestation: A scientific approach to restoring native forests by planting indigenous species of plants and trees.

Reserve: An area that serves as a primary site for the protection, restoration, and maintenance of native landscapes and ecosystems and associated biological diversity.

Resource-based recreation: Outdoor recreation activities that occur on sites that are to a large extent unmodified by human activity, including hiking and horseback riding on conserved lands as well as fishing on rivers, boating on lakes, hunting in forests, and so forth. Also known as *nature-based recreation.*

Rewilding: A scientific approach to protecting and restoring large wilderness areas and native ecosystems based on the regulatory roles of large predators.

Riparian: Living or located on the bank of a natural watercourse; a riparian corridor is a corridor adjacent to and/or including the banks of a body of water functioning to protect water resources and environmental integrity.

Site: In a green infrastructure network, a small feature that provides a place for native species and/or human activities and serve as a point of origin or destination but may or may not be physically linked with other system components.

Smart conservation: Conservation strategies and practices that promote resource planning, protection, and management in a way that is proactive not reactive, systematic not haphazard, holistic not piecemeal, multi-jurisdictional not single jurisdictional, multifunctional not single purpose, and at multiple scales not at single scales.

Smart growth: Strategies for planning development in ways that are economically sound, environmentally friendly, supportive of community livability, and that enhance quality of life.

Social capital: The norms and networks of social relationships that build mutual trust and a spirit of reciprocity among community residents, organizations, and institutions.

Special assessment bond: A bond payable from the proceeds of assessments imposed on properties that have benefited from the construction of public improvements such as water, sewer, transportation, and irrigation systems.

Special district: An independent unit of local government organized to perform and pay for a single governmental function or a limited number of related functions; special districts usually have the power to incur debt and levy taxes.

Steward: Anyone acting with a sense of responsibility for, desire to participate in, or take charge of the protection of land and water resources.

Stewardship: Sense of responsibility for, desire to participate in, or taking charge of the protection and management of land and water resources.

Suitability surface: A graphic developed by characterizing all landscape features with respect to their suitability or appropriateness for a particular type of ecological linkage, trail corridor, or other land use.

Sustainability: Making sure present needs are met without compromising the needs of future generations; maintaining resources in such a way to be able to renew themselves over time or to keep in existence and supply with necessities.

Systems approach: A way of holistically thinking about systems and the structures, functions, and processes in which systems are made up of sets of components that work together for the overall objective of the whole and thereby achieve a behavior or

performance that is different than the sum of each of the components taken separately.

Trail: A linear corridor on land or water that provides public access for recreation or
authorized alternative modes of transportation.

Transfer of development rights (TDR): A tool for preserving rural or undeveloped land
while allowing landowners to reap the full value for their property by allowing
landowners to sell assigned rights to developers at a mutually agreed upon price.

Urban growth boundary (UGB): A legal boundary, required by some states and used by
other local governments, that separates urban land from rural land by designating
the area inside the boundary for high-density development and restricting the area
outside the boundary for low-density rural development.

Watershed: A topographically discrete unit or stream basin, including the headwaters,
main channel, slopes leading from the channel, tributaries, and mouth area, all
defined by a common drainage pattern.

Wetlands: Swamps, marshes, fens, and bogs.

Wildlife corridor: Stretches of land that connect otherwise disconnected wildlife habitat;
wildlife corridors contribute to greater biodiversity and increased long-term genetic
viability and are needed by some species to survive.

Working lands: Land that has been modified by humans to produce food, fiber, or other
materials; working lands include lands used for agricultural protection, forestry,
ranching, and mining; also called *working landscapes.*

SELECTED BIBLIOGRAPHY

Arendt, Randall G. 1996. *Conservation Design for Subdivisions: A Practical Guide to Creating Open Space Networks.* Washington, D.C.: Island Press.

Beatley, Timothy. 2000. *Green Urbanism: Learning from European Cities.* Washington, D.C.: Island Press.

Benedict, Mark A. 2000. *Green Infrastructure: A Strategic Approach to Land Conservation.* Chicago: American Planning Association PAS Memo.

Benedict, Mark A. and Edward T. McMahon. 2002. *Green Infrastructure: Smart Conservation for the 21st Century.* Washington, D.C.: Sprawl Watch Clearinghouse. See also the condensed version of this article in *Renewable Resources Journal* 20, 3:12–17.

Dramstad, Wenche E., James D. Olson, and Richard T. T. Forman. 1996. *Landscape Ecology Principles in Landscape Architecture and Land-Use Planning.* Washington, D.C.: Island Press.

Durbrow, B. Richard, Neil B. Burns, John R. Richardson, and Cory W. Berish. 2001. "Southeastern ecological framework: a planning tool for managing ecosystem integrity." *Proceedings of the 2001 Georgia Water Resources Conference*, J. Hatcher, ed., Institute of Ecology, The University of Georgia, Athens, Georgia.

Flink, Charles A. and Robert M. Searns. 1993. *Greenways: A Guide to Planning, Design and Development.* Washington, D.C.: Island Press.

Forman, Richard T. T. 1995. *Land Mosaics: The Ecology of Landscapes and Regions.* Cambridge, UK: Cambridge University Press.

Groves, Craig R. 2003. *Drafting a Conservation Blueprint: A Practitioner's Guide to Planning for Biodiversity.* Washington, D.C.: Island Press.

Harris, Larry D. 1984. *The Fragmented Forest: Island Biogeography Theory and the Preservation of Biotic Diversity.* Chicago: The University of Chicago Press.

Hoctor, Thomas S., Margaret H. Carr, and Paul D. Zwick. 2000. "Identifying a Linked Reserve System Using a Regional Landscape Approach: the Florida Ecological Network." *Conservation Biology* 14, 4:984–1000.

Hudson, Wendy E., ed. 1991. *Landscape Linkages and Biodiversity.* Washington, D.C.: Defenders of Wildlife/Island Press.

Lewis, Philip H. 1996. *Tomorrow by Design: Regional Design Process for Sustainability.* New York: John Wiley & Sons, Inc.

Little, Charles E. 1990. *Greenways for America.* Baltimore: The Johns Hopkins Press.

Maryland Department of Natural Resources. 2001. *Maryland's GreenPrint Program: Summary of Methods to Identify and Evaluate Maryland's Green Infrastructure.* Annapolis, MD: State of Maryland.

McHarg, Ian. 1969. *Design with Nature.* Philadelphia, PA: The Falcon Press.

McMahon, Edward T. 2000. "Green Infrastructure." *Planning Commissioners Journal* 37.

McMahon, Ed and Mark Benedict. 2003. *How Cities Use Parks for Green Infrastructure.* City Parks Forum Briefing Paper no. 5. Chicago: American Planning Association.

McQueen, Mike and Ed McMahon. 2003. *Land Conservation Financing.* Washington, D.C.: Island Press.

Meffe, Gary K. and C. Ronald Carroll. 1997. *Principles of Conservation Biology.* Sunderland, MA: Sinauer Associates Inc.

Noss, Reed F. and A. Y. Cooperrider. 1994. *Saving Nature's Legacy.* Washington, D.C.: Defenders of Wildlife/Island Press.

Noss, Reed F., Michael A. O'Connell, and Dennis D. Murphy. 1997. *The Science of Conservation Planning: Habitat Conservation under the Endangered Species Act.* Washington, D.C.: Island Press.

Shafer, Craig L. 1990. *Nature Reserves: Island Theory and Conservation Practice.* Washington, D.C.: Smithsonian Institution Press.

Smith, Daniel S. and Paul Cawood Hullmund, eds. 1993. *Ecology of Greenways—Design and Function of Linear Conservation Areas.* Minneapolis: University of Minnesota Press.

Soulé, Michael E. and John Terborgh, eds. 1999. *Continental Conservation: Scientific Foundations of Regional Reserve Networks.* Washington, D.C.: Island Press.

Stein, Susan M., Ronald E. McRoberts, Ralph J. Alig, Mark D. Nelson, David M. Thebald, Mike Eley, and Mary Carr. 2005. *Forests on the Edge—Housing Development on America's Private Forests.* USDA Forest Service, Pacific Northwest Research Station, General Technical Report PNW-STR-636.

Weber, Theodore and John Wolf. 2000. "Maryland's Green Infrastructure—Using Landscape Assessment Tools to Identify a Regional Conservation Strategy." *Environmental Monitoring and Assessment* 63:265–277.

INDEX

Note: Italicized page numbers followed by *b*, *f*, or *t* indicate boxes, figures, or tables. "Green infrastructure" is abbreviated as "GI," except when it is used as the key term in main headings.